# Marital Separation

# MARITAL

# SEPARATION

---

## Robert S. Weiss

---

BasicBooks
*A Division of* HarperCollins*Publishers*

Library of Congress Cataloging in Publication Data

Weiss, Robert Stuart, 1925–
    Marital separation.

    Bibliography:  p.
    Includes index.
      1.  Divorce–United States.  2.  Marriage–United
States.  I.  Title.
HQ834.W48        301.42'8        74-78307
ISBN: 0-465-04388-7 (cloth)
ISBN: 0-465-09723-5 (paper)

For

Stephen, Christopher, Peter, and Douglas

Each in his own way a witness

I wonder if there are ways of making the process that people go through, in separation, more widely known. Because there is a vast ignorance of what the experience is among people who are, I don't know, social workers, psychologists. They don't understand. I think people don't realize the extent of the crisis in somebody's life. They feel that you made the choice, or the choice was forced on you, and you make an adjustment to it, and that is that.

(Woman, early thirties, three months after leaving her husband)

# CONTENTS

*Contents*

# PREFACE

Marital separation has become almost a commonplace, if unanticipated and undesired, experience in American lives. Extrapolating from current trends, we can reasonably expect roughly half the marriages now being made to sustain a separation at some point in their future. Most of the husbands and wives involved will thereupon enter a prolonged period of social and personal upset.

This book is addressed to people contemplating or undergoing separation and to professionals working with them. Its aim is to make available the information I have gathered as a sociologist who has conducted research on marital separation and has provided transition counseling for the separated.

To suggest the kind of work that lies behind this book, I think it may be useful to describe my research experience. About twelve years ago I began to explore the question of the provisions of social relationships: What do we gain from relating to others, and what goes wrong in our lives when our relationships with others fail? I was particularly concerned with marriage because it is a relationship of central importance to most people, and so I asked: What does marriage provide that makes it so important?

The standard sociological answer to this question is that marriage contributes to tension management and makes possible a division of household labor; in addition, it may help to establish one's role in society and, in consequence, one's self-definition. But I could find little systematic empirical work to support this view: rather it seemed to rest on common sense and everyday observation.

It seemed to me that there were two approaches that might develop empirical materials which would reveal the provisions of marriage. One would be to compare a group of married people with a group of unmarried. But this would pose problems of matching: how could we insure that the married and unmarried were the same kinds of people? Better, it seemed, to begin by trying to infer the provisions of marriage from the provisions newly sought or the deficits newly displayed by people from whose lives marriage had recently been removed. For example, if marriage provides "intimacy," whatever that might be, and "intimacy" is truly needed, then people from whose lives marriage had been removed should display a lack they had not suffered when married.

I had come this far in my thinking when I realized that a population of such people was available in the membership of the Parents Without Partners organization. I got in touch with the president of the local chapter and asked his permission to attend meetings and to interview some of the members. He passed my request on to a committee. The committee asked about my research aims, my academic affiliations, and my publication plans. But what finally decided them in my favor, I think, was that I, too, was a parent without a partner. They saw no reason to fear that I would disparage them just because their marriages had ended.

I began the study assuming that the contributions marriage makes to emotional well-being can also be found in a number of other relationships, especially friendships and dates. I expected that only those members of Parents Without Partners who were without these presumably substitutive relationships would feel their lives to be defective. This assumption, as it turned out, was only partially correct; it woefully underestimated both the uniqueness of marriage (it is only marriage, for example, that makes continued accessibility an intimate's legal obligation) and the role played by marriage in organizing the rest of a person's life. But the Parents Without Partners study did suggest the different provisions made by marriage and other relationships; moreover, it led me to consider the different ways in which the no-longer-married, on the one hand, and the married, on the other, establish and organize social relationships. I thereupon embarked on an intensive interview study of a small sample of single parents and a comparison group of married parents. That study provided the materials reported in Chapter 9, on single parents.

At about the same time I became associated with a study of the social and emotional impact of the death of a spouse and the processes by which bereaved persons reconstruct their lives. The experience of the bereaved and of the separated differ in many ways, and I would not try to equate them. Yet individuals in both groups are subjected to traumatic loss (although the loss is sometimes complicated, among the separated, by its having been largely voluntary) and are often distressed by the confusions of moving from one life organization to another.

Many among both the separated and the bereaved, recognizing that they are managing badly, blame themselves for not having returned to effective functioning more quickly. This self-blame seemed to me undeserved as well as unfortunate. The difficulties members of these groups experience result not from weakness or inadequacy but are instead *situational difficulties;* anyone in their situations would be equally troubled.

A program that would make available to the separated and the bereaved information about their situation might, it seemed to me, fend off this tendency toward self-blame and perhaps prove useful to them in other respects as well. I first implemented this idea with a program which my colleagues and I later called Seminars for the Separated. I am now developing a similar program for the bereaved. My experience within Seminars for the Separated led me to believe that information is indeed useful; that belief, in turn, led me to write this book.

I am myself a veteran of marital separation, though I do not want to claim too much for this special status. Those who have undergone an experience are not necessarily more understanding or more helpful to those for whom the experience is a current reality. Indeed, to the extent that the veteran protects his or her present self by minimizing its vulnerability, he or she may be impatient with others who are still dealing with disruption and distress. But I note that I am a veteran to disclaim at the very beginning any intrinsic moral superiority. Marital separation can happen to anyone, and has happened to me.

The materials in this book are presented in the order in which they might become concerns for someone trying to grasp the phenomena of marital separation. I shall first consider why separations take place, then discuss the emotional impact of separation, move on to various aspects of the relationship between the separating spouses and the relationships of each with kin and friends. Finally I shall discuss the problems likely to arise in their relationships with their children. Subsequent chapters discuss issues associated with establishing a new life: the time required to start over and the strategies that might be adopted, legal matters, dating, and the nature of reliable cross-sex relationships.

The materials for the book derive from studies with which I have been associated, beginning with the study of Parents Without Partners,[1] and continuing through the studies of single parents [2] and of conjugal bereavement.[3] I learned a great deal from participants in Seminars for the Separated, though it was not a formal research project. At this writing I have served as director and lecturer for seven series of Seminars for the Separated and have helped to organize a number of series that were conducted by others.

Although this book has, I believe, a strong empirical foundation, I cannot draw on the kind of survey data necessary for quantitative statements: for estimates, for example, of the proportion of separated individuals who have had specific experiences. Nor can I say with confidence which of various fairly common experiences occur most frequently, although I may be able to say that some experiences appear to occur often and others to be rare.

[1] See Robert S. Weiss, "The Contributions of an Organization of Single Parents to the Well-Being of Its Members," *The Family Coordinator* 22 (July 1973): 321–326.

[2] For the theoretical preconceptions of the study, see Robert S. Weiss, "The Fund of Sociability," *Transactions* 6 (July/August 1969): 36–43. The major report from the study is in preparation. One section of it appears in idem, "Helping Relationships: Relationships of Clients with Physicians, Social Workers, Priests, and Others," *Social Problems* 20 (Winter, 1973): 319–328. Case histories from the study appear in idem, *Loneliness: The Experience of Emotional and Social Isolation* (Cambridge, Mass.: M.I.T. Press, 1973), and some tentative conclusions in Hugh Heclo, Lee Rainwater, Martin Rein, and Robert S. Weiss, *Single Parent Families: Issues and Policies*, a report for the Office of Child Development (Washington, D.C.: Department of Health, Education, and Welfare, 1973). Chapter 9 of this book is based in part on this study.

[3] The bereavement study is reported in Ira O. Glick, Robert S. Weiss, and C. Murray Parkes, *The First Year of Bereavement* (New York: Wiley-Interscience, 1974). Further reports are planned.

Much in this book is theoretical in nature, especially Chapter 3, on the role of attachment in love and marriage; Chapter 5, on the impact of separation on identity; and Chapter 11, on strategies of recovery. Other theoretical material is implicit, as in the discussion of the different responses to separation of kin and friends. Almost all these theoretical formulations seem to me to be supported by my own observations and by those of others.

Theories are inherently uncertain. It may well be, for example, that some of my propositions hold true only for some people in some circumstances. Nevertheless, I think the theoretical materials can, at the least, provide a starting place for thinking about what might otherwise be endlessly perplexing events. Even if the reader feels a particular theory is off the mark, it may suggest an idea worth considering.

I have consistently referred to the separated as "he or she." Though awkward, this construction recognizes explicitly that the separated comprise both men and women, and this point seems to me important. On the other hand, in referring to a child or to a professional, I have often used the generic "he."

I have included many direct quotations—most of them statements made by participants in Seminars for the Separated, others made by respondents in the earlier studies—to illuminate or exemplify some point made more abstractly in the text. All identifying information in this quoted material has been removed or disguised. Because of the need to protect the anonymity of the speakers, I cannot say as much about them as the reader might like. For instance, I cannot routinely report occupation or number of children. Only when such information is necessary to understanding the material and also provides no key to the speaker's identity have I included it. I have at times omitted intervening material within a quotation, but unless that material was significant or represented movement to another topic, I have not noted this with ellipses.

# ACKNOWLEDGMENTS

A good many friends and colleagues have contributed to the work on which this book is based. Drs. Ralph Hirschowitz, Bernard Fisher, and Maurits van Nieuwenhuysen helped develop Seminars for the Separated, Dr. Hirschowitz providing ideas, support, and energy at the very beginning, and Drs. Fisher and van Nieuwenhuysen helping to develop the program's format. Mr. Andrew Selig, Mr. Gerald Brocklesby, Mrs. Belle-Ruth Naparstak, and the Reverend Justus Fennel took early responsibility for the court-associated groups, and Mr. Brocklesby and Reverend Mr. Fennel kept them going. Mrs. Dorothy Burlage conducted an analysis of already gathered evaluation material and augmented it with her own evaluation study. Mrs. Barbara Altman made possible clerical support for Mrs. Burlage's work.

I would like to thank Dr. John Bowlby, Dr. C. Murray Parkes, and Dr. Martin Rein for helpful and clarifying discussions, and Mrs. Joyce Brinton, Mrs. Burlage, Dr. Arlene Daniels, Miss Dolores Hayden, Mrs. Marlene Hindley, Dr. Mary Howell, Dr. Susan Krinsky, and Mr. Peter Marris for comments and criticisms in response to an earlier draft of the book. I want especially to thank Dr. Daniels for her careful and critical reading. Mr. Erwin Glikes, of Basic Books, Mrs. June MacArthur, and Miss Laura Kent offered useful editorial advice. I want to thank for instruction regarding legal matters Mr. Brocklesby, Mr. Michael Wheeler, Mr. Wells Henshaw, and Mr. Paul Pearson; none, however, should be held responsible for my errors. Mr. Arthur Norton and Dr. Paul Glick of the Census Bureau and Dr. Alexander Plateris of the Office of Vital Statistics provided statistical material. Mrs. Mary Coffey, as she has in the past, took responsibility for typing and retyping. Dr. Gerald Caplan, director of the Laboratory of Community Psychiatry, unfailingly provided support and guidance. I am deeply indebted to my wife, Joan, who has been a friend and colleague throughout my work. I would also like to thank those leaders of discussion groups for Seminars for the Separated whom I have not already named in another connection, including Dr. David Epley, Dr. Clark Johnson, Dr. Sophie Lowenstein, and Dr. Alan Siskind. Last, but far from least, I would like to thank the many individuals who described to me the events of their separation and patiently, and sometimes impatiently, listened to hypotheses regarding the causes of those events.

Financial support for my work was provided by a National Institute of Mental Health Research Scientist Award, No. MH 45731.

# Marital Separation

# 1

# The Rising Rate of Separation

Few events in the life-cycle require more extensive changes in
activities, responsibilities, and living habits (or cause greater
alterations in attitudes, reranking of values, and alterations of
outlook on life) than does a change from one marital status to
another.
                    Donald T. Bogue, *The Population of the United States*
                    (Glencoe, Ill.: Free Press, 1949, p. 212.)

Last week one girl in my office came in to say she was separating
and the day after another one came in to say the same thing.
Apparently it doesn't matter how many other people it has happened to, it hurts just as much. Like being hit by an automobile.
                                        (Business executive)

### Separation and Divorce

Brief, unavoidable separations occur in every marriage: the husband goes on a business trip or the wife enters the hospital to have
a child. Despite evening telephone calls or daily visits, the couple
may miss each other. But they know they will soon be together
again; their marriage continues. This is not the case in the separations I discuss in this book. The hallmark of the marital separations to be dealt with here is that they truly suspend the couple's
marriage. The couple may eventually reconcile, but they cannot

(3)

be sure of this during the separation: Their marriage, so far as they know, is over. Not only have they established different households, but they have done so with the understanding that they will no longer honor the vows they once took to love and to cherish one another.

Because separation depends partly on a couple's state of mind, situations may arise in which the couple is not sure whether a time apart is truly a separation. After a quarrel a husband or wife may leave for a vacation alone, intending to think things over. Or a husband and wife in pursuit of separate educational careers may attend schools in different cities, without either being committed to return to their unhappy marriage. Yet undecided marital status seems rare—much more unusual than a situation where a couple's definition of their status shifts, where the couple decides one day that they have separated and the next that they are only apart. No one can live long with marital uncertainty; we are called on too frequently to define our status in interchanges with others and in planning for ourselves.

A decision to separate does not necessarily mean that the couple will never again live together; it may mean only that they have no positive plans to do so. This suspension of marital vows appears adequate to produce the withdrawal of emotional and physical accessibility that underlies the phenomena of marital separation.

Many of those who have not themselves been through it think of the end of a marriage in terms of divorce rather than separation. Divorce does sometimes have great emotional significance, as the ceremony that ends the marriage as a legal entity. But it is separation, not divorce, that disrupts the structure of the individual's social and emotional life.

Separations are, of course, more frequent than divorces: every divorce implies a separation, but the converse most definitely is not true. And separations, like divorces, have become increasingly common in recent years. Why this might be so has puzzled many observers of American life. Before actually attempting to estimate their current rate, it may be useful to consider how we might explain it.

## Why the Rise in Separations and Divorces?

The question of why the rate of marital disruption is so high may hold interest for the newly separated in the same way that a discussion of the causes of our economic recession may interest someone who has just lost a job. It is reasonable to want to know what large-scale forces have shaped one's personal troubles.

We can quickly reject the theory that increased longevity is to blame. Fifty years ago a man of twenty could expect to live to be sixty-six; a woman of twenty could expect to live a bit longer, to age sixty-seven or sixty-eight. Thirty years later, in 1956, a man of twenty could expect to live to be seventy and a woman of twenty could expect to live to be seventy-six.[1] Men had gained about 6 percent, women about 14 percent, in the length of their adult lives. These are not insubstantial gains. In that same period, however, the divorce rate increased by about 40 percent, or almost seven times as much as the increase in adult life for men, three times as much as the increase in adult life for women.[2] Furthermore, from 1960 to 1971, a period when life expectancy hardly changed at all, the divorce rate increased by more than 70 percent.[3]

If not by greater longevity, then how might we explain our increasing rate of marital disruption? The most plausible explanation is socioeconomic: The demands of our modern economy for mobile and adaptive citizens whose first loyalty is to their own functioning has led to greater emphasis on the individual's right —almost duty—to maximize his capabilities and has at the same time led to a weakening of barriers to self-development and self-determination. Goode notes that industrialization seems to produce roughly the same magnitude of divorce rate wherever it appears.

[1] U.S. Bureau of the Census, *Historical Statistics of the United States, Colonial Times to 1957* (Washington, D.C.: Government Printing Office, 1961), p. 24.

[2] *Ibid.*, p. 30.

[3] Paul C. Glick, "Dissolution of Marriage by Divorce and its Demographic Consequences," in *International Population Conference*, Vol. 2 (Liege, Belgium: International Union for the Scientific Study of Population, 1973), pp. 65–79.

In Western countries it has been accompanied by a marked increase in divorce. But in some non-Western countries, such as Japan, industrialization has reduced a previously very high rate.[4]

In our own country a number of developments stemming from our concern for self-realization and our unwillingness to impose restrictions on the private lives of our citizenry may have contributed further to the increased rate. Primary among these are the lowering of legal barriers to divorce and modifications in our understanding of the nature of marriage.

Only forty years ago divorce was scandalous, as novels and articles of that time demonstrate. Today the separations and divorces of the great or the glamorous occupy the news only briefly, and those of others pass unnoticed except by their friends. Just twenty-five years ago Margaret Mead commented on the fading but still visible image of the divorced person as selfish, irresponsible, or shady.[5] Today the older person who has been divorced is held in at least as much regard as the older person who never married. Certainly divorce no longer means the end of a political career, as our many divorced and divorcing Congressmen demonstrate.

Organized religion, too, has become more permissive. The Roman Catholic church, once immovable in its opposition to divorce, is in slow process of change. Some Roman Catholic priests have proposed increased acceptance of secular divorce in instances in which continuation of the marriage would be intolerable. A few now achieve the same end by application of the doctrine that to be religiously valid, a marriage must be entered into wholeheartedly by both partners: unhappy marriages are likely not to have been entered without reservation.

One indication that wider acceptance of divorce may be a major factor in the increasing divorce rate is that first divorces—divorces among people with no previous divorce—increased twice as much between 1960 and 1970 as did divorces among those who had

---

[4] See William J. Goode, *World Revolution and Family Patterns* (New York: Free Press, 1963), pp. 358–365.

[5] Margaret Mead, *Male and Female: A Study of Sexes in a Changing World* (New York: William Morrow, 1949).

already divorced once and then remarried.[6] What this means is that people who had not previously shown that they were willing to get divorced now have developed a divorce rate nearly as high as those who have demonstrated, by getting one, that they have no fundamental objection to divorce.

Not only the attitudinal but also the economic barriers against divorce have been weakened. At one time the great majority of married women were financially dependent on their husbands. Unless they could count on alimony as part of the divorce settlement, they could hardly dare to divorce. Today many more women feel themselves able to manage on their own, if need be. Partly as a result of the various women's rights movements that have periodically developed in our country's history, partly as a result of such other developments as our national need for women's labor during and immediately after the two world wars, more women have come to feel that it is appropriate for them to work, and more job opportunities have become available to them. The woman with small children may still find it difficult to make the child-care arrangements that would allow her to be self-supporting, and the older woman with little previous work experience may find it hard even to imagine where she might fit into the labor force, but most women now have reason to believe that they can achieve economic independence if they want it.

Some married women already make enough money to assure their economic independence. Not only are they working but their incomes approach or exceed the incomes of their husbands. It has been found that these women, should they decide on a divorce, are less likely than others to change their minds.[7] It is not known whether the divorce rate is actually higher in such cases, but it seems evident that the woman's fear of getting a divorce is lessened.

Reduction of the various pressures against getting divorced has been facilitated by a declining veneration of marriage as a kind

6 Glick, "Dissolution of Marriage."
7 George Levinger, in an as yet unpublished study of divorce actions in the Cleveland courts, found that women whose incomes compared favorably with those of their husbands were less likely than other women to drop a suit for divorce once they had initiated it.

of calling, almost like the ministry, a service to the society, if not to God; the keystone of the family, on which in turn Western civilization rests. In our present view marriage is solely a source of individual benefits, not a social responsibility. We have de-sacralized marriage. By doing so, we have made it easier for those couples who feel that their marriages are not going well to jetti-son them. Some may stay together nevertheless, for the children's sake, or because they cannot financially afford to separate, but fewer will stay together because they regard marriage as a sacrament.

The desacralization of marriage makes it no less important to us. Indeed, considering the near universality of marriage in this country, we might surmise that most Americans consider it criti-cal to their well-being. But the belief that a good marriage is im-portant for a good life does not necessarily lead to a strengthening of marital bonds. Instead it may lead to a refusal to tolerate a marriage that is other than satisfactory.

In addition to all this, there may be elements within the Ameri-can value system that contribute to our high divorce rate. For although several other Western nations have achieved as high a level of industrialization, no other has as high a divorce rate.[8] We might consider, in particular, the intensity of our impatience with barriers to self-realization.

To a greater extent than seems true elsewhere in the world, we Americans seem to cherish our right to the unimpeded pursuit of happiness, no matter how much sorrow that pursuit may en-gender. It makes perfect sense to us, in consequence, that we not have our actions and emotions constrained by "the ink on some long-forgotten paper." We want the freedom to continue to choose a marriage, rather than having that continuation forced on us. But along with this goes the freedom to end the marriage. Margaret Mead has written:

The emphasis on choice carried to its final limits means in marriage, as it does at every other point in American life, that no choice is irrevocable.

[8] In 1970 divorce rates per 1,000 population (not the best measure, but the only one available) were, at the high end of the list: U.S. 3.50; U.S.S.R., 2.63; Hungary, 2.26; Denmark, 1.94. The rate in the U.S.S.R. was increasing twice as fast as the rate in the U.S. These figures were reported by Glick in "Dissolution of Marriage."

All persons should be allowed to move if they don't like their present home, change schools, change friends, change political parties, change religious affiliations. With freedom to choose goes the right to change one's mind. If past mistakes are to be reparable in every other field of human relations, why should marriage be the exception? [9]

Often accompanying our discomfort with restriction is a sense that we are obligated to realize our potential for growth, development, experience, or expression—whatever would make us feel we have given scope to the strivings within us. This sense of obligation might be termed the *ethic of self-realization*. More and more, it would seem, men and women give some version of this ethical position as a reason for impatience with their marriages.

Although few subscribe to it unreservedly, the ethic of self-realization would seem to have a good deal of appeal, if articles in popular magazines can be taken as a guide. For instance, *New York* magazine recently included an autobiographical account by a writer-editor who had left a good job and an unsatisfactory marriage to fulfill his longstanding fantasy of living on a South Sea island. It was by no means clear that he was glad he had done so; actually things seemed to have worked out rather badly. But his repudiation of responsibility in a quest for self-fulfillment was published, presumably, to interest readers who had their own comparable fantasies. In another issue of the same magazine a woman told of leaving her comfortable suburban home and equally comfortable marriage to realize herself as a writer amid the challenges of New York City. She was quite sure she was right to have done so, despite the insecurity and recurrent unhappiness of her new life.

Although it is unusual for someone to leave a marriage solely to achieve self-realization, it does happen occasionally. One woman within our Seminars for the Separated, who had for years been a dutiful housewife and mother, left her husband—and her children, since they would not accompany her—to return to the profession she had earlier relinquished for the marriage. She felt that if she waited any longer to make the break, she would not

[9] Mead, *Male and Female*, p. 334.

make it at all but would instead stagnate until her death. Another woman reported that her husband had left their marriage in order to adopt what he termed "a new, more congenial life style."

In several instances in which the pursuit of self-realization did not itself produce the separation, it seemed nevertheless to have contributed to marital strife. In a few cases, a spouse who also subscribed to the ethic felt it wrong to interfere with the other's freedom to grow, though the expression of that freedom was injurious to the marriage. In others, a husband or wife felt it a personal failure, and a justification for the spouse's departure from the marriage, that he or she had not contributed to the spouse's growth.

**There was considerable growth in my marriage for me. I got a lot of things, did a lot of things, that I never would have done. Just simple things, like trying out a new sport, or being pushed to go back to school. I don't think I could have done without it. But I don't think my husband could say the same thing. I can't see him saying that he got anything out of the marriage, out of the association with me. Which is one reason, I think, that he walked out on it.**
**(Woman, thirties, formerly married to a highly successful businessman)**

These several factors taken together seem to me to offer the most plausible explanation for our high rate of marital disruption. They are phenomena that affect most members of our society: those in marriages that remain intact as well as those in marriages that do not. They insure that husbands and wives in marriages that continue, as well as in marriages that do not, have now and again wondered whether it is better to go on or to take advantage of our increasing acceptance of starting over; they make the implications of marital separation a personal concern for the great majority of us.

## What Are the Rates?

Arriving at reliable estimates of the rate of marital separation is no easy task. Statistics on divorce are, of course, available. But not every separation ends in divorce. Many, perhaps most, end in reconciliation, although many of these reconciliations will later give way to new separations. Still other separations continue until one of the partners dies and the survivor becomes a widow or a widower. Almost certainly not more than half of all separations go on to divorce.[10]

Simply judging from the divorce rate, we can be confident that a significant separation will occur in many American marriages. Indeed, if we assume that the rate of separation in the future will be the same as it is now, it is a safe prediction that about half of the American marriages now being made will at some point sustain a separation.

The proportion may well be higher. The divorce rate in this country has increased steadily since before the turn of the century, with the exception of a period of near stability in the 1920s and a sharp rise during the years of World War II, followed by a drop to a much lower level and another time of near stability during most of the 1950s.[11] The steady increase in the rate resumed in 1962, picked up speed by 1965, and by 1971 had moved beyond the peak of 1946.[12] It is still rising.[13]

If in the future couples who have been married a given number of years are no more likely to divorce than were couples in 1971, then we might expect 40 percent of newly formed marriages eventually to end in divorce.[14] If the frequency of divorce in the

[10] The observation that the number of separations is considerably greater than the number of divorces has been made by Goode, among others. See William J. Goode, *After Divorce* (Glencoe, Ill.: Free Press, 1956), p. 174. George Levinger found in the study of divorce actions in the Cleveland courts referred to earlier that between 20 and 30 percent of suits for divorce were withdrawn, with the couples returning to their marriage. It would seem plausible that at least the same proportion of separations end in reconciliation without any court action whatsoever.

[11] Arthur J. Norton and Paul C. Glick, "Marital Instability: Past, Present, and Future, *Journal of Social Issues*, in press.

[12] Glick, "Dissolution of Marriage."

[13] For the twelve months ending December 1974, 970,000 divorces were granted. The rate of divorce in the total population was 4.5 percent higher than it had been the year earlier: "Births, Marriages, Divorces, and Deaths for 1974," *Monthly Vital Statistics Report* (Washington, D.C.: Department of Health, Education, and Welfare, 1975).

[14] Glick, "Dissolution of Marriage."

future should be more nearly that of 1965, about 30 percent of newly formed marriages can be expected to end in divorce.[15] Conservatively, we may expect the divorce rate to lie within the range of these estimates. But if the divorce rate continues to increase, a marriage may be more likely to end in divorce than not.

If there is a separation that ends in reconciliation for every separation that ends in divorce, and if about half of those that end in reconciliation eventually go on to a new separation that this time ends in divorce, then—taking the more conservative prediction of the future divorce rate—we would expect that somewhere between 45 percent and 60 percent of marriages now being formed will at some point sustain a separation. Taking the higher estimate of the future divorce rate, and assuming that the ratio of separation to divorce remains nearly what it is now, it may be more usual than not for a marriage at some point to sustain a significant separation.

Newly separated people, however, are likely to feel that they have become distinctly different from everyone else in their circle of friends. They may, in consequence, find it difficult to believe that marital separation is so common a marital event. There are two explanations for this apparent paradox, the first statistical and the second sociological.

The statistical explanation is that though the likelihood of separation in marriage is fairly high, the likelihood of separation occurring in any particular year is fairly low. At present the average annual probability of separation is about five in a hundred.[16] Thus, if a couple have about fifty other couples in their friendship network, they will know an average of only one or two who also separate in any given year. As time goes on, of course, many more of the couples in their friendship circle will separate.

But what of all the couples who separated in the preceding years? Why does the newly separated person not know a good many people who have already separated? The answer would seem

[15] Paul C. Glick and Arthur J. Norton, "Perspectives on the Recent Upturn in Divorce and Remarriage," *Demography* 10, no. 3 (1973): 301–314.

[16] This is about 150 percent of the rate of divorce. See Norton and Glick, "Marital Instability."

to be that friendships tend to form among people in similar situations. Married couples tend to restrict their friendships to other married couples. Thus, the married person who separates will know married people, not others who have separated.

As a consequence of these two factors, the newly separated may for a time feel themselves to be nearly alone in the path they have taken, although it is a path that will be taken, sooner or later, by a large proportion of our population.

Our high rate of separation and divorce will seem to many sure evidence of a fundamental flaw in our society. And, as subsequent chapters will make clear, marital disruption is indeed likely to produce pain and impaired functioning. Perhaps there *is* something fundamentally wrong in a society whose values and institutional arrangements encourage so much distress.

Yet there is another way to look at the matter. In no society, not even those which absolutely prohibited divorce, have citizens not occasionally contracted marriages that sooner or later proved unhappy, that became empty or depleting, and impossible to continue. A certain proportion of marriages are bound to fail, no matter what. This fact should be neither surprising nor alarming. After all, we acknowledge easily enough that other human relationships besides marriage may fail, with no one at fault for the failure: Attempts at friendship may founder, and working partnerships dissolve in dispute, although the participants entered the relationships with the best intentions and were throughout reasonable in their expectations. Not every pair of people who think they can get along with each other turn out to be right. It may be one expression of our respect for these uncertainties, as well as for individual autonomy, that our social understandings permit the unhappily married to divorce and try again, rather than, as in an earlier time, requiring that they remain forever faithful, at least in public, to their marital vows. It is to the credit of American society that we are willing to forgo the image of a society whose domestic arrangements are entirely stable when this image no longer corresponds to the wishes of our citizens as individuals.

# 2

# Aspects of the Failing Marriage

My husband wasn't planning to stay with me. He was going to go away to a new job and leave me with the child. Because he was very much in love with a much younger girl. I told him to get out. I just didn't want him around talking about her all the time.

(Woman, thirties)

My wife had me believing that the whole thing was my fault. But I started going to this minister, and the more we kept hashing things out, the more I saw that my wife was so immature it wasn't funny. She wasn't ready for a family and responsibilities.

(Man, about thirty)

## Accounts

For months after the end of the marriage, the events leading to its breakdown are likely to occupy the thoughts of the separated husband and wife. Again and again they review what went wrong, justify or regret the actions they took, consider and reconsider their own words and those of their spouse. Endlessly they replay actual scenes in their minds or create scenes that did not happen but could have, in which they said different things or took different actions so that the separation was averted or the spouse was told off once and for all.

Gradually the separated come to terms with the events of their marriage. They develop an *account*, a history of the marital failure, a story of what their spouse did and what they did and what happened in consequence. Often the account focuses on a few significant events that dramatize what went wrong, or on a few themes that ran through the marriage; in addition it allocates blame among the self, the spouse, and any third parties who may have entered their lives, and so settles the moral issues of the separation.

The account is of major psychological importance to the separated, not only because it settles the issue of who was responsible for what, but also because it imposes on the confused marital events that preceded the separation a plot structure with a beginning, middle, and end and so organizes the events into a conceptually manageable unity. Once understood in this way, the events can be dealt with: They can be seen as outcomes of identifiable causes and, eventually, can be seen as past, over, and external to the individual's present self. Those who cannot construct accounts sometimes feel that their perplexity keeps them from detaching themselves from the distressing experiences. They may say, "If only I knew what happened, if only I could understand why...."

An account is not the same as an objective and impartial description, assuming that any such thing could be constructed. The accounts of a failed marriage offered by a husband and by a wife are likely to disagree, not only in that they report different versions of the same events, but even more in that they report different events. A listener who heard first the husband's account and then heard the wife's might not realize he had been told about the same marriage. In one instance the wife complained that her husband had tried to stop her from improving herself by taking college courses and had attacked her love of books. She talked about how little tolerance her husband had for her studies. Her husband, she said, could not comprehend her wanting to stay up to work on a paper or to finish a book. But her husband complained not about her studiousness nor about her passion for literature but rather about her flirtatiousness. He said that whenever they went to a party there were men around or, worse, a single other man. He said that he was constantly competing for her attention and that sometimes he lost the competition. None of the events significant to him appeared in her account, nor were any of the events significant for her included in his account.

The account is a selection, from a bewilderingly complex tangle of events preceding and surrounding a separation, of certain events that together can constitute an explanation. Here, for example, is the account of one separated man. It leaves out, among other things, the deepening estrangement between him and his wife that preceded his wife's involvement with someone new.

One of the events that led to my divorce was my brother's death. No question in my mind about it. That's a very tough thing, the first time you lose somebody you are close to. I mean friends die, but I was never affected by it, not like that. But my brother was the closest person I had. I was very, very grief-stricken when he died. And my reaction was to bury myself in work. I took on a very heavy project which I should never have taken on. It took me two and a half years, during which I paid no attention to my wife's needs, all I did was work.

I'm sure of it. There is no question in my mind that that is what happened in my relationship with my wife. And then she found a lover, because I wasn't home.

(Man, thirties, owner of a small electronics firm)

Certain themes tend to recur in accounts. One is that the marriage was wrong from the start: from the beginning it was unwanted and unsatisfactory; ending it was simply rectifying an error.

The few months before the day we were married weren't that good. Differences already had come up and there were problems and we weren't as happy as we were before. But the wheels of marriage had already started working and we were already buying silverware and dishes and it was too late. . . .

After being married a couple of months, at least subconsciously we realized that we were too different to be living together or even to be going out together. But divorce never really crossed our minds because we had just gotten married and sent out thank-you notes. You know, we couldn't very well say, "Thanks for the money. By the way, we are not married any more."

(Man, late twenties)

Some people said it had taken them years to accomplish a separation although they had wanted it almost from the beginning.

For some, practical considerations slowed their departure. One woman, afraid that she would be unable to support herself, had waited until she completed the college work required for a nursing degree before leaving her husband. Other women reported waiting until they had paid employment, and both women and men reported waiting until their children were in school. For others, the delay in departing was caused by the need to first reorganize themselves emotionally.

**For years I really wanted to be out of the marriage and wasn't able to do it. Cutting loose was a torturous thing. I knew that I wanted a divorce and couldn't look at it, because there was guilt and fear and, you know, shit going on inside me, so I just couldn't face it.**

**(Man, about forty)**

Many of those who had tried for years to make the best of a bad marriage mourned not the marriage itself but rather the years they had given to it. They wondered at their having tolerated the marriage for so long and congratulated themselves for, at last, having emerged from it.

**It was just a rotten marriage to start with, and it just kept getting worse. But so slowly, over fifteen years, just living in the same house, that you just don't realize how yucky it is. I didn't particularly like the way it ended, but I'm glad that it's over.**

**(Woman, late thirties)**

Another recurrent theme in accounts was each spouse's wanting different things in life. Occasionally one partner wanted greater autonomy than the other could permit: In one instance the desire of one for freedom to develop clashed with the other's desire for a settled life.

**I was trying to find myself, and she wanted to have babies. Well, I did and I didn't. She would have been quite happy with ten children living in a little place. It was a clash of values.**

**(Man, about thirty)**

A woman described a conflict between her own wish for a traditional life style and her husband's desires for a communitarian life:

I think what happened was that our interests were growing in different ways. I don't know, you'd think at this point I could put my finger on exactly what it was. He had this dream, everybody having a community with each other. He wanted to form a commune with some friends. And I realized that I just did not want that.

(Woman, early thirties)

Some accounts stressed a chronic failing in the spouse, a trait with which it was impossible to live. One woman had been married to a compulsive gambler whose changes of fortune kept her life and the lives of her children in turmoil. Women and men who had been married to alcoholics reported deciding after years of misery that they could continue no longer.

Although in most cases nothing less than a grievous and apparently incorrigible fault was offered as an explanation for separation, in a few, persistent inaccessibility or inattention were mentioned. One woman said that she had been made distraught by her husband's coolness; although he was dutiful enough, he had acted toward her as though she was a distant cousin. When she confronted him with this charge and asked him if he loved her, his answer was "No." A few days later, she told him to leave.

In a few instances other faults, such as stinginess or sexual inadequacy, were cited as having contributed to the frustrations of marriage, but rarely did they seem sufficient in themselves to justify separation. Arguments over the fault, however, might lead to estrangement and eventually to separation. One man said that he had been burdened by his wife's inability to make decisions. Exasperated, he had insisted that she manage her life herself. After a few months of increasing estrangement his wife left, to his dismay.

When I came home from work, what she did was to present a thing like, say, "The refrigerator is busted." And I'd say, "What the hell, I've got fifty problems! Can't you take care of that?" Now she says, "You wouldn't listen to me. I came to you, I wanted to talk, but you wouldn't listen." And it is true. I probably should have listened.

(18)

But she didn't come out and say, "Look, our marriage is falling apart." You bet *that* would have got me listening.

(Man, early forties)

Serious depression figured in several accounts as a cause of separation. One man reported that his wife had been recurrently depressed until—almost at wit's end—he asked her whether the marriage could be responsible. She said she thought it might be, and the next day was gone. In another instance a woman reported that she had been the depressed one and felt her marriage was at least partially responsible.

I got very depressed, and the psychiatrist I was seeing suggested that I move out. Initially I felt much better.

The psychiatrist seemed to think I didn't love my husband, but I finally established that I loved him for certain things and certain things I didn't. In many aspects my husband is a marvelous person. But there were a lot of problems.

I still go back for a few hours to see how things are, hoping they have changed, but they haven't. I've gone back for a few hours, and I guess for a night, but I was extremely depressed the next morning. Things are always as awful as I am afraid they'll be.

(Woman, early thirties)

One woman reported having been unable to tolerate her husband's depression.

My husband had lost a series of jobs and was very depressed. He just couldn't keep a job. He had a job for a couple of years, and that ended, and then he had another for a year, and that ended, and then he had another. And then he was really depressed, and he saw a social worker, but it didn't seem to be helping. And he was sleeping a lot. And I think one day I just came to the end of the line with his sleeping. I think I went out one night and came back and he hadn't even been able to get out of bed to put the children to bed. I left them watching television and there they were when I came back. The next day I asked him to leave. Very forcefully.

(Woman, late twenties)

Those who end a marriage because of their spouse's failings often suffer intense guilt and remorse. Only when the spouse's shortcomings are truly unbearable do they feel justified in leaving, and even then they may continue to feel that they have done wrong in deserting their spouse. The following report by a woman who had left a man hospitalized for depression suggests the level of justification that may be required before a troubled spouse can be forsaken:

My husband had to go into a mental hospital. And I had to decide that there was just a point where I could no longer be responsible for him. I care what happens to him. And I stayed with him as long as I could. I took our marriage very seriously. But I finally had to realize that if it went on I would go down the drain and my children too, and it was a matter of survival.

(Woman, about forty)

In some accounts a marriage that had at one point been satisfactory became hopeless not because of any identifiable fault in either spouse but because the couple had lost their ability to talk with one another. Instead, they bickered. Each spouse felt bruised by the other and, when opportunity presented, retaliated. As one man said, "Both of you are reacting after a while, and the more you react, the worse it gets." Though husband and wife may each have recognized that the marriage was rapidly becoming insupportable, each was too irritated with the other to talk without malice or to listen with sympathy.

I felt too threatened in my marriage to say, "My God, our marriage isn't going right," and get down to the nitty-gritty. When I was very unhappy I would begin to nag about certain things that he hadn't done, like the garbage had been left in the garage for about a week. You know, "When are you going to get it out?" I would blast away, and then he would blast away, "I'll get to it when I feel like it." I was afraid to talk to him. When I did I'd feel I was so desolate. I didn't know how to say, "Our marriage isn't going right," without us ending up having a royal battle.

(Woman, late thirties)

Infidelity appeared as a theme in many accounts, though its implications were not always the same. Sometimes its discovery seemed enough in itself to have precipitated the separation.

He's out of the house because I found out he's been running around for two years that I didn't know about. And I said to him, "Are you willing to give up this girl and start over again?" And he said, "No." So I said, "Well, you can't live here and live there."

(Woman, about thirty)

In other instances discovery of infidelity served merely to make a bad situation worse. The husband or wife might at first try to live with knowledge of the spouse's unfaithfulness, and perhaps only after months give the marriage up.

The last few years were just terrible. I couldn't do anything right. When he was home, which wasn't very often, he just sat in front of the television set and stared at it. I knew there was something wrong, but you don't realize. It happens so gradually. Then I found out that for over a year he had a little honey stashed away who was treated royally, who was wined and dined. He'd call me at night and say he had to work overtime.

I was really broken up. I'd sit at work and the tears would come. I'd run in the washroom and cry. I lost so much weight I didn't have any clothes to wear. Finally I said, "See you later. Off you go."

(Woman, mid-thirties)

Some tried to build separate lives so they would not be so hurt by their spouse's new involvement. Some attempted to compete with the other person for the spouse's affections. Such approaches may in some marriages eventually succeed. In the marriages described to us, they did not:

Well, my husband had a mistress. And he was quite comfortable comparing me to her culinarily, sexually, in every way. He'd been telling me about her for weeks, and I wanted him so badly that I tried to manage that. I thought, "I will bring him back"; you know, the old female competition. "I will be intelligent and understanding. I will tolerate and I will live through this. And I will be a gourmet cook or whatever it takes." Because I was raised in the South, where you fry everything. Well, he would have let it go on forever. And finally I just had to decide that he had to leave.

(Woman, early thirties)

Sometimes it was not the infidelity alone, but also the duplicity that had accompanied it, that caused pain. The attempt to conceal an affair could introduce so much mystification into the marital relationship that the spouse's confidence in his or her grip on reality was weakened. One woman reported finding a new wallet on her husband's bureau soon after his birthday. It could only have been a birthday present, yet her husband insisted that he bought it for himself. Later, after learning of his infidelity, the woman realized that it had come from his girlfriend, and felt that she should have guessed this at the time. Instead she had been confused, although she had said to herself that he had a right to buy himself a new wallet if he wanted to.

The following account has a similar theme:

When I normally wasn't going to be home, like if I delayed my departure for work in the morning, the telephone would ring, and there would be nobody there. Nobody would answer it at the other end. I'd pick up the phone and say "Hello," and there would be no dial tone, and obviously there had to be somebody at the other end of the phone, and there would be nobody there. So you say, "What in the hell is going on?" And my wife says, "I don't know what it is." You begin to distrust your own ability to reason, to think. It would have been a hell of a lot better if she had just leveled.

Well, I found out this had been going on for about a year. Meanwhile she had told me I was the source of all her tensions. Well, I discovered that I wasn't the source of her tensions. My presence in the home while this was going on on the outside, this was the source of her tensions, not me.

(Man, thirties)

A few husbands—and fewer wives—who were themselves either carrying on an affair or being repeatedly unfaithful were reported to have encouraged the spouse to a similar sexual style. Sometimes the results were as much comic as tragic.

When my husband heard that I had a sexual relationship. he sort of congratulated me, he was so delighted about it. But then it turned out that when I wanted to see this man, my husband wasn't able to make a date with the person he was seeing. And he had to quick find somebody else to fill the void. And it was just kind of an unbelievable thing. I look back on it and it is ludicrous.

(Woman, mid-thirties)

Some husbands and wives admitted that they had been unfaithful yet blamed the disruption of their marriage not on their infidelity but rather on their spouse's overreaction to it.

I had an affair with a younger man and it didn't amount to anything. My husband could have just let it pass. But he felt that I was open to other relationships and I don't think he could handle that.
(Woman, late thirties)

One woman was bitter that her husband had become almost violent when he learned that she was having an affair—one she had entered only reluctantly—although unbeknownst to her he was at the time himself involved with someone else.

I fought this affair for three years and wound up with a rash on my arms before I could break the bonds of my religious upbringing. I didn't have the guts to have an affair. I went through hell before making the damned decision. And then when he finds out, I'm totally condemned. And then I find out he had been having one right along with me!
(Woman, late thirties)

A few men and women reported that they had had only mild reactions to the discovery of a spouse's infidelity. One man explained this by saying that he already knew his marriage was over. "Had that man not been there, she might not have found anybody else, but her feelings would not have been substantially different toward me." A woman who had known for two years that her husband was involved with someone else managed to keep her knowledge from intruding on her consciousness until the other woman called, out of bitterness and spite, to tell her that the affair was over. At first the wife was intensely upset, but then she became quite calm—to her husband's consternation.

The biggest thing my husband won't forgive me for is that when I found out that he had had a two-year affair I didn't slit my wrists or jump out a window or do something. The thing that he can't emotionally conceive is that I reacted to it two years ago and

(23)

learned to deal with it then. Finding out now was, you know, a formality.

(Woman, mid-thirties)

Most of those who learned of a spouse's infidelity were hurt; some were almost devastated. This was generally true even when the marriage was known to be in trouble for other reasons. Indeed, infidelity seemed to be the most hurtful of the afflictions of a failing marriage. Why this might be so is one concern of the following section.

### The Afflictions of a Failing Marriage

No matter what else they have in their lives—successes at work, warm friendships, rich and absorbing interests—people caught in an unhappy marriage tend to feel isolated and beset. The morning's harsh words echo as they conduct their daily round; anticipation of an evening spent in strained silence makes returning home a chore. Their sense of isolation may be intensified as they find it necessary to dissimulate when meeting others during the day: "How's the family?" "Fine."

If the couple are quarrelsome, much of their energy may be given to reviewing the last fight and preparing for the next. They vacillate between wanting to make up and wanting to get even. Their thoughts dwell on their misery and their work suffers. Colleagues and coworkers may notice, perhaps without knowing the source, their tension, distraction, persistent preoccupation, and intermittent depression.

The couple may want the marriage to continue. There are so many reasons for trying to save a marriage: continued attachment, feelings of obligation to the children, unwillingness to hurt or shame the parents, fear of being alone, fear of the unknown problems of single life, financial uncertainty, unwillingness to admit to failure, and the simple determination to be faithful to one's marital vows. And yet the couple may hurt one another con-

(24)

stantly, as they communicate their frustration by look, posture, and tone of voice. Repeatedly they may recognize their situation and say to one another, in dismay, "We can't go on like this."

The couple may seek professional counseling, individually or together. Or they may experiment with partial separation, such as separate bedrooms, separate vacations, or separate lives within the same household. They may try to talk it out and discover that there is so much anger or there are differences so fundamental that no bridge can be built between them. They may try to avoid one another; yet how can this be managed with the two living in the same household?

The possibility of separation may be blurted out impulsively during a quarrel, or it may be brandished as one more weapon in the domestic war, a disguised threat of abandonment intended to intimidate. Gradually it may come to be seen as a realistic alternative to the continued abrasion of the marriage. The man or woman may begin to look appraisingly at "Apartment for Rent" notices in the windows of real estate offices, to think about how the furniture might be divided, to wonder how the children might be told. Now separation may be mentioned not just during quarrels but at other times as well.

Yet as separation approaches, each spouse may become anxious at the prospect. One woman described her feelings in this way:

**When the idea occurred to me that I could live without Dave and be happier, my immediate next feeling was just gut fear. It's really hard to explain. It was just terror. I would think that you would start feeling happy if you would feel you could maybe make a better life without somebody. But my whole instinct was just fear.**

**(Woman, about thirty)**

It is natural that the thought of separation frightens people. Separation means starting over, alone. It means setting off without the partner on whom one has, perhaps for years, relied. It means new vulnerability, and perhaps isolation and loneliness. One cannot anticipate everything it will mean, and this too can be frightening.

The couple may recognize how moribund their marriage is, how close to expiration. They may not be sure from week to week that it will continue. Planning for the future can now become mired in uncertainty: "If we are together, we might go to the beach for a week at the end of the summer. Do you think we should rent a place?" It is easier not to plan at all.

There may be impulsive, only partially intended separations. The husband may walk out and return; the wife may call her closest friends to say that it is all over and then call again to say that she was mistaken. Fights and separations and reconciliations may follow hard on one another. The couple may find that they can neither live with one another nor give one another up.

**We are talking, my husband and myself, and we know we've got to make a final decision, and you know, it has led to blows and all kinds of other things. It has led also to very sane talk at the same time. I keep going over and over in my head what is really the best thing to do. When I'm away from home, my head says to me I should separate, and when I'm back in the home scene, even though I see a lot of things that are wrong, I see other things that hold me. A fifteen-year marriage is a long time. And it is just very hard to kiss it goodbye. And the closer you get to the breakup, the harder it is.**

**(Woman, about forty, still married)**

There may be conflict over the separation itself: one partner may want the marriage to continue, while the other wants to pull away:

**I remember going to a marriage counselor at that time and I said, "Gee, at this stage of the game you'd think we could talk to each other and work something out compatible to both of us." And he said, "My dear, it takes two and he just does not want to be married."**

**(Woman, late forties)**

Because of the uncertainty of their situation, and because they dislike planning things together, the couple may almost stop asking friends to their home. In turn their friends, newly uncomfortable with them, may be hesitant to invite them. Before the separation actually takes place, they may feel themselves isolated, no longer a part of their previous social world.

Now the husband and wife may try a separation within the home, each going places alone, sleeping alone. Because each is withdrawn and inaccessible to the other, each becomes lonely even though both remain in the same house. Or their separateness may be incomplete, established enough to remind them that things are going badly, but interrupted as their need for one another becomes overwhelming.

**We are sleeping in separate bedrooms. It is helping to establish the fact that we have got to do something about the problem. But there are still invitations, and sometimes we wind up in the same bed.**
                    **(Woman, about forty, still married)**

There may be fights, the style varying from marriage to marriage but often sudden and violent, shattering to the emotional equilibrium of each spouse, forcing each to wonder about his or her stability, frightening them both and alienating them from themselves and each other. And in the intervals between fights a war of attrition may be waged: abrasive, demeaning, embarrassing before the children.

The children become a cause for worry. What should they be told? When? By whom? Can they be shielded from the tension? Sometimes it is only when the children grow withdrawn or tense because of the deteriorating marriage that the parents finally decide that they must act, that they cannot inflict their own distress on their children.

Not all failing marriages follow this course. In some marriages one partner feels compelled to leave to find freedom or growth or self-realization, and the other sadly, but with understanding, agrees. These may be marriages in which anger has been dissipated in rational discussion, and the couple can almost cooperatively set about establishing separate households.

**Right now we're just friends. We're not sleeping together. But we live in the same house. He goes to work, he kisses me in the morning, calls me in the afternoon, kisses me goodnight. And as soon as the house is sold, we're separating. I'm really not as upset as I was last month. Whether or not I have accepted it, I don't know yet.**
                    **(Woman, mid-thirties, still living with husband)**

Other marriages end without warning, when one partner departs suddenly, after the briefest of explanations, leaving the other partner dumbfounded and desolate. One man was surprised to be told by his wife that she was unhappy and wanted a divorce. By the following morning she had packed and was gone.

**I didn't know anything was really wrong. It was like a bomb dropping. Oh, we had been married a lot of years, and I knew we had a couple of problems, but I would say, "I feel sorry for all these people who are married and the marriage gets very dull. We still love each other." And we did, you know, in terms of sex. That is why it was such a bomb falling on me. Now I see it was there all the time, but our way of communicating was so poor that it just never got to me.**
**(Man, late thirties)**

Most separations, however, are neither amicable nor unanticipated. Rather they come about only after a long and anguished process of mutual alienation from which both partners emerge bruised, their morale depleted, their self-esteem low, their ability to function damaged by the varied assaults of the failing marriage.

*Attacks on Self-Assurance*

All married couples have interchanges in which one spouse acts to dampen the anxiety or enthusiasm of the other by questioning or denying an appraisal made by the other. For example, one spouse might try to assuage the other's worry about the hours their adolescent children keep by saying, "I don't think we have to be that concerned. We stayed out just as late when we were their age." In marriages in which the husband and wife have scores to even, however, this dampening feedback normal to marriage moves to bickering. Each questions the other's assertions almost automatically, and the questioning is often implicitly derogatory: "Can't you trust anybody at all, not even your own children?"

Systematic invalidation of a spouse's perceptions and concerns, even without the added freight of derogation, can be disabling. The film *Gaslight* turned on a husband's deliberate attempt to weaken his wife's confidence in her perceptions by (among other techniques) secretly dimming the lights and then insisting that there had been no change. Participants in a failing marriage can, without conscious intent, subject one another to similar sorts of systematic invalidation. Each may question not only the other's judgment but also the other's memory of what each promised the other before their marriage, of what rules they agreed on for the children, of what happened on their last vacation.

Bickering may contain comments intended to diminish the spouse, motivated by the desire to reduce the spouse's capacity to hurt, for a diminished, invalidated spouse may seem less dangerous. And so the husband becomes critical of the wife's housekeeping and cooking, her appearance and sexual performance, her mothering, relationships with friends, ability as a decorator and hostess, and quality as a human being. And the wife becomes critical of the husband as a father, provider, companion, sexual partner, mate, and person. Each provides the other with criticisms of the other's frailties, often reaching back to observations each had made earlier in the marriage and resolutely suppressed. Now the cruel comments come tumbling out, one after another.

Rejection assumes almost endless forms, appearing now as open disapproval, now as wit or kidding. All-out confrontations are interspersed with random sniping; as one man put it, "We kept needling each other." And discontent may be expressed in still other ways: in an ironic tone of voice, in icy politeness, in wary or unfriendly glances, in silence and avoidance.

Neither spouse can entirely discount the other's disparaging appraisals. Eventually the man may find himself partially agreeing that he is self-centered, unable to care for others, immature, and irresponsible; the woman may almost accept that she is slovenly, cold, unsupportive, or competitive with men. Each spouse is likely to tailor the indictments to the other's actual characteristics, and may draw support for them from confidences given in better times. Thus, the indictments are difficult to shrug off: They seem to be based on strong evidence; they are made by the person in the best position to know; and they are repeated at every opportunity.

My husband asked me how this group was going. I said, "Fine, I really like it, and I'm really getting a lot out of it." And he said, "Gee, I'm surprised. You're so cold and distant with me, I'm surprised you can relate to anyone."

(Woman, about thirty)

The husband and wife may have still another compelling reason to lose trust in themselves and, especially, in their own judgment: the fact that they entered the marriage to begin with. If contracting this marriage is a sample of their judgment, they may think, they clearly can't be trusted to cross the street. Furthermore, they may suspect they are idiots to put up with it. To clinch matters, they may recognize their desire to repair their marriage, to conciliate, to talk things out, even though every similar effort in the past has led to further bitterness and hostility.

By the time they actually separate, both husband and wife badly need the reassurance provided by a trustworthy supportive relationship. But the failing marriage may have so shaken their belief in their acceptability that for some time afterward they may not entirely credit affection and respect displayed toward them.

### Betrayal in the Failing Marriage

In our society it is assumed that married individuals act as an economic and social unit, a partnership, sharing economic gain or loss, social position, and social esteem, and therefore we expect them to be loyal to one another and to protect one another's interests. Husbands and wives share this expectation: Whatever the state of feeling between them, they believe, each should be able to count on the other not to broadcast embarrassing information, not to demean him or her before others, to be on his or her side in a dispute with a neighbor or with kin. In a failing marriage this normal expectation that the spouse will be a trustworthy ally tends to be frustrated in small and sometimes large respects. Spouses may tell friends damaging stories "in confidence," may publicly display their disrespect or dislike, and may be sympathetic to the other side of a conflict.

A failing marriage offers endless temptations to minor betrayals:

(30)

responding with blame rather than comfort to the spouse's story of a disastrous day; withholding support from a spouse embroiled in a dispute with the children; or refusing to accompany the spouse to a party given by the spouse's family, friends, or colleagues. Simply trying to maintain one's own equilibrium by explaining to others how one feels may constitute a minor betrayal, since to let kin and friends know that the marriage is in trouble violates the understanding that one spouse will withhold from outsiders information embarrassing to the other.

There may be large betrayals, too, notably infidelity. But why is infidelity so regularly treated as a betrayal, an attack by someone previously trusted? Most of us are so accustomed to this interpretation that we fail to recognize that it needs explaining.

Of critical importance, certainly, is the symbolic meaning of a sexual relationship. Sexual accessibility implies to us emotional accessibility; therefore when a husband or wife learns that the spouse is sexually accessible to another, the spouse's emotional commitment becomes questionable. Further, the spouse's sexual involvement with another suggests that the husband or wife is sexually inadequate. Still further, the affair not only implicitly disparages the wronged husband or wife but suggests indifference to the potential damage this disparagement may inflict on his or her standing among others and self-esteem.

To the extent that the unfaithful husband or wife has become emotionally engaged with the third person, the wronged spouse may be isolated emotionally. The unfaithful husband or wife may be preoccupied, at times remote, his or her thoughts absorbed by the affair. The wronged spouse is being left out and may sense this, if not actually recognize it consciously.

As was noted earlier, infidelity tends to be accompanied by duplicity. Almost inevitably the wronged spouse will have been lied to, given false explanations for evening or weekend hours spent away from home, for changes in mood or manner or style of dress for which the affair is responsible. Indeed, carrying on a secret affair in itself constitutes a major deception. The wronged spouse may now and again recognize instances of deceit. The eventual consequence is an erosion of his or her ability to believe anything the other says or to trust his or her own capacity to distinguish truth from falsehood.

After my husband left I screamed and yelled that I wanted him back. "I don't care what you do, just don't go see her. Come back. Everything will be fine." So there was a whole year of just lies, terrible, terrible lies. Then finally I said, "Please, just tell me the truth." Everytime he left the house he left me in hysterics, crying.

I still love him. But I have decided that if he ever decided to come back, it can't be. I can't just take him back, even if he came back, and start over again. Who knows, after being lied to for so long, whether I could ever believe him.

(Woman, mid-thirties)

But while lying is injurious to the spouse in many ways, informing him or her of the affair may be no better. For one thing, it suggests a callous disregard for the spouse's feelings.

The first reactions of husbands and wives on learning of a spouse's affair are often similar to reactions to a spouse's sudden departure from the marriage. Indeed, for the reasons already given, being informed of infidelity is equivalent to learning of the loss of an attachment figure, in which the individual responsible for the loss *is* the attachment figure. Infidelity is partial abandonment. One woman said that when she learned of her husband's affair she shook all over. Another woman cried uncontrollably for days. A man was both physically ill and furious.

Later the wronged spouse may be intensely angry not only with the betraying spouse but also with the third person. The two have colluded to remove a critically important figure from his or her life. One woman was amazed at the intensity of her fury. Nothing in her past had prepared her for it.

I've never felt this way about another human being. Even my aunt who raised me after my mother died, who abused me, beat me, for ten years, I never felt that way about her. I can't understand it. I have urges I never dreamed I'd have.

(Woman, mid-thirties)

The wronged spouse's anger with the third member of the marital triangle may be especially strong if the third person had an independent relationship to the wronged spouse: if the third person was a friend or neighbor or coworker. Then two relationships are lost at once, and two sectors of the wronged spouse's life become immediately painful.

**Not only do I feel bad about my wife, but one of the things that I really enjoy, that sort of sustained me a little bit, was this club that I belong to, and this guy is in the club. I know that I can't go back to that club because if I do I'll kill him, I'll physically destroy him.**
**(Man, late forties)**

The anger felt by the wronged spouse is likely to be intensified by the injury done to his or her self-esteem. He or she has been made a fool. Certainly the other man or other woman, this new ally of the faithless spouse, must be triumphant. The husband or wife may want to know just how extensive the betrayal was: What was the third person told about him or her? There may be an intense desire to become equally knowledgeable, to insist on one's right as a spouse to learn about the details of the affair.

Even a brief sexual contact without emotional implications can shake some marriages. The wronged spouse may feel that the other's commitment can no longer be trusted. What if another opportunity should present itself? In addition, almost any infidelity, apart from its implications for the trustworthiness of the marital alliance, raises issues of fairness. At the time one was conscientiously meeting one's own obligations to the marriage, the spouse was playing around: While the woman was home, tending to the dirty dishes and runny noses, her husband was with another woman; or while the man was hard at work, earning the money to support her, his wife was with another man. There may be rivalry with the spouse, expressed as resentment that the spouse has more freedom or more opportunity for self-indulgence.

### Reluctance to Separate

Despite the injuries the partners inflict on one another in a disintegrating marriage, separation is ordinarily accepted only after long and anguishing debate. Indeed, it is because partners are loath to separate that they remain together so long, despite the discomforts they suffer.

We are still living together. We can't live with each other and we can't live without each other. The sexual thing is a very powerful force between us. It has always worked very, very well. But everything is antagonistic. It is weird . . . .
   It is really a crazy, mixed-up thing. Because I love him, but I know I can't live with him, and I know it is going to destroy us both if we don't break up. I want to have the strength to make a decision. We both know it has been impossible, and we both don't want to be the one to initiate the final break. And yet we know that it is necessary.
   (Woman, about forty)

Sex is not the only bond holding a disintegrating marriage together. The couple may feel a need for one another that may appear almost mysterious in origin.

I lived through a celibate marriage for two years, and yet I didn't want him to leave. Now you figure that one out! I still to this day can't figure out why I didn't want him to leave, and yet I didn't! I don't know. There's something missing without a man in the house.
   (Woman, early forties)

Even when the couple finally decide to live apart, they may almost immediately negate their decision by brief reconciliations, or even briefer returns to one another that are understood as not undoing the separation. The marriage seems not to have ended but rather to have entered a new phase—one that is odd and obviously unstable.

He'd been talking about leaving and he had this woman, and all this kind of crap. And just one night we had an awful fight, and he left. And I wanted him to come back, and then we did things like spend holidays together, all that sort of stuff. But just recently I thought, "Gosh, do I really want this?"
   (Woman, about thirty)

Eventually couples tend to move either toward reconciliation or toward a complete break. The on-again, off-again arrangement is too painful to be sustained.

(34)

I've been on a yo-yo. My wife would come up for the weekend and wow, we'd have a hell of a time. And then Monday she'd go back to her school, leaving me with the children. And I know she has somebody there. And then I wouldn't hear anything, no phone call. So I would say, "Jesus, it must have been lousy." I must have been a terrible lover, or I just didn't do this right or that right or, you know, all kinds of thoughts go through your head. And you feel really lousy. And no phone calls, no nothing. And this went on until just recently. And then she came up and she was in such a hurry to get back that I said, "Once you leave, just stay away."

(Man, late thirties)

Although there are exceptions, the majority of separating couples began with love for one another and only after a time did their marriage become unhappy. What happened to their initial love? And, when it is gone, why do they remain so important to one another? These questions are considered in the next chapter.

# 3

# The Erosion of Love and the Persistence of Attachment

He, who was the cause of my despair, was the only available human being, the only person I felt close to.
(Woman, mid-forties)

I am at once torn between the desire to be free of all the drudgery and bitterness of this marriage and an incredible fear of separation and loneliness.
(Woman, early twenties, contemplating separation)

*Man, early forties:* Isn't it amazing how much our sense of security, identity, and self-esteem seem to depend upon this relationship with one person?
*Woman, mid-thirties:* It shouldn't. It should be possible for a person to be strong enough that they don't need another person to fullfill themselves or to complete their lives.
*Woman, mid-thirties:* But it does.

## Love

By the time a couple separate, their fondness for one another will in large part have been dissipated. The other's faults will be as clear as his or her virtues; trust may have given way to mistrust; identification may have changed to alienation; instead of desire to be nurturant or supportive to the other there may be anger and the wish to be revenged. The couple may wonder how the fondness that was once present could have been so totally lost; they may question whether it ever existed. But although their love for one another has faded, oddly enough their sense of connection, of being emotionally bound to the other, may remain. They may still thrill at the sight of the other; they may still feel comfortable only when with the other. This may be true even though they squabble whenever they talk. Yet how perplexing: Why, after all that happened, with all the bitterness they feel, with so much of their love entirely gone, should a feeling of connection remain?

This is the question to which this chapter addresses itself. It is not a question that can be answered with certainty in the present state of social psychological knowledge. But it is possible to offer a tentative explanation.

Most marriages begin with the two partners believing that they love one another,[1] although cautious young people, perhaps aided by parental guidance, may arrange to fall in love with individuals who appear suitable marital choices on grounds of similarity of background and brightness of promise. Feelings that would otherwise be called love, if directed toward someone apparently unsuitable, may be disparaged as "infatuation." Love may not be the only reason for marriage, but by and large those who marry declare themselves to be in love and give every evidence that their declaration is honest.

When we examine what young people, and others, mean by "love," the term appears to refer to a complex of attitudes and emotional states, but not always to the same complex. Emotions and attitudes that together constitute one instance of "love" may be quite different from those that constitute another. Different people may mean quite different things by "love" and, indeed, the same people may mean different things at different points in their lives. For example, one instance of "love" might include regard for the other approaching idealization, whereas another might in-

---

[1] This assertion is supported by studies we have conducted at the Laboratory of Community Psychiatry, including a study of courtship directed by Dr. Rhona Rapoport as well as my own work with the separated and bereaved. The assertion seems to me to be true for working-class couples as well as middle-class couples, although the stresses on an inadequately funded marriage may hasten the erosion of love within it. See also William J. Goode, "The Theoretical Importance of Love," *American Sociological Review* 24, no. 1 (February, 1959): 38–47.

clude no idealization at all, but instead a nurturant indulgence of the other's frailties.

"Love" appears to be a term we use to convey that the accessibility of the other seems important to our well-being, and that, in addition, reasons for positive regard, such as respect, admiration, or desire to nurture, are present. These "reasons for positive regard" can be of different kinds, and generally more than one is present at a time.[2] The particular combination of elements may be unique to an individual experience.

One among the forms of positive regard that may enter into love is a sense that the other person is as good or capable or trustworthy as is possible. The underlying mechanism of such *idealization* undoubtedly involves projection onto the other of some aspect of one's wished-for self. Although there are different kinds of idealization, depending on what aspect of the wished-for self is projected, any of them may make the individual feel that association with the idealized figure is self-enhancing.

Another form of positive regard may be *trust*, unquestioning belief in the other's commitment. Being with someone trusted allays anxiety and, in addition, may augment the individual's feelings of self-assurance; there are now two to deal with whatever arises.

Another possible component of love is *identification*, the sense that one's essential self is associated with the other, so that when the other does well one feels pleased for oneself, and when the other does badly one suffers. If the other seems in need of guidance or nurturance, then caring for the other and seeing the other happy can have the quality of caring for oneself, just as caring for one's children can gratify one's own dependent needs.

There can be a sense of *complementarity*, in which the other is seen as having capacities missing in the self, such as adeptness in social affairs or firmness of purpose, so that association with the

[2] I am indebted for recognition of the componential character of love to Zick Rubin. See his *Liking and Loving: An Invitation to Social Psychology* (New York: Holt, Rinehart and Winston, 1973), chap. 10, "The Nature of Love," esp. pp. 212–216.

other in some way completes the self. Sometimes individuals talking about the loss of someone they love will say, "I feel as though I had lost part of myself." But complementarity may act in another way, too; an individual may be reassured of his or her worth because he or she is needed by the loved one. The ability to remedy the other's incompleteness can also become a part of love.

Each of these elements may be present in some instances of love and absent in others. But in most instances of love one finds *attachment*, a bonding to the other that gives rise to feelings of at-homeness and ease when the other is present or, if not actually present, is felt to be accessible. The integration of attachment seems to account for the sense of no longer being lost or lonely that may accompany the formation of a new love relationship.[3]

In a marriage that is going badly, almost every component of the couple's initial love may come under attack. Idealization is apt to fade under the constant exposure of daily life. Trust may be eroded by small and large disappointments and betrayals. Feelings of identification may give way to a view of the other as critic and antagonist. Instead of feeling reassured and augmented by their relationship, the partners may feel oppressed and diminished by it.

Yet with love seemingly ended, the husband and wife may continue to feel uncomfortable, edgy, or restless when the other is inaccessible. Contrary to what they believe they want, they may be drawn to one another.

I was gone for a week and I came back and I had no intention at all of going home to my wife. I went to a bar and sat there and drank. And, well, at ten o'clock, I decided to go home. . . . And then, Sunday, things started up again: the bickering, the whole thing.

(Man, about forty)

[3] For still other emotional elements that may enter into love, and for further discussion of these, see Lilly Oppenheimer, "Psychodynamics of the Choice of Mate," in *The Marriage Relationship: Psychoanalytic Perspectives*, ed. Salo Rosenbaum and Ian Alter (New York: Basic Books, 1968), pp. 59–69. See also Sigmund Freud, "On Narcissism: An Introduction" and "Contributions to the Psychology of Love: A Special Type of Choice of Object Made by Men," in *Collected Papers*, ed. Ernest Jones, trans. Joan Riviere (New York: Basic Books, 1959), vol. 4, pp. 30–59 and 192–202. See also Rubin, *Liking and Loving*, chap. 10.

Attachment gives rise to a sense that home is where the other is. It persists even in bad marriages, even when the ultimate result of going home is that things start up again.

Because attachment persists, the ending of a marriage—or just the recognition that it is about to end—may give rise to a condition associated with loss of attachment that I call "separation distress." To explain both the persistence of attachment and the character of separation distress, let us consider the nature of attachment.

## A Natural History of Attachment

The presence or at least the accessibility of some specific other person seems necessary for our security almost from the very beginning. Infants at six months of age appear content when their mother is in sight, restless and disturbed when she is absent for some time, or for that matter when she only leaves them through an unaccustomed door—suggesting, presumably, that their previous experience of her regular return is not now applicable.[4]

The attachment figure for infants is not always the mother; fathers or others sometimes serve in this role. And there may be attachment figures in addition to the mother, although the relative importance of secondary attachment figures such as the father (when the mother is a primary figure) or siblings is still uncertain.

[4]My discussion of attachment in children is based on John Bowlby, *Attachment and Loss* (New York: Basic Books, 1969–73), vol. 1, *Attachment*, and vol. 2, *Separation: Anxiety and Anger*. A critical review of recent studies of attachment in infants is presented by Leslie J. Cohen, "The Operational Definition of Human Attachment," *Psychological Bulletin* 81 (April 1974): 207–217. The importance of "the unfamiliar exit" is noted by Milton Kotulchuk, "The Nature of the Child's Tie to His Father" (Ph.D. diss., Harvard University, 1972). Kotulchuk draws on the work of R. Littenberg, S. Tulkin, and J. Kagan, "Cognitive Components of Separation Anxiety," *Developmental Psychology* 6 (1971): 387–388. There has been very little systematic work on attachment in adults. Materials on related topics may be found in C. Murray Parkes, *Bereavement: Studies of Grief in Adult Life* (New York: International Universities Press, 1973), and in Robert S. Weiss, *Loneliness: The Experience of Emotional and Social Isolation* (Cambridge: M.I.T. Press, 1973).

It appears that secondary figures can often function as temporary substitutes for the primary figure, but the extent to which they can replace the primary figure, and the extent to which they may be required figures in their own right, are not known.

Development of attachment behavior as the child moves through the years before adolescence is marked by increased capacity to tolerate separation from the attachment figure, so long as that figure is understood as accessible. A two-year-old taken to the playground can toddle off to explore so long as he is sure that whenever he looks back he will see his mother sitting on the bench where he left her. A somewhat older child may be able to play happily in front of his home, knowing his mother to be within. A still older child can go off to school in the morning and return late in the afternoon without experiencing distress. It is, however, easy to recognize the continued importance to this older child of the accessibility of the mother should the child arrive home to an unexpectedly empty house. If time goes by and the mother still does not appear, the child may experience panic.

Fundamental changes in the functioning of attachment appear to develop in adolescence. There is a progressive, though at times halting and often stressful, withdrawal of attachment from the parents, and development in its place of attachment directed toward peers: perhaps an inseparable best friend, perhaps a peer of the other sex, perhaps a group of peers in which the group is experienced as a single figure. Parents may remain important to the child's security, but in a different way than was true during the child's earlier years. Now they are important because they can provide a firm base from which the child can move into independence; their accessibility may still matter, but not so much.

As the individual emerges from adolescence and begins to establish an adult identity, to become more nearly the person he or she will be as an adult, attachment feelings direct themselves toward someone with whom later life may be shared. In early adolescence there begins a convergence of attachment feelings and sexual strivings, so that the same person might be an object for both. In late adolescence and early adulthood it may in addition be important that a prospective attachment figure be someone compatible with the individual's newly developing identity. The prospective figure will have to make sense as a life partner, given the person the individual is and wants to be. Indeed, the attachment choice may help to crystallize a particular identity.

There may be two or more attachment figures in early adulthood. Each time an attachment relationship ends, no matter how sensible its ending may be, there are likely to be feelings of desolation and self-questioning. Eventually most individuals marry, and with marriage assume that finally they are assured a permanently accessible attachment figure. This belief that marriage will insure the accessibility of the attachment figure is very likely one of the attractions of marriage; disappointment of this belief is one source of bitterness in separation.

### Separation Distress and Loneliness

Just as comfort and a sense of security tend to be associated with the accessibility of an attachment figure, so distress tends to be associated with that figure's inaccessibility. Among infants a sense of the attachment figure's almost immediate availability seems necessary to fend off distress. As individuals mature, they increasingly can tolerate separation in time and space if the attachment figure's accessibility when needed is assured.

Separation distress is a response to intolerable inaccessibility of the attachment figure. It is displayed in a child by withdrawal of attention from other matters, by tension, sadness, and perhaps tears. There may be pining for the lost figure, or angry or tearful demands for its return. The child may become diffusely apprehensive, worried by both noise and stillness. The child may resist falling into sleep and may wake early. If separation is protracted the child may enter into despair.

Many of these same symptoms, perhaps less obvious in their expression, occur in adult separation distress. And in both child and adult there may be anger with the attachment figure, who may be seen as somehow responsible for the separation.[5]

Until adolescence, separation distress is a response to a parental absence. With adolescence and the relinquishing of parents as attachment figures, separation distress can be experienced on loss of a new attachment figure. The relinquishment of parents as attachment figures also provides opportunity for there to be a total lack of attachment figures; beginning in adolescence it becomes possible for there to be no figure in an individual's life whose accessibility would provide the comfort and security associated with attachment. The parents will not serve, and no replacement may have appeared. The adolescent can now experience all the symptoms of separation distress, but without an object. This is *loneliness*. The symptoms of loneliness are like those of separation distress, except that instead of pining for a particular figure the individual pines for anyone who could love and be loved, and instead of angrily or tearfully demanding the return of a particular figure, the individual laments the barrenness of the world.

With adolescence, then, individuals become able to experience loneliness as well as separation distress.[6] This capacity remains through their later lives. The ending of a love affair—or a marriage—may in consequence first produce separation distress, and then, as the other is relinquished as an object of attachment, loneliness.

## The Persistence of Attachment

Children become attached to parents whatever the parents' characteristics, so long as the parents are adequately accessible and attentive. It does not matter to the intensity of the children's attachment, though it may matter greatly in the development of

[5] Bowlby, *Attachment and Loss*, vol. 2. See esp. "Prototypes of Human Sorrow," pp. 3–24.

[6] See Harry Stack Sullivan, *The Interpersonal Theory of Psychiatry* (New York: W. W. Norton, 1953), p. 290.

their personalities, whether their parents are reliable, consistently loving, or considerate of the children's health and welfare. Nor does it matter whether the children admire their parents or even whether they feel friendly toward them. Children who are battered and bruised by parents will continue to feel attached to them. Attachment, like walking or talking, is an intrinsic capacity that is developed under appropriate circumstances; it is not willed into being after a calculation of its advantages.

In a similar fashion, attachment seems to develop regularly in marriage so long as the spouse is adequately accessible and attentive. Most of those who marry have become attached to one another during their courtship, and most of the remainder become attached early in marriage. The highly charged positive emotions of courtship and early marriage may facilitate the development of attachment. So, it would seem, does the constant mutual accessibility and relative inaccessibility to others imposed by marriage. In truth, however, we know little about the processes by which attachment is formed. We do know that marriages without attachment are exceptional: A study of widows and widowers, middle-aged or younger, found no more than 5 percent who had not suffered intense grief, in which separation distress was a major component, on the death of their spouse.[7] "Empty shell" marriages seem to be rare.

Once developed, attachment seems to persist. Even when marriages turn bad and the other components of love fade or turn into their opposites, attachment is likely to remain. The spouses resemble battered children in their feelings: They may be angry, even furious, with one another; they may hate one another for past injuries and fear one another's next outburst of rage; after a quarrel they may find consolation in fantasies of confrontation and revenge in which they imagine themselves saying, "You can just take your things and get out of here" or "Don't try to find me because I'm not coming back." But when they actually consider leaving their marriage they become almost paralyzed with fear.

The continued attachment of each spouse makes it possible for

[7] Ira O. Glick, Robert S. Weiss, and C. Murray Parkes, *The First Year of Bereavement* (New York: Wiley-Interscience, 1974).

the other to use threat of separation as a weapon. Each can provoke separation distress in the other by the threat that if the other does not change, if things go on as they have, the marriage will be over. The threat is, of course, two-edged; the separation, if it came, would hurt both parties. But there is security in being the one momentarily in control of the possibility of separation.

Some couples attempt to undo their attachment to one another while still living together. They agree that each must be free to go his or her own way, without obligation to the other, and therefore that neither must rely on the other. Or they may insist to themselves that emotional separation has already occurred. This stance may provide protection from the other's threats, but at the cost of painful loneliness; the marriage, although itself empty of attachment, remains as a barrier to formation of new attachment. Men and women who were emotionally alienated from their spouses during the last months of their marriages later report that they have at no other time been so lonely as they were then.

In most marriages headed for separation the partners seem not to relinquish their attachment for one another. It would be too painful to do so, and even if they wanted to, they cannot control their feelings. But often for reasons of pride, because of hurt and anger, or from impulses toward self-protection, they attempt to hide their attachment behind a mask of indifference. Yearning for the other may nevertheless at times break through and result in a declaration of need if not love, which may in turn lead to a temporary and grudging reconciliation. Or there may be quarrels in which anger is fueled by feelings of rejection, and in which an undertone to bitter accusations is a plea that the other change and become loving.

Often individuals in marriages they believe to be hopeless, who recognize their continued attachment to a spouse they feel they must leave, curse themselves for their weakness and dependence. They should not. Attachment can be extraordinarily resistive to dissipation. Even individuals who have been long separated, who believe their marriages to be finished and have found someone new, may discover on meeting the spouse that dormant feelings of attachment are reawakened.

The following story was told by a woman who had left her husband after years of almost desperate unhappiness. She had not seen him for about a month and then had seen him twice on succeeding days in her lawyer's office.

**Wednesday afternoon I had the second of two conferences with my husband and his lawyer and my lawyer and myself. At the end of the second one I told my lawyer that I was not going to do that any more. In preparation for seeing him I had gotten myself as beautiful as I could. And I felt that as long as my husband was in the room, I felt protected, and that it was just the two of us, not the lawyers. And, midnight, I was sitting in bed, eating vegetable soup, my first meal of the day, and I wanted to call him and say, "What a colossal mistake we've made. I only feel together when I'm with you."**

The potential for such an experience appears to remain, no matter how much time passes. One respondent in our study of single parents felt a happy, hopeful, excitement, despite her better judgment, when her husband called her after a three-year disappearance. (What she expressed to him in the phone call, however, was her anger with him for his disappearance and his equally unfeeling attempt to start things up again.) Attachment seems, at least in many individuals, to have an imprinted quality; once a certain other has been accepted as an attachment figure, that person can again elicit attachment feelings, at least until he or she is understood as having become intrinsically different. At that point the individual may be able to say, as did a single parent mother who claimed that she no longer had any feeling for her former husband, "I loved him once, but he was a different person then."

# 4

# Distress, Euphoria, and Other Emotional Reactions to Loss of Attachment

I'd start with an anxiety attack, about five o'clock in the morning, like if I would have it early enough, then by nine o'clock I would be ready to go to work.

(Woman, late twenties, separated about five months)

The marriage has been going badly for months or years until the couple can endure it no longer and the husband leaves for a motel or a friend's apartment, or the wife packs the children and a few clothes and goes to stay with her mother or sister or a friend. Or the separation may have resulted from a different process. The couple may have accepted sadly that one or both would be happier alone, and they then together looked for a room or apartment to which one of them could move. Or just one member of the couple may have planned the separation. In one instance the wife secretly rented an apartment and then chose a propitious moment to tell her husband that she was going; in another the husband mentioned to an older child that he was leaving, and the child then broke the news to his mother.

What happens next? Among those for whom the separation was unexpected, who had no reason for imagining it might happen until the spouse announced his or her departure, there may be a brief period of shock and disbelief. But for most people, separation almost at once ushers in a time of upset, both emotional and social.

## Separation Distress

A man in his mid-forties who had left home at his wife's insistence kept a diary of the first days of his separation. On one of those days he had returned home to pick up some clothes and to see his children. He had hoped that while there he might somehow engineer a reconciliation, but he had no more than suggested to his wife that they talk out their differences than they were again in a fight. The following excerpt from his diary describes his feelings after that encounter:

My hands are shaky. I want to call her again but I know it is no good. She'll only yell and scream. It makes me feel lousy. I have work to do but I can't do it. I can't concentrate. I want to call people up, go see them, but I'm afraid they'll see that I'm shaky. I just want to talk. I can't think about anything besides this trouble with Nina. I think I want to cry.

I just went to make myself some coffee. I hardly knew what I was doing. I tried to drink it and couldn't, and poured it down the sink. I started out to walk, changed my mind, started out to walk again, changed my mind again.

The only thing I seem to be able to do is to write this. As long as I'm concentrating on how I feel, I feel almost all right. I wonder why. I'm scared. I feel almost hunted.

This is separation distress. It is marked by a focusing of attention on the lost figure, together with intense discomfort because of that figure's inaccessibility. There is likely to be unhappiness stemming from feelings of desolation. There may also be apprehensiveness, anxiety, or panic.

Because of his or her discomfort and frustration, the individual is readily angered. A later entry from the same diary describes this:

I got into a shouting match with a counterman at the cafeteria over having to wait to be served. That's not like me. I've gotten short-tempered. I don't give a damn. I *want* a fight, almost. Maybe I can forget the misery if I'm fighting. I realized I was taking it out on the poor guy and I stopped. But I can't take much more. I'm close to spilling over.

(48)

As is noted in the preceding chapter, separation distress is an analogue in the adult to the child's response to threat of abandonment. A few among the newly separated recognize the correspondences:

When my husband left I had this panicky feeling which was out of proportion to what was really happening. I was afraid I was being abandoned. I couldn't shake the feeling.

I remembered later that the first time I had that feeling was when I had pneumonia and my mother left me in the hospital, in a private room, in the winter. And this picture came back of this huge hospital and these old gray rooms and it was winter and every night at five o'clock, when the shadows would come across my bed, my mother would put on her coat and say, "Goodbye, I will see you tomorrow." And I had such a feeling of panic and fear at being left.

(Woman, about thirty)

Separation distress stems from the inaccessibility of a specific person, the spouse, rather than simply from being alone. It may be relieved, but is unlikely to be cured, by finding someone new. A man whose wife had left him after a stormy marriage and who thereupon traveled across the continent to see a former girlfriend was nevertheless assailed by separation distress:

Here I was, three days with someone of the opposite sex, trying to start rebuilding, and I just got overwhelmed with panic at being three thousand miles from Laura. And these waves built up until I was just white. It is an unbearable feeling.

The specific symptoms of separation distress are, as was noted in Chapter 3, understandable as responses to the inaccessibility of the figure to whom the individual is attached. *Apprehensiveness, anxiety, fear, or panic* are expressions of the individual's sense of new vulnerability. In reality the individual may be no less equipped to cope with threat than had been true when the spouse was present, but to the individual's emotional understanding a security-providing partner has been lost.

Apprehensiveness and related states give rise to *tension and vigilance*. The individual is alert to promise of relief or threat of

(49)

attack. Loss of confidence in the self may increase foreboding and consequent tension.

Tension and vigilance often produce *difficulties in sleeping*, which then lead to further distress. The individual lies wide awake in bed for what seems hours. When sleep finally comes, it may be fitful and end with waking at four or five in the morning. Some attempt to overcome these sleep difficulties with tranquilizers or barbiturates or alcohol. Others prefer to battle sleeplessness rather than risk addiction. And some find that not even drugs will work. The following is one woman's report:

I am having the most vicious time, not because of anything going wrong in my life especially; there seems to be no problem, except I can't sleep. I can't sleep, and it keeps building and building until I feel really absolutely devastated. I function all right in my job. And I try to schedule things every evening, social things, things like that. But even when I think I've done well, I still can't sleep at night. And I feel awful.

It gets to be just so unbelievably terrifying to believe that you are not going to be able to get to sleep. I've taken sleeping pills and they don't work. And that is so unbelievably terrifying, that they don't work. It just shows the power that your mind has over your body, that these things don't work at all.

There may be other expressions of tension, including appetite loss (though some combine this with compulsive nibbling), irritability, and susceptibility to sudden anger or sudden tears. Some report increased use of alcohol, apart from its possible value as a soporific, and also of cigarettes.

The individual may be unable to concentrate attention on matters unrelated to the separation. Tasks requiring sustained, thoughtful attention cannot be completed. Driving may become less skillful; some among the separated report having minor auto accidents for the first time in their lives.

Throughout, the spouse and the unhappy marital relationship occupy the separated individual's mind. Many among the separated report pining for the spouse, though they may ruefully admit they cannot understand why they should.

*First man:* I remember all the good things in my marriage. Really the good things occupied only 5 percent of the whole time, but

> when I think about it they occupy nearly 100 percent of what
> I think.
> *Second man:* I miss the things I didn't have. But I still miss them.
> *First man:* I had things, but they were very transient. But I still miss
> her. Even though I know perfectly well we are never going to
> get together again.

Many want to hear about their husbands or wives, to learn how
they are doing. If they learn that the spouse is seeing someone new,
they may be deeply hurt. If they accidentally encounter the spouse,
they feel excitement, almost a thrill. Should the spouse be among
those at a party, or in the audience at a public event, even though
some distance away, they can direct their attention to little else.

They may seek reassurance that the spouse remains accessible,
without quite recognizing that it is this reassurance they are seeking. It is not unusual for a separated man to attempt to relax in
the evening by going for a walk or a drive that happens to take
him down the street on which his wife now lives. Nor is it unusual
for a separated woman to call her husband because she misses him,
but when he answers find another reason for the call, perhaps
concern regarding the children, or anger because a support check
has not arrived.

Separation also often produces episodes of deep sadness and
regret for the lost chances of happiness. And although we cannot
be sure that the separation should be held responsible, severe depression is much more frequent among those who have recently
been separated than among individuals of similar ages and socioeconomic status who have not.[1] What is not clear is whether the
separation produced the depression or whether early symptoms of
depression produced the separation. The accounts we have of
failed marriages suggest that depression can burden a marriage in
many ways: the depressed spouse is likely to appear ungratified
by the marriage, to have limited energy for the give and take of

---

[1] This was the finding of a study of hospitalized depressives and a matched
sample of individuals living in the community. About 12 percent of the hospitalized
depressives had separated in the six months preceding the date of their hospitaliza-
tion, compared with just 1 percent of the matched sample. See Eugene S. Paykel
et al., "Life Events and Depression," *Archives of General Psychiatry* 21, December
1969: 753–760.

family life, and to be sufficiently withdrawn to make the other spouse feel uncared for. The failing marriage may then produce an upsurge in quarreling that itself fosters depression, even without separation having taken place.[2]

There are a number of reasons why marital separation might increase the likelihood of depression. Feelings of worthlessness that are residues from the battering of the failing marriage, and perhaps from rejection at the hands of the spouse, may be intensified by separation distress. It is easy to blame one's abandonment on oneself, to believe that one was abandoned because of one's own unacceptability.

**There's somebody that knows you the best of anyone, and because of that knowledge he has made a decision about you, and you just have this idea that if everybody else knew you as well as he did, they too would feel the same way.**

(Woman, about thirty)

Blaming the self may be self-protective—if one already blames oneself, additional criticism has been robbed of much of its power to hurt. Or it may be felt to be propitiating toward the spouse. "Look how terrible I feel," the spouse who is depressed seems to say. "How can you be angry at me?" Or blaming the self can in its own way be a form of retaliation: "See how thoroughly you have convinced me that it was my fault. Aren't you ashamed?" All these maneuvers may take place without the spouse being physically present to witness them. The internalized image of the spouse may be witness enough.

A variety of losses may contribute further to depression. There may be perceived or actual loss of social standing as a consequence of the separation. Some, because of lessened access to friends, may feel they have become like pariahs. Inevitable material losses may remove much of what the individual had achieved in years of struggle: income, property, savings, perhaps home, car, and articles of furniture. The parent who relinquishes custody may lose access to the children.

The fact that the world of the separated individual may be

[2] Ibid.

without social supports can give to depression a most dangerous edge. Many among the separated have suicidal fantasies. Some plan future suicides only as a way of cajoling themselves through a miserable present: "In two months, if things don't improve, I can always turn on the gas." But some are quite serious. They feel desperate enough, despairing enough, and angry enough to do it.

## Euphoria

Sometimes loss of attachment gives rise not to separation distress, but rather to its opposite, euphoria; or it may alternate with or be interrupted by euphoria. Some among the separated report that for brief or more extended intervals they felt just marvelous, as though they were walking on air. They had new confidence in themselves, liked themselves better than ever before, and with these changes in self-regard felt that the world was open to them, that anything was possible. Life had become an adventure through which they could confidently sail. They reveled in their sense of freedom.

Individuals caught up in this euphoric mood may be untroubled by minor reverses that might once have left them distraught, such as a parking ticket or a missed appointment. They may become more active and outgoing than they had been before. They may insist that the separation was the best thing they had ever done, and their only regret is that they hadn't done it sooner.

This mood, seemingly so different from separation distress, may yet be connected to it. Here is another excerpt from the diary quoted earlier which suggests how:

For a while last night I thought we were going to get back together. Then she said, "This doesn't change anything." I woke up about four, thinking about this. I wondered what I might have done to provoke it. I couldn't get back to sleep. I got out of bed and made myself follow my morning routine. I straightened out the apartment and washed the dishes. I got dressed and went out. It was still early so I started to walk, instead of taking the bus. It was a brisk, snowy, morning, just after dawn. I suddenly felt happy. I had gotten myself through the night. I was going to see people during the day. I was all right. It was a fine world.

The euphoria results from the appraisal that the attachment figure is not needed after all, that one can do very well alone. It is another way of managing loss, in which the individual rearranges his or her emotions so that the loss is without significance. Instead of needing the other, the individual feels that he or she needs only the self. Furthermore, removal of the other has made available to the self new opportunities for gratification and self-realization.

This euphoria does not generally seem to be an integrated or lasting aspect of the separated individual's personality. A very few report having been sustained by euphoria for a period of months, after which they returned to normalcy without any bad times along the way. Most who experienced euphoria report that it proved fragile; when a reverse was encountered that made them question themselves, it gave way to separation distress or object-less depression. One such reverse might be rejection in a dating situation. Another might be criticism at work. So fragile can euphoria be that some participants in Seminars for the Separated reported its loss just from hearing in a lecture that it might not last.

Sometimes euphoria seems to end spontaneously, perhaps on recognition that life without attachment is unsatisfying. No matter how it ends, it tends to be replaced by separation distress, which includes, among its other symptoms, pining for the former spouse.

I found that I felt quite euphoric for about three months. I sort of did everything that I wanted to do. I hadn't gone out much, so I went to the theatre. I didn't do these things before I was married. I sat in a bar, drinking, just talking to anybody. I met just lots of different people.

After three months and having met just one or two people who were really interesting, I found it was an empty life. I realized that my family meant a great deal to me and that there was no family any more. There was just the kids and myself. And the things I had done with my husband, I could no longer do them.

(Woman, early forties, separated
after a marriage of about twenty years)

When I have talked with individuals describing themselves as euphoric, it has seemed to me that they often displayed tension and anxiety without being aware of it. Sometimes a rush of speech or a nervous mannerism belied their insistence that everything was fine. But euphoria seems to be more than just whistling in the dark; euphoric individuals did appear to be doing more, and managing more effectively, than others. A woman who said in the first months of her separation that she felt on top of the world, two years later described those first months as miserable; yet she seemed unusually active and effective in those first months, despite what later appeared to have been denial of intermittent depression.

There may be two psychological mechanisms involved in the production of euphoria, one which leads the individual to feel independent of the former attachment figure, and one which results in an increase in available energy. The first may be the reorganization of attachment feelings so that they are directed to the self instead of to the former attachment figure. It is as though individuals who were disappointed in their previous attachment now direct attachment feelings to a new figure that is competent and attractive, and, in addition, absolutely trustworthy, because the new figure is themselves. This mechanism might be described as *narcissistic attachment.*

Accompanying narcissistic attachment may be the release of energy that had been previously absorbed during the unhappy marriage by attempts to avoid confrontations (or survive those not avoided) and by worry and despair. Ordinarily, separation distress is able to absorb as much energy as did the marriage. Euphoria, by fending off separation distress, may make this energy available for other uses.

Euphoria is certainly a more pleasant state than separation distress, and anyone experiencing it ought to enjoy it while it lasts. Realizing that one is able to keep one's spirits up can contribute to morale and augment self-confidence. To this extent, euphoria can be self-sustaining.

But even though individuals may feel heartened by how well they seem to be doing and may thus be encouraged to continue to do well, postmarital euphoria is inherently fragile. In this lies its danger, for when the individual comes down, he or she comes all the way down. The attachment to self is seen to be without value for security. The world appears suddenly barren, and the individual alone. The resultant distress may be the worse for following so closely a state in which the individual felt entirely self-sufficient.

Some among the separated report a single experience of euphoria which, once ended, did not recur. Others report repeated experiences of euphoria alternating with separation distress. For them separation is a time of extreme volatility in mood, an emotional roller coaster in which their spirits plunge in response to a reverse, soar as self-confidence and self-esteem are renewed, and then plunge again when a new reverse is encountered.

## Loneliness

In Chapter 3 loneliness is described as different from separation distress in that it involves no image of a figure whose accessibility would restore comfort. To put it in a formula, loneliness is separation distress without an object. The separated are vulnerable both to loneliness and to separation distress. Loneliness usually becomes the more prominent as the separation continues.

A second kind of loneliness may be encountered in separation, in addition to this "separation distress without an object." This is the loneliness that is a response to social isolation. To distinguish between the two, the first might be called *loneliness of emotional isolation*, the second *loneliness of social isolation*.[3] The second kind of loneliness is discussed in Chapter 8.

The loneliness of emotional isolation gives rise to symptoms much the same as those of separation distress. These include anxiety, tension, vigilance, and their physical correlates, including sleep difficulties and loss of appetite. In addition, loneliness has symptoms peculiarly its own. The world seems desolate of po-

[3] See Robert S. Weiss, *Loneliness: The Experience of Emotional and Social Isolation* (Cambridge, Mass.: M.I.T. Press, 1973).

tential attachment; it seems barren, silent, dead. Sometimes it is not so much the external world which seems blighted but rather the world within oneself. The community of one's representations of others, one's internal community, has been depleted. The lonely individual may say he or she feels empty or hollow.

Loneliness can give rise to powerful driving forces that may cause individuals to behave in ways usually foreign to them.[4] Both men and women who in their marriages were conservative, even staid, report that under the press of loneliness they have explored singles bars and public dances. Often their experience is that they feel out of place; nevertheless they may return several times before giving up. Or they may enter affairs, appropriate or inappropriate, to gain some respite from loneliness.

Some attempt to escape their loneliness by getting away. Occasionally this works; more often, it would seem, it does not.

I wanted to get away from the situation and be with the kids in another country. So we left the country. I mean we really got away. And the feeling I had was of even more acute loneliness. Like I was walking through Barcelona. The kids didn't want to hang around, and they took off. So I was walking down a street and trying to visit some of the sites. And it was a very kind of empty feeling, having nobody to share any of these places with, not even the kids. It was very hard.

(Woman, early forties)

Friends of long standing who can tolerate the lonely person's unhappiness can sometimes be helpful. Their home may serve as a haven, a place of escape when the walls of an empty house or apartment seem about to close in. But being with friends who are securely coupled can also exacerbate the distress of the lonely by intensifying their feelings of marginality. An evening with married acquaintances can lead the lonely to feel themselves "a fifth wheel," awkward and superfluous. Being with other lonely people, on the other hand, can reduce their feelings of marginality. Even if they do not feel any less lonely as a result of the contact, it can be helpful to know that others are in the same boat.

[4] This is Sullivan's perception. See Harry Stack Sullivan, *The Interpersonal Theory of Psychiatry* (New York: W. W. Norton, 1953).

## Holidays

Certain holidays celebrate family life: Thanksgiving, Christmas, and, for the religious, Easter or Passover. The separated are especially vulnerable to sadness on these days, which, before separation, their family would have spent together. These are times when everyone else seems to be together with family, and the separated may feel themselves to be different from all others in the society—nonparticipants, outsiders.

Holidays are impossible. As a matter of fact there were times when I thought, well, why don't I go do volunteer work at a hospital or something? Just so I not be alone. Or why don't I get a part-time job for those days?

(Woman, about fifty)

If there are children, arranging a holiday celebration may be felt to be a parental responsibility. Provision of a festive Christmas, especially, may be seen as an obligation to one's children. Yet just preparing for the holiday may be depressing.

I found that decorating the tree was just joyless. And I used to love cooking and preparing all those things. This time it was just a big effort. I felt like taking the tree and shoving it right out the window.

(Woman, late thirties)

Actually, children seem better able to accept a changed holiday than their parents. Several participants in Seminars for the Separated reported that their children were perfectly content with two Christmases, one with mother, one with father. It was the parents who found the change to be hard.

I found Christmas to be devastating for me. I was miserable. Christmas was always big for us. We got lots of little gifts and it took four days to unwrap them. It was devastating not to get those little gifts this year.

(Man, late twenties)

This past Christmas was my first Christmas alone, and in addition to having a first Christmas alone, my husband told me he was getting married. I really was crushed.

(Woman, late thirties)

The separated who did best over holidays seemed to be those who spent at least part of the day with other adults. Some shared their parents' holiday. Some temporarily reconstituted their marriages, just for the day. (Chapter 6 briefly presents the generally mixed experiences of those who rejoined their spouse for a holiday.) Those who spent Thanksgiving or Christmas alone seemed to have had the worst time. Christmas especially cannot be shut out of one's life: it declares itself on radio and television, at work, on the street. Not to participate in Christmas means to be joyless, Scrooge-like, rejecting, and rejected. To be with others on Christmas at least defends one from feeling ostracized from life.[5]

Thanksgiving was the hardest holiday for me. Christmas wasn't bad. I dated someone Christmas Eve, and then I went to my sister's Christmas Day.

(Woman, mid-thirties)

## A Note Regarding Work

Certain kinds of work seem to help individuals reduce or avoid some of the pain of separation distress, whereas other kinds may prove all but impossible to accomplish. Work that requires active engagement with others or with a nonintellectual task seems often to be both manageable and helpful. But work that requires solitary concentration may be beyond the individual's powers. Here is one man's description of his reaction to the two kinds of work:

[5] A few among the separated, who have no children, choose to work during Christmas and so free someone else for a Christmas at home. This altruistic behavior is not always rewarded by a sense of having participated indirectly in the other's Christmas; instead it may be felt to be further confirmation of one's difference. See Mark Benney, Robert S. Weiss, Rolf Meyersohn, and David Riesman, "Christmas in an Apartment-Hotel," *American Journal of Sociology* 65 (November 1959): 233–240.

I'm holding two jobs and in one of them I have to go out and talk with all kinds of people and the other one is very technical. The one where I go talk with people, that is easy. I go in, I function, I do all those things. But the other one I just can't do. It has just gone. I just sit there and do nothing.

(Man, about forty)

The mind of an individual who is newly separated returns insistently to the separation and its attendant events. The individual cannot redirect it. *That* is the problem it wants to deal with, not editorial copy or a balance sheet.

Some days I'd go to my office and look at a piece of paper for hours and all of a sudden look up and somebody would come and say, "Hey, it's twelve o'clock, let's go for lunch." And I'd just sit there and look down and I'd just realize that I had got in at nine o'clock and I'd sat there for three hours.

(Man, about thirty)

Jobs that require frequent but superficial engagements with others, however, may be ideally suited to the recently separated. The interactions required by such jobs as administration or selling demand the redirection of attention from the events of the separation, and so may provide some relief from obsessive review. They may also provide reassurance of the individual's continued acceptability. The quality of one's judgment may, however, be reduced temporarily. The man quoted above on the two types of work went on to say that although he could do the "people job," he wasn't confident that he did it well:

The way I was, I would hate like Hell to get on an airplane where the guy flying it was like I was. Because he's not really thinking about what he's doing.

(Man, about forty)

### Factors Affecting Separation Distress

Although most among the separated experience distress at the end of their marriage, there are differences in the intensity, duration, and quality of their distress. On the basis of reports from participants in Seminars for the Separated it seems possible to suggest some determinants of these differences.

*Forewarning*

Separations that occur, not after a long and painful period of marital disharmony, but rather after what had seemed to one partner to be a reasonably satisfactory marriage, appear to be unusually painful for the unprepared partner.

There are any number of ways in which previously unanticipated separations occur. One husband waited until the children were asleep, then said to his wife that he had fallen in love with another woman, with whom he now intended to live. A wife, after weeks of brooding over the callous indifference of her husband, fixed a casserole, put it on the kitchen table, propped a goodbye note against it, and left before her husband returned from work. Another wife had repeatedly been depressed during the marriage until one evening the husband, at wits' end, asked if possibly the marriage itself was to blame; the wife said that it was, and the next morning was gone.

It may seem unbelievable that the husband or wife who is visited by these sudden announcements really could not have anticipated them. Yet individuals whose marriages ended in this way insist that they had no warning, received no hint or threat that they felt they should have taken seriously. And they appeared to be no less sensitive, no more given to denial, than others among the separated. Some of them knew their spouse to be dissatisfied or unhappy, although they did not suspect that the spouse was contemplating departure, but others had thought their marriage a good one—perhaps not as close as some, but reasonably satisfactory—until they were told it was over. Marriage, though it forces husbands and wives to be aware of one another's moods, apparently does not require that they know one another's plans. And most spouses can maintain areas of reserve from one another that make it possible for each to develop plans of which the other has no suspicion.

Individuals abandoned without forewarning often cannot immediately grasp what has happened. It is as though they had been out on a clear sunny day when suddenly everything about them collapsed, and then their footing also gave way.[6] Those who endured the harrowing last months of a failing marriage at least can be grateful that when the marriage ended they knew why. They may feel disoriented on first finding themselves alone, but that is nothing like the shock of unforewarned loss. It can take days for the spouse whose marriage ended without forewarning to accept that it is indeed over. Meanwhile, that spouse is aware that when acceptance comes, he or she will enter into a nightmare.

Not only will individuals who experience an unanticipated separation recover more slowly, but they also will have to surmount special difficulties. They will have to learn that not every organization of their lives is vulnerable to unanticipated devastation. In addition, they may have to overcome a more persistent distrust of their judgment and perceptions than that which confronts other separated individuals.

### Length of Time Married

It would seem reasonable to suppose that the longer a marriage had lasted, the more upsetting to the partners would be its ending. Our experience in Seminars for the Separated suggests that this is only partially true.

Participants in the Seminars who had been married many years did not appear to be more distressed than those who had been married only a few years. However, of the approximately 150 separated individuals who attended the Seminars, few had been married less than two years, and none had been married less than one year. Yet separations in the first or second year of marriage are frequent; indeed, more separations take place in those two years than in any other two-year period. The only possible conclusion is that separation soon after marriage does not give rise to sufficient disruption of social and emotional life (whatever it may

[6] After I used this image in a talk to a community group, a man said, "No, that's not what it's like. It's like you're just there, you know, talking, and everything is all right, and then you're hit on the side of your jaw, and you shake your head and you're hit on the other side of your jaw, and that's it. You're down, and you can't come back."

cost in loss of face) to make a program such as Seminars for the Separated attractive.[7]

We might surmise that it takes about two years after marriage before individuals fully integrate the marriage into their emotional and social lives, and that prior to this full integration the end of the marriage is less disruptive to well-being. But once the marriage is fully integrated into the individual's life, additional years of marriage seem to matter little: the social and emotional impact of separation would be as great after three years as after thirty.

### The Leaver and the Left

There do seem to be differences in the impact of separation on those who define themselves as leavers and those who define themselves as left, but the differences seem to be more nearly in the character of the resultant distress than in its intensity.

In most separations the definition of which spouse is the more responsible for the separation appears to be largely arbitrary. The marriage became nearly intolerable for both partners; somehow one partner rather than the other decided finally to call it quits. Sometimes husband and wife alternated in the initiation of preliminary separations, with first the husband storming out of the house, then the wife insisting that he go. Sometimes a spouse who had been unwilling to accept responsibility for ending the marriage behaved so outrageously that the other spouse could not go on with it. And sometimes a husband or wife who had insisted on separation later had a change of heart and wanted to become reconciled, but the other spouse now refused. In all these circumstances the identification of one spouse as leaver and the other as left oversimplifies a complex interactive process.

Nevertheless, in a minority of instances, one spouse is determined throughout on the separation while the other opposes it or only reluctantly acquiesces. However, when we compare those

---

[7] Goode found that, compared with other respondents, a distinctly smaller proportion of respondents who had been married four years or less said that their separation had been highly traumatic. See William J. Goode, *After Divorce* (New York: Free Press, 1956), p. 191.

who were determined on the separation and those who had it imposed on them in terms of the level of postmarital discomfort they experienced, there seems not to be much difference. Separation distress appears in both groups. Both groups have to cope with all the problems resulting from social dislocation and the need to establish a new social identity. One woman who had left her husband after years of unhappy marriage said, in a comment that could have been made by many others among the "leavers," "I don't want to return to my marriage, although my husband wants me to. But I hadn't guessed separation would be this hard." [8]

An exception to the generalization that about the same level of postmarital distress affects those who initiate separation as those who have it imposed on them might be made for the husbands and wives who leave their marriage for another love. If they have entirely shifted their attachment feelings to the new figure, they may escape separation distress. More likely they will experience intermittent separation distress, but at a much reduced level. More is said about this below.

Although there do not generally seem to be great differences in the level of postmarital distress between those who initiate separation and those on whom separation is imposed, there do seem to be distinct differences in the *kinds* of distress the two groups experience. Those who initiated the separation tend to feel guilty, even anguished, at the damage their departure inflicted on those they were pledged to cherish. They may anticipate the condemnation of others and feel such condemnation to be partially deserved. They may also question their capacity to meet emotional obligations.

Those on whom separation was imposed, in contrast, have been the recipients of traumatic rejection, with what may seem to have been inadequate opportunity to retaliate. They may feel

[8] Goode's female respondents reported that separation gave rise to a high level of trauma most often when it was the husband who had first suggested the divorce, then most often when it was the respondent herself, and least often when the idea had been mutually arrived at. Of equal significance, differences among the groups were not great. It might be concluded that where separation is not mutually agreed on, it may be better to be the one to make the break, but not a great deal better. See Goode, *After Divorce*, pp. 193–194.

aggrieved, misused not only by the one man or woman who ended the marriage to them but by the entire human race. They may feel that friends and neighbors who know they were left or forced to leave may have lost respect for them. And they may have lost respect for themselves; they may question their capacity to hold the love of anyone. They may accept their spouse's accusations that they are unattractive or cold or doltish or sexually inadequate, and decide that they are utterly without value. In addition, they may feel so hurt by the ending of their marriage that they are for a time reluctant to trust themselves to another relationship.

### Someone New

A new attachment can reduce separation distress and virtually prevent the loneliness of emotional isolation. In addition, the respect of the new person can combat feelings of worthlessness and unacceptability, and his or her support can reduce the anxiety that is a natural response to the threats and insecurities of change.

I think a new relationship, if you keep your eyes open, can be very healthy. I mean it can be very self-affirming. I mean if you come out of a marriage where the image you're getting back from your spouse is something hideous, you're a bitch, you're everything horrible, and then all of a sudden there is someone else who respects you and likes you, and you see a very nice person reflected back to you, it just makes you feel much, much better.

(Woman, late twenties)

Many fewer of those who attended Seminars for the Separated had themselves established new attachments than reported that their spouses had established new attachments. Having someone new would appear to provide some defense against the emotional assaults of separation.

Yet it would exaggerate the value of a new relationship to suggest that it will deflect all postmarital distress. It will not reduce disruptions in relationships with kin, friends, and children. Nor will establishing a new relationship end an individual's continued moral obligations to the other spouse, obligations that may be disowned after separation, but that are likely, nevertheless, to weigh on the individual's conscience. And, despite the new relationship, attachment to the spouse may continue. The individual may recurrently feel that home is where the spouse is and may experience periods when the new love will seem a stranger and the new relationship a terrible mistake.

**When I was with him, all I could think of was running home to Burt.**
**(Woman, about thirty)**

The new relationship may make the spouse unreachable not only because of the separation but because of the new commitments that have been made. These commitments may be felt to be real, even though the former spouse may scoff at them. One man called the wife he had left two months earlier to tell her that it was she whom he really loved, and not the woman for whom he had left her. But because of his obligations to the new woman, he could not return immediately. His wife responded, acidly, that he also had obligations to her and to his children, and later reported the phone call to her friends as additional evidence that her husband had taken leave of his senses.

The contrary tugs of marriage and a new attachment may lead an individual into shuttling between the relationships. A responsible executive, after twenty years of marriage in which he had been tormented by the impracticality and impulsivity of his rather fey wife, left her for his younger, more attractive, and less unsettling secretary. Then he discovered that he could not refuse his wife's calls for help, and so returned to her. He then pined for the new woman in his life—with whom he had daily contact at work—and after an interval again left his wife for her. But his wife pleaded that she could not manage without him, and so again he returned to his wife. His work, needless to say, did not go well during this period, and he was refused a promotion.

New attachments may themselves become sources of distress. The pressure of need that can make any new relationship seem attractive to the separated increases the likelihood that a new relationship will be a mistake.

Immediately after we broke up I threw myself into a relationship with somebody else which was a mistake. The relationship is still going on, but like it just seemed like such a beautiful thing and, oh, great, all my problems are solved and here's my answer of a dream man, and all of a sudden you wake up one morning and it's not a dream man, and you're just more disillusioned than you were with the marriage.

(**Woman, about thirty**)

### The Quality of the Postmarital Relationship

Husbands and wives treat one another after separation in ways that range from mutual considerateness to open warfare. There are definite advantages for couples who locate themselves at the mutually considerate end of the continuum.

The "friendly divorce" has its poignancies, and may require from the spouses a generosity they may not have brought to their marriage. But it can provide them with the assurance that their married years were not totally wasted, that despite separation they can, within limits, still count on one another. The husband and wife can offer each other company and solace, and in so doing can help each other manage the apprehensiveness that is a part of separation distress. If there are children, it becomes possible for the wife, if she has custody, to call her husband for help or relief, and for the husband to see the children within their usual home.

Unfortunately, more separations seem to be at the other extreme, with one spouse or both acting as the other's enemy and persecutor. Husbands charge their wives in court with being unfit to mother, call them in the middle of the night to threaten them, or follow them when they leave their homes; wives refuse to allow their husbands to visit the children, or are forever demanding additional support from them, or embarrass their husbands by appearing, wild with outrage, at the husbands' offices. Couples who have not quite moved to warfare may nevertheless in the phone conversations necessary to arrange visiting be icy or bitter, so that each is deeply upset on replacing the receiver.

A postmarital relationship in which the spouses, despite all, try to remain considerate of each other can make separation easier for both to manage. A postmarital relationship in which one spouse is determined to punish or frustrate the other can consume the energy of the persecutor and sap the morale of the target.

*Personal Resources*

In separation, as everywhere else, those who are better provided for do better. The individual in separation may need to call on resources of many kinds, social as well as personal, including but not limited to money. The more such resources exist, the better off the individual is likely to be. They do better who have a more resilient character, better job skills, and greater ingenuity and energy; who have loyal kin and supportive friends; and who have adequate financial resources. The woman who accompanies her husband to a new job in a strange part of the country and then, before setting down new roots, separates from him, may have more than the normal quota of trouble. And so, irrespective of social situation, will the man or woman whose personality integration is fragile, who has a tendency to severe withdrawal, depression, or panic in response to frustration or threat.

Separation often produces financial stress, even when the couple enjoy an above-average income. Two living spaces have to be paid for instead of one. New capital equipment may have to be obtained—perhaps a second car, very likely a second television set. There may be legal fees, and perhaps fees for counseling. To those already financially pressed, separation may mean financial disaster. This can provide an entirely realistic justification for the apprehensiveness that is one aspect of separation distress.

Separation distress is difficult enough to manage for individuals who can call on old friends and kin for support, who are sufficiently well-off financially to retain counselors and therapists as they need them and to defend themselves from the anxieties induced by dunning letters. Those who are without these resources may be expected to find separation distress that much more difficult to manage.

# 5

# Separation
# and Identity Change

I feel this total lack of any direction. You know, I'm flailing around, "What am I going to do? What am I going to be when I grow up?" You know, one would like to know before one got one foot in the grave.

(Woman, about thirty-five)

A woman has her family, her home. A man has to go home to a room, or to a relative, or something like that. . . . You can go to a bar, and you can pick up a girl or something like that, but it's artificial. A woman has got the children. She's got something to satisfy her.

(Man, about forty)

With the end of their marriages, most among the separated suffer the loss of some of the social scaffolding on which their self-definition had rested. They lose the spouse as a partner, and they also lose the social definitions that are associated with marriage, of settled respectability and limited social freedom. The woman may lose that access to the occupational world she had had as a vicarious participant in her husband's work. The man may lose his children's daily testimony that to them he is a father. In consequence, both the woman and the man, after separation, may no longer feel themselves to be quite the same people they had been when they were married.

But while individuals after separation experience some loss of their former self-definitions, they have not yet gained new ones. They are, as it were, between selves. There are any number of ways they display this uncomfortable status. They now are willing to consider, indeed to perform, actions that would previously have been foreign to them: quitting a job; moving to another part of the country; talking with reckless frankness to friends with whom they had previously maintained reserve. Yet while they recognize fewer constraints, they also suffer from aimlessness that may express itself in inconsistency or impulsiveness or apathy. They have as yet no new coherent self in terms of which they can evaluate alternatives.

Some among the separated welcome the chance to become different. They may have accepted their spouse's view of them as reprehensible or unappealing. They may themselves have been dismayed as they witnessed their own behavior, which included, perhaps, violent or hysterical outbursts or irresponsible impulsivities they might have preferred not to have had to recognize as within their repertoire.

**I'd sit there at home at night and I'd be depressed and I'd say to myself my wife is right, I'm such a terrible person, I'm such a bastard.**
**(Man, late twenties)**

For many among the separated alienation from self began before the actual end of their marriage. They felt inauthentic when with friends whom they permitted to accept their marriage as no different from the marriages of others: good enough, and likely to be permanent. They treated their misery as a secret stigma, a blemish they could not admit to friends without embarrassing and alienating them. They may have accustomed themselves to describing a vacation as pleasant when it had been filled with tension and bickering. They may have repeatedly assured parents and other kin that things were fine even as they smarted from an evening's argument.

With separation, there is no further need for pretending: it is possible to be one's self. But what self that is may now have become uncertain.

(70)

## The Disruption of Identity

Our marital status is used as a basis for our classification not only by survey interviewers and the Internal Revenue Service, but by new acquaintances as well. We ourselves recognize and accept the social implications of being a married man or woman; we became different when married. Our marriage ended, we recognize the social meanings of being separated; again we become different.

There is a deeper way in which marriage contributes to our identity. A marriage that is beyond its first two years or so, a marriage that has had time to infiltrate the most remote sectors of our lives, has become part of what we are. Loss of the marriage may be experienced by us as akin to loss of a limb. This is true even if our marriage had been largely unhappy, or had been one in which we were distant or reserved when with our spouse. It is the constant, uninterrupted custom of years together, not whether husband or wife like one another or have access to the other's secret thoughts, that produces interdependence. It is the years of going places together, sitting down to dinner together, consulting each other on management of the children and the house, presenting ourselves to others as a couple, sharing a house, a car, a bedroom, that makes our marriage a part of ourselves.

Some go beyond the more usual integration of the marriage into the self; they feel they have meaning and worth only as they are linked to the spouse. When their marriages end they feel that they have lost more than just a part of themselves; they feel they have lost themselves almost entirely.

My husband was in graduate school and we had three babies and I was really up to my neck in diapers. And I was doing part-time work, very menial types of things, secretarial and typing, that sort of thing. And what he was doing was so much more interesting than what I was doing. Who wanted to hear about loads of dirty diapers and my fascinating clerical jobs? So when we broke up I felt that for all those years he had been sort of developing. And my identity was so mixed up with that, that I would find it very hard to describe myself apart from him.

(Woman, about thirty-five)

Not only does an individual's marriage become part of his or her identity, but because of the marriage the individual is in constant contact with someone who almost requires the individual to maintain a particular self-image. Among the issues decided fairly early in every marriage is the kind of person each spouse believes the other to be: reliable or unpredictable, stodgy or exciting, someone to lean on or someone to guide. This image is constantly communicated, implicitly by what is taken for granted and explicitly by the spouse's characterizations.

**When we were first going together I was vivacious, but then I became loudmouth Dotty.**

(Woman, about forty)

Sometimes the beginnings of a marriage's decline can be found in the unwillingness of one partner to modify his or her presumptions regarding the other. A professional man who married while a student, or a successful business executive who married on obtaining his first job, may have a wife who, years later, still relates to him as an insecure beginner rather than as the established figure he has become. Or a woman may want to become someone other than the person her husband insists on believing her to be. Nora's complaint in *A Doll's House* is that her husband will not change his perceptions of her.

Yet, though they may be at times disparaging or minimizing, the images of the individual communicated by the spouse help stabilize the individual's identity. Loss of the spouse's support for a particular view of the self can be relieving, but for a time the individual may have no support for a new view with which to replace it. Without stabilizing input, his or her self-definition can change abruptly, producing equally abrupt shifts in mood and in planning.

Beyond this, the separation is likely to bring about changes in almost every sector of the individual's life, from relatively minor changes in the organization of time to major changes in the individual's relationships with others. After separation, an individual's work may continue to structure his or her day, as it did during the marriage, but the silent and solitary mornings and the empty evenings will be new. New tasks will become necessary as the individual becomes responsible for what had previously been the spouse's domain. It may be some time before the man feels comfortable shopping for food in the supermarket or the woman is at ease driving alone to visit friends or family in the evening. The problem is not that the new tasks are difficult so much as that they are out of keeping with what had been understood to be appropriate responsibilities, with what had been the self.

Some among the separated complain, during the period before they once again develop a coherent self, that their motives and behaviors seem oddly alien to themselves. They watch themselves do something and then wonder whether they are doing it because they want to, or because they feel they ought to, or to avoid the spouse's criticism—although the spouse will never know—or because of the sheer persistence of marital habit.

**I found myself in the kitchen cleaning my oven, and in the middle of it I was saying, "Am I doing this because Nancy would have wanted me to clean the oven?" Or was it that I really wanted to because the oven was dirty? Or using the brand of toothpaste that she bought, or other little things. I hope that when I'm through it will be me more than someone else.**

**(Man, about thirty)**

Some feel that the major task of their separation is to battle through to an autonomous self, distinct from the self they had maintained during their marriage. They want to become able to speak with their own voice and pursue their own interests.

**You know I taught music for six years before I married. I was married at twenty-nine. He was a musician, and we went to New York for four years, and the babies started to come, and we went through that bit. And I had to give him space for evolving. I had to give him space to compose. And I discovered that I had married him for his creative ability. That was his attraction. Since our marriage ended I've discovered that I have creative ability myself.**

**But I have to work against his style. It was like first I entered his world and then I had to extract myself.**

**(Woman, about forty)**

Many among the separated had relied on their marriages to support their sense of worth, and after separation need to find other supports. Women are likely to have felt that marriage provided the significant tasks in their lives, that their marriage had been a career as well as a relationship. Their jobs in the working world had been incidental to their service to home, husband, and children; they may well have minimized their paid employment as "helping out."

Separation for these women is like losing a career. Their homemaking tasks might remain, especially if they have children, but they no longer receive adult recognition for their performance. Nor can they expect to be supported because of their work in the home. With the end of their marriages, they have to look for something new. At that point they might feel that there is nothing else they are prepared for.

**I didn't know where to turn. I had no handles. I didn't know what I was going to do. Whereas my husband had a career, a good job. I didn't feel that I wanted to pursue teaching—teaching little children, because I had been in elementary education. I just didn't want that. I had been doing a lot of volunteer work. But it had been several years since I'd worked. And I'd never been a career person. I'd been just raising children.**

**(Woman, late thirties)**

Separation is apt to mean loss of many of the possessions or capacities that had reassured the husband or wife during the marriage that they had achieved position or security. Just how this expresses itself depends on the initial income level of the couple. But virtually all couples whose expenses had consumed most of their income have to reduce their standard of living.

The man in middle-income circumstances may lose his suburban home and lawn and return from work instead to a dreary two-room apartment. Many such men had found reassurance of their worth in the products of their work: their home, family, and financial standing. Separation might wipe out much of their achievement.

**In the ten years that we were married I went from twenty-four to thirty-four and they were a very significant ten years. I started a career, started to succeed, bought my first house, had a child, you know, very significant years. And then all of a sudden every god- damn thing, I'm back to zero! I have no house. I don't have a child. I don't have a wife. I don't have the same family. My eco- nomic position has been shattered. And nothing recoverable. All those goals which I had struggled for, every goddamn one of them, is gone.**

**(Man, mid-thirties)**

Middle-income women may lose their ability to buy small items carelessly and to pay their bills with credit cards. Instead of rela- tive security they may be faced with chronic financial worries. And they may have reason to fear that their contribution to the success of their husbands will now go unrewarded, that whatever position they helped the husbands to obtain will not be shared with them.

## Changes in Social Role and in Identity

Some separated individuals feel that their separation has changed so much in their lives that the formerly familiar now seems quite remarkable. They feel themselves almost to have become marginal to the world they inhabit. They may find themselves looking at its features with curiosity, like travelers in their own country, with a traveler's curiosity about the inner lives of the people they pass in streets and shops. Their own lives have changed dramatically, despire lack of outward indication of change; now they wonder about the lives of others.

**I went into the supermarket—I go into the supermarket almost every day because I have three kids—and everything looked different. The**

people looked different. I looked at all their faces and I wondered what their lives were like.

(Woman, early thirties, newly separated)

Separated individuals are made aware by others, as if that were necessary, that they have entered a new social role. Friends may protest that things will be no different, but there may be fewer invitations to attend a specific social occasion and more to "just drop in any time." And the separated individual is now the odd person for dinner, the one who leaves alone at the end of the evening.

There is change, too, in the separated individual's attitudes toward work, in his or her daily routines, and in his or her planning for the immediate and distant future. Functioning in all these areas depends on the individual's self-definition, and with separation this has been disrupted. Eventually the individual will develop a new coherent self, but its formation is a slow process, and for a time the separated may feel confused and without direction.

## Sense of Discreditation

Continuing self-deprecation and guilt can slow movement toward the formation of a new postmarital identity. The accusations and disparagements of the spouse, some of which are likely to remain vivid for months after the actual break, may constitute only the lesser half of it. More burdensome is likely to be the individual's self-condemnation for having failed to maintain a home for the children, or simply for having failed at marriage. This self-condemnation can be fueled by the assumption of responsibility for the difficulties of the children or the sorrows of the spouse.

A lessened ability to command the respect of others often lends support to such self-condemnation. Women, especially, may be treated differently by service personnel and thus perceive that their standing in the community has been lowered. One woman reported that the moving men she had hired, on learning that she was newly separated, suggested that they return in the evening to help her "rearrange the furniture." Several women reported janitors scolding their children in a way they would not have if the children's fathers were at home. Several others reported being questioned closely by prospective landlords regarding their ability to pay the rent. And one woman said that a real estate agent had refused to rent an apartment to her when he learned that she was separated because he feared that she might introduce an element of instability into a building occupied primarily by two-parent families.

**There is no dignity, no honor, in divorce. The divorced woman is pictured as a sleazy character. Men think a divorced woman is horny, or else that she's hard and cold. No landlord wants a divorced woman floating around. He has this picture of men going in and out at all hours.**

**(Woman, late thirties)**

Eventually some women become briskly businesslike in their dealings with service personnel and landlords and, where possible, hide their newly separated status.

### Problems in Planning

Until a new coherent identity develops, choice and planning become difficult. How can anyone choose a dress or dwelling, an occupation or a life style without knowing who he or she is? In the absence of a firm identity every decision is a statement about an intended self and so is weighty with implications. Deciding on a neighborhood to move to or the purchase of a new home is also deciding on a self.

Absence of a coherent and stable self to which to refer decisions makes possible a variety of pathologies of decision making. Newly separated individuals may be unable to decide on anything at all, or they may act impulsively, since any action seems as good as, and no better than, any other. Or they may vacillate, deciding on one course and then on another. Many among the newly separated are highly suggestible and can quickly modify their definitions of themselves in response to the comments of others.

A woman, herself separated, described helping a newly separated male friend choose furniture for the apartment into which he was about to move:

He decided he was going to get a narrow single bed. You know, if you're married you need a double bed, and if you're single you have a single bed. This was the way he was thinking. So I said, "Walter, you know, sometime you might want to have somebody in your bed with you. You don't feel that way now, but you might feel that way in the future." So he thought that was a great idea, and he was going to order a water bed. So I had to tell him to take it easy, that it wasn't one or the other.

Unwise decisions are sometimes made for the sake of strengthening a particular identity. For example, a man determined to retain the sense of maturity his marriage had provided bought a home in a suburban area in which he became the one unmarried man. As might have been predicted, he soon felt miserably out of place.

Separated individuals may want not to retain their former selves, but rather to change in some respect. Many explore experiences or procedures that promise to make them better people. Traditional psychotherapy is only one among several possibilities; others include encounter groups, bioenergetics, and fundamentalist religion. Some among the separated may take apparently irreversible action that is intended to impose a new identity on themselves. They may give up their jobs, move to a new part of the country, or to a different country entirely. An insurance agent may decide to become a lawyer, or a businessman may drop out to paint. One man gave up his office job to devote a year to building a house. A woman spent all the money that came to her in the property settlement to buy a rock-filled farm where she felt that she and her children would return to fundamentals.

Some degree of uncertainty and vacillation may continue to afflict the separated individual despite apparently irreversible action. After such action, however, it may be focused not on what to do, but on what was done.

*Obsessive Review*

Obsessive review seems to be a normal concomitant of identity change. It is a reaction to events that would be inconceivable, given the person one thought one was. Somehow the events and the self have to be made consistent, and obsessive review is the process by which this takes place.

**I'm trying to relive the past, looking back to see what I should have done, what might have turned out differently, especially focusing on the last few days. How I could have changed it by making some gestures or by doing something that might have changed the outcome.**

**(Woman, about fifty)**

Obsessive review is a constant, absorbing, sometimes maddening preoccupation that refuses to accept any conclusion. Often the preoccupation seems to have control of the individual's mind. His or her determination to think about other things is again and again frustrated as the preoccupation reenters with its own images and feelings.

Obsessive review seems to occur whenever there is a major relational loss—not only when there has been a separation, but when a spouse or a child dies; when, for whatever reason, there is a loss of someone loved. It seems to occur as well in response to any serious reverse, such as loss of a job or financial loss. The more a reverse is felt to be inexplicable, given the person one believed oneself to be, the more the reverse resists the individual's efforts to "come to terms with it," and the more marked seems to be obsessive review.

Enmeshed in obsessive review, the separated may find their thoughts returning repeatedly to the events of their marriage, trying to identify what went wrong, to imagine what else might have happened, to speculate on how they could have acted differently and what might then have followed. They may imagine how they might have been more forceful, or the spouse more reasonable. Or they may review the incidents and thoughts that led them to enter the marriage to begin with, and allow themselves to imagine what might have happened had they remained single or married someone with whom they could have remained in love. Or they may review the humiliations they endured within the marriage, only to have the marriage end anyway. They may

(79)

imagine having refused to accept them, and instead forcing the spouse to leave, or walking out themselves.

Obsessive review provides a means for gradual acceptance of an unpalatable reality. It allows the separated to incorporate their experience into their new selves. When this process becomes too painful, they can interrupt their unhappy memories with the relief of fantasy; imagination provides them with an alternative scenario more in keeping with the person they believed they were. Then, after this respite, they can recognize the scenario as imaginary, and return to what actually happened.

Yet obsessive review can also fix on just those events that were most excruciatingly painful and refuse to relinquish them. One man replayed in his mind, as on an endless loop of film, the scene in which he had come home late one night to discover parked in front of his house a car belonging to his wife's boyfriend, and in the back seat of the car his wife and the boyfriend in an embrace. He could not accept the scene, nor could he forget it. It fit with nothing else; it made no sense; and yet it was more real for him than anything happening around him. Others sometimes reported that lesser humiliations, insults, slights, and inattentions, despite their more ordinary quality, refused to fade from their minds. Some endlessly reviewed the event of parting, perhaps berating themselves for having left, or justifying the leaving, or trying to find the explanatory clue in the scene in which the spouse left, after a quarrel that seemed no different from any other quarrel.

Some feel persecuted by their inability to escape obsessive review. They try by an act of will to think of other things, yet as they drive or read or try to concentrate on work, their mind and feelings continually return to the incidents of their separation. Some attempt to free themselves from obsessive review by decisive action. They may leave the area, hoping that by so doing they can also leave their memories. And indeed, a number who did this later reported that to a limited extent the strategy worked; away from the scenes and people associated with their marriage, and among others for whom their new identity was the only one that was known, they were freer of the past.

Some among the separated attempt to end obsessive review by

arranging a last, hopefully definitive, interchange with the spouse. They want to clarify for themselves the nature of their feelings about the spouse, and to assess and perhaps terminate the possibility of reconciliation. Unfortunately this maneuver may only result in the provision of new material for obsessive review.

The only entirely adequate remedy for obsessive review seems to be the passage of time. With time a new identity forms and the past loses its grip. Some events of the past and the potential for behavior exhibited in them are incorporated into the new self-image. Some past events are seen as belonging to a self that has been disposed of, or as having been inexplicable aberrations; or they may be blamed on the spouse, or on the peculiar circumstances of the time. In any case, they are treated as without importance for the present self. With this management of the past by partial acceptance or repudiation, the individual can again function with self-confidence.

## The New Identity

One of the many ironies of marital separation is that the crisis of identity occurs when many decisions simply must be made: decisions about where to live, about legal steps, about how to relate to the former spouse, about how to reorganize one's life. As decisions are made, and steps taken to implement them, they contribute to a restructuring of the individual's identity. But false starts occur with some frequency. Many among the newly separated explore a variety of tentative identities before establishing a persisting direction. An individual may decide that with the end of what had been a stultifying marriage, he or she wants more than anything else to be socially active, adventuresome, and extroverted—only to discover belatedly that this self-assessment was mistaken, and that a quieter life is more congenial. Or the individual may be absorbed by a sequence of compelling interests, each for a time engaging all of his or her attention, each in turn dropped for a new absorbing interest. Nor will there necessarily be any connection among the interests: One woman moved from intense investment in yoga to total absorption in social action to graduate study in a technical field.

Separated individuals often take evening courses in art or poetry, only partly because they want to fill otherwise empty time, but more because now they can give serious attention to a talent formerly neglected. Sometimes these explorations constitute false starts; sometimes not. Often this is a time when individuals decide to complete previously postponed educational plans. Schools that offer opportunities for adults to complete a college degree or that offer any sort of "second chance," such as graduate schools that will accept men and women in middle age, may draw a large proportion of their student body from among the recently separated.

As decisions are reached and, finally, felt to be right, and as new decisions and new commitments are made that fit with them, the individual's life again assumes stable form. It becomes possible again to relate the present to the past and to see the present as moving consistently toward a desired future. The individual becomes once again the same person from day to day, just as was true before separation. Now, however, the individual is a different person from the one he or she was then.

# 6

# The Continuing Relationship of Husbands and Wives

I can't make the complete surgery that everybody tells me I
should.                                                    (Woman, mid-forties)

I can't understand why my husband cried and wanted to come
back to me after all I have done to him.
                                                          (Woman, late thirties)

My wife works Tuesday nights and I was babysitting last Tuesday night for her, and she came in and we started talking and
I told her that I thought I should come back. And she said she
had thought about it and she wasn't really sure about the separation at all. And all of a sudden I really felt like I wanted to try.
So I said things like that, and we agreed on it, sometime about
four in the morning, and really felt good, both of us. And we
hugged and kissed and she said, "Goodbye, come for dinner
Friday night." And that was really great. And I got into the car
and drove away feeling really fantastic. And then I said to myself, "What the hell am I doing? Why do I want to go back?
Why do I want to go back at all?" So I called her up and I
said, "Are you still planning for me to come Friday night?"
And she said, "Well, no, I guess I've decided against it."
                                                          (Man, early forties)

Separation is an incident in the relationship of spouses, rather than
an ending of that relationship. It is a critically important incident,
to be sure: an incident that ushers in fundamental changes in the
relationship. But it is not an ending. Months after the individual
has moved to a hotel room, furnished flat, friend's apartment, or
back to the parental home, the spouse is likely to remain the most

important figure in his or her world. Even if the spouse has disappeared, as occasionally happens, he or she will remain vivid in the individual's internal world, there to be harangued, entreated, and called on to witness the devastation produced by his or her departure.

The postmarital relationship of former husbands and wives is unique among relationships. It is unique only partly because of its resilience, a characteristic it shares with other kin ties. More singular is its extraordinary ambivalence, a characteristic it shares with no other relationship. Within the postmarital relationship of a formerly married pair one may observe in close succession anger and attachment, quarrels and remorse, vicious fighting and passionate rejoining, each state crowded by its opposite, so that whichever is the manifest state, its opposite is pressing almost visibly for expression. True, all relationships, and not only those of ex-spouses, contain ambivalences: faithful lovers are now and again bored with one another; fierce competitors can harbor a grudging mutual admiration. But elsewhere one affect in the relationship is dominant, and its contrary is only weakly developed. In the relationship of former spouses, as in no other, intense and persistent positive feelings coexist with equally intense and persistent negative feelings; yearning for the other person mixes or alternates with anger and, sometimes, hatred.

In this chapter I shall consider the source of this simultaneity of contraries and speculate about its implications. I will speak again of the persistence of attachment and consider how it can paradoxically give force to negative feeling: If the spouse were not so needed, his or her absence would elicit less rage. I shall also describe other bonds holding together a no-longer-married pair, and other reasons for the husband and wife to be angry with one another. Finally, I shall discuss some alternative resolutions of this most peculiar, and disturbing, relationship.

### The Persistence of Marital Bonds

Marriages are formed of the intertwining of many separate strands: sexual intimacy, shared parenting, companionship, mutual obligation, collaboration in furnishing and maintaining a home, love. All of these tend to resist severance for longer or shorter periods after the couple have announced their separation to themselves and others. Even the sense of maintaining a shared home, which on logical grounds should end abruptly on separation—indeed, what else could separation mean?—often remains, frayed but intact, for a few days or weeks.

A man who has agreed to move to a room may feel that despite his new residence he has a right to keep a key to his former home; that he helped to pay for it for years, perhaps continues to pay for it, and that it is partly his.

**I told him that I wanted the key. And he said that it is our house and he won't give me the key.**

**(Woman, late twenties)**

Some men return to their former home at intervals—perhaps without calling to let their wives know they are coming—to see the children, pick up possessions, shower, or use the laundry facilities. One man who regularly returned to use the washing machine complained to his wife when she was out of detergent.

The spouse who has moved out may not be the only one reluctant to accept that separation implies separate domiciles, each closed to the other spouse. Often there is collusion between the two spouses in not insisting on the formal ceremony of giving up the key. Neither may want to interrupt a connection that makes it possible for each to continue to feel still married, while at the same time their marriage moves toward a legal ending.

The collusion may be largely unconscious. One woman was asked why she tolerated a husband who continued, a month after their separation, to let himself into her home when he came to see the children. She replied that if she demanded his key or changed the lock, the children would let him in anyway. Then she laughed, as she recognized that the point wasn't her husband's ability to gain entry into the home, but rather his right to a key, and the fact that she did not want to take it from him.

There can be embarrassments because the separation is incomplete; the couple themselves may hardly understand it, and friends and neighbors may not understand it at all. Visiting friends may not be prepared for the unexpected arrival of the supposedly banished husband, letting himself in with his own key.

**I went in there to use some tools and I walked in the house totally unexpected and I hadn't noticed that there was a car parked there because the car was parked not in front of the house where most visitors park but across the street. And it was a friend of ours— a friend of hers, more—a lady friend. And they were just sitting there, sort of in a conference. And I knew that I was intruding, and I felt very bad about it. I apologized to both my wife and her friend. I said, "I'm really sorry I intruded on you, but I just wanted to use the tools."**

**(Man, thirties, separated about a month)**

In another instance a husband was about to enter his former home early one evening, just fifteen minutes after his wife had admitted a date. The wife caught him at the door and sent him away, but the husband, unabashed, telephoned late that same evening to say that there had been no need for alarm—and, possibly, to ascertain whether her date had left.

**He came in the front door, Monday, and I had a date. I said he couldn't come in. He said he just needed water for the car. I said he had to go away. Later he called and he said, "You seemed to be so upset." So I said, "I had a date." So he said, "Well, if you have a date I will just come in and shake hands with the guy."**

**(Woman, about thirty)**

As the separation becomes more firmly established, the spouse who departed from the home ordinarily stops using his or her house key. Some do this voluntarily, to communicate that they no longer consider themselves household members. But others continue until finally the spouse in the home demands that they stop. One husband had formed the habit of coming to his former home every morning to have breakfast with his children and also to shower and prepare for the day. For a while his wife was pleased that she could sleep late, since the husband was there for the children. But the sound of the daily shower and the image of her husband soaping and dripping in the downstairs bath became too much for her, and one morning she descended in a fury and ended the arrangement.

Here is a man's description of the process by which he was led to relinquish his right of entry into the previously shared household:

I was being a pain in the ass, going in the house, and I was hassling the kids and a few words would start and we'd get into a fight. Finally she threw me out. Now the last couple of weeks I take the kids and I bring them back and I go to the garage, maybe fix one of the kids' bikes, maybe there's something else like that to do. And it seems to be working out fairly well.

(Man, about forty)

It usually takes only a few weeks for each member of the couple to accept that the departed spouse no longer has rights of access to the previously shared household. The obligation of the departing spouse to contribute to its maintenance may end somewhat more slowly.

*Continued Partnering*

As an unhappy couple see their marriage approaching its end, both may become anxious about their subsequent lives. Especially if their marriage has been a long one, each may fear that without the other he or she will be unable to function—that the services the other performs are essential to living. The woman contemplating separation may worry that without her husband she will be unable to manage the mechanics of banking and bill paying, that salesmen will exploit her, that the car will go untended and the house will sink into disrepair. The man may worry that without his wife he will be helpless to cook or clean or furnish his apartment, that when the children are with him he will not know how to keep them warm or healthy or amused, and that except for the women he may date he will be socially isolated because of his inability to entertain.

Almost always these fears of inability to perform the tasks that had been the other's responsibility turn out to be exaggerated: Partnering, while it may have made each spouse's life marginally more efficient proves not to have been essential. The woman discovers that managing a bank account requires little skill and can provide a not unwelcome sense of awareness, if not control, of her household economy. She may regret her helplessness to question the recommendations of garage mechanics, but she can nevertheless arrange to have her car cared for. She can learn to do some of the small repairs required around the house, and the remainder she can manage by calling in a carpenter or electrician. The man, on his part, is apt to find that cooking is much easier than high school chemistry; that methods for dealing with most child-care problems can be arrived at by common sense or suggested by easily procured advice; and that there are female friends, both single and married, happy to help furnish his apartment and his social life. Only if he has custody of the children, and must add responsibility for them to responsibility for a job, may the man feel a desperate need for a wife's services; even then he can apply for help to female kin, if he has any living nearby, or he can try his luck with paid housekeepers.

The newly separated spouses may even find some advantage in not having to coordinate their activities. Both now have freedom to suit their chores to their mood, rather than being hemmed in by commitments to the other to pick up milk on the way home or to take the car in for servicing. The woman no longer must organize her afternoon to have the man's dinner ready for his return in the evening, and the man no longer must interrupt his work so that he can come home to eat it. Freedom from obligation to a partner can feel like a blessing. Now there is no one to be critical if one errs or forgets—other than the children, who may not notice, and whose criticism in any event is less wounding. And one need not constantly confront the obstructive noncooperativeness of the other.

Nevertheless, a limited partnering persists after separation. Immediately after separation the husband and wife may not be aware of their capacity to manage for themselves. In addition, each may feel continued responsibility for the other and for the previously shared household; it may seem unnatural suddenly to stop contributing. And so the couple may briefly, through inertia, continue to perform those shared household tasks that are still possible to people living apart. The man may arrive on the weekend to mow a lawn or repair a lamp. The woman may continue to take calls for her husband. In one instance a bat entered the wife's home and she telephoned her husband to come deal with it. Another woman finished knitting a sweater for her husband, though they had separated before she got to the sleeves. A woman was baffled by how to install screens and when her husband, with whom she was ordinarily furious, arrived to pick up the children, she prevailed on him to show her how it was done.

Obligation to perform specific services for the other tends to fade rather soon. In the first weeks after separation a man might continue to feel responsibility to fix a lamp for his wife; a month later he might feel that fixing the lamp was a favor. Yet even when they no longer feel responsible to the other spouse for specific tasks, husbands and wives may feel a lingering sense of concern for the other's well-being.

I'm really worried about my wife. I'm firmly convinced that she will really not do very well by herself. Although the evidence doesn't seem to support this. I will say to others that it really isn't her I care about, it is my children, but I'm coming to wonder whether in fact that's it. All of a sudden I find myself wondering about whether she should keep the apartment, whether it would be better for her to move.

(Man, late twenties)

One man, who had been willing briefly to do household repairs for his wife, stopped because he felt foolish caring for a house in which he did not live. But he continued to try to help his wife with advice.

I don't come around the house and do chores anymore. I don't do husband things. I've told her that if she doesn't want me in the role of a husband I will not do husband things. But she calls me up to say, "I just had an accident and I need some help," or a tradesman has been ripping her off. So I give her some advice on how to handle the man and how to negotiate, and things like that.

(Man, mid-thirties)

Occasionally, one hears of couples who, years after a marriage has ended, continue to display responsibility for one another. A man or woman may lend a long-separated spouse money to tide him or her over a thin time, or to finance an operation or an education. Others may find it odd that anyone should feel responsible for an ex-spouse, but despite all, many among the separated do.

*Companionship*

When a marriage is going badly companionship between the spouses seems to wilt. The spouses may accompany one another on evenings out, but they hardly talk. Each is wary of giving the other an opportunity for attack and neither can, in truth, listen to the other with much sympathy. They communicate mostly mutual distrust and dissatisfaction, and often they do so through silences and avoidances. Except when a quarrel occurs, at which time they may shout their hurt and anger, they may try to insulate themselves from each other.

Separation, oddly enough, sometimes seems to improve matters. Husband and wife have in common their new independence. Each may be curious about the problems the other encounters, and about the other's feelings, plans, and hopes. Each may be fascinated to learn how friends or kin are reacting to their separation. The two may exchange information about what this one said and that one did and so enhance their sense of still being allied to one another, though now secretly.

After separation there is no longer any need to be irritated by the spouse's mannerisms, to be made anxious by his or her impulsivity, or to feel suffocated by his or her caution. It becomes easier to enjoy the spouse.

**When we see each other now we get along famously. If I could see her two hours a day, I'd be quite happy.**

**(Man, late twenties)**

It can also be easier to be candid with the spouse. Unless there are legal negotiations that might be affected, it is no longer absolutely necessary to hide an affair.

**We had this conversation one night which turned out to clear the air a lot when she told me she had this guy and I told her about this woman.**

**(Man, thirties)**

A few couples after separation become good friends. They may talk regularly with each other by phone, see each other frequently, consult one another regarding important problems, and spend Christmas or a child's birthday together. But most couples who experience an upsurge of companionship after their separation have mixed feelings about it. The new friendliness and mutual interest is bittersweet, painful as well as rewarding. It carries unhappy memories and is itself a reminder that things might have been different, and better, if only the couple had been able to be friendly earlier.

There are still other problems in postmarital companionship in addition to its tardiness. Ambivalence toward the other may express itself in failing to appear when expected, in letting the other sit unoccupied while a telephone call to a girlfriend or boyfriend is completed, in unanticipated irritation with the other's accounts of postmarital life. The couple are likely to find that the new companionship, while engaging, leaves them upset, for the spouse is not simply a secret friend but also an attachment figure who is now being relinquished. After seeing the spouse his or her voice remains in one's ears, his or her image fills one's mind. Finally each may decide that there is too much feeling ready to be elicited to permit easy companionship and that, everything considered, it is not worth it.

Some couples are too angry after their marriage ends to be civil to one another. They may not believe that others can be friendly to a former spouse. On the basis of their own experience they do not see how a couple can break up, yet like one another enough to remain friendly; indeed, the idea may seem unnatural and repellent. Yet they, too, years later, may find occasion to talk with their former spouse; they may be surprised to discover that not only anger and resentment, but also an interest in the other akin to friendliness remains as a residue of their marriage.

*Feeling of Connection and the Persistence of Guilt*

One essential difference between a married couple and a couple only living together is that the married couple are next of kin to one another in the eye of their neighbors, the law, and their other kin, while the couple who live together, however they may feel about one another, are understood to be unrelated. Just as a sibling from whom one is estranged remains a sibling, still entitled to ask for help in an emergency, a spouse from whom one is separated remains almost—perhaps not quite—a family connection who still has some right to ask for help.

The sense of continued connection to the former spouse may be submerged in the upset that follows the separation, but after the initial anger and yearning have subsided it can reassert iself. Though there may be caution in its expression, there may then be recognition of continued obligation to someone who once was one's husband or wife.

Unless there is real pain or you are still in the grips of a very negative feeling period, you are concerned for the other one. At least—I am talking just personally—once you get over that pit of negativism, you do tend to have a concern. It is qualified. You don't want to get too concerned because you don't want to get hurt again. But you still maintain that interest in the other person.

(Woman, about thirty)

Feelings of continued obligation to help are especially likely to appear in response to a former spouse in great need. One woman whose former husband was unemployed and ill gave him what she had left of her housekeeping money (she had remarried) to help him reestablish himself. But obligation to help does not imply wanting the other in one's life. Later this woman tried to prevent her former husband from seeing their children.

In another incident a woman, divorced about seven years, had planned to remarry. A few weeks before the wedding was to take place her fiancé died of a heart attack. She was overcome by grief and called her former husband to ask him to take the children for the weekend. Her former husband canceled his engagements, drove to the city in which the woman lived, stayed in her apartment, cared for the children, prepared meals, and at one point shoveled her car out of the snow. When the weekend was over he and his former wife returned to their previous relationship of rather tense civility.

One spouse may call on the other for help in managing the emotional effects of reverse: a man on being left by a girl friend may, for example, turn to his former wife for solace. Or a spouse who is feeling low may call the other just to talk.

My ex-husband called me last week and I said, "What's the matter?" I can tell from his voice. And he said, "I'm depressed." And I said, "Well, what's wrong?" He said, "You are the only one I know who I can call and complain to." And it's true. No one else would listen or be interested. Not that I am, but I can still pretend.

(Woman, late thirties)

Guilt often assails those who feel responsible for the separation. Inability to respond to the other spouse's desire for continued contact can then give rise to further guilt.

If your spouse says, "I love you and I need you," you feel so guilty because all you have to do is be nice to this person and it will make them happy. That puts incredible guilt on you. He says, "How can you leave me when I love you so much?"

(Woman, late twenties)

Those who left a spouse despite the spouse's pleas may afterward be anguished by guilt. One woman had been married to an alcoholic and had survived one marital horror after another: sporadic financial crises; senseless, violent, fights; embarrassing scenes with friends and kin. She finally left her husband when he continued drinking after a physician had told him that it would be fatal to do so. Now she received calls from him several times a week, pleading with her to return. She could not, if it meant watching him kill himself. Yet she was distraught at his plight.

A woman whose husband had encountered a serious business reverse about the time she decided to leave him was also beset by guilt afterward.

The first six months were a nightmare. There was no keeping him out of the house. It was just unreal. He was there all the time. He was lost. Talk about guilt! I went around one whole year feeling so guilty; it was like I had deserted one of my children.

(Woman, mid-forties)

Some men and women, under the press of guilt, agree to a grotesquely uneven property division as partial reparation. Many for a time do not permit themselves a satisfactory relationship with someone new. It is in some ways the fortunate husband or wife who feels absolved of responsibility because his or her spouse took initiative for the break or demonstrated faults grievous enough to justify departure.

I've come to grips with this terrible feeling of guilt that I had. I did a lot of thinking about it and I realized that my wife was not perfect. There were a lot of things wrong with her. And this relieved a lot of my guilt.

(Man, about thirty)

Some among the separated, in order to still their sense of guilt, seek a final repudiation by their spouse:

I called my husband and I said I wanted to see him. And I think what I would have liked him to do is reject me. Because this other relationship I'm in is getting more intense as time goes on. It is going to become more committed . . . . So I wanted to see him as a way of validating my feelings, I think, and reassuring myself that it was over. And to relieve me of the guilt, because I was the one who was getting the divorce. So I think I would have liked him to reject me. Then I'd be relieved of the guilt and responsibility.

(Woman, about thirty)

The spouse who is understood to have been left may attempt to retain access to the departing spouse by eliciting that spouse's guilt. The departing spouse can be baffled by this. He or she is apt to continue to feel obligated to support the other's well-being, yet is unwilling to meet the other's implicit demands, especially if these require return to the marriage.

My husband is contemplating suicide. He's been telling me this, and it is a hard thing to live with. He's going to be very methodical. The house will be sold, the car fixed, I will have my money. And he will just do it very quietly. [Said sarcastically.] It's very scary. I don't know whether he's bluffing—I don't know. I have mixed feelings. I love him. I don't want the separation. But he wouldn't talk, he wouldn't go out, and when he wanted to stay in he also wanted me to stay in. He didn't want me to have a life of my own. It was a whole bunch of things.

(Woman, about thirty)

In time, individuals who previously displayed a sense of continued obligation to the spouse may decide to disclaim it. They reach a level of exasperation with the spouse sufficient to justify his or her rejection.

He called me and he said he [had ended an affair]. He said "I've got to talk with you." And I was on my way out of town and I said, "I can't talk to you now, I'm going out of town. I can talk to you when I get home." And he said, "I still have the same problem. I'm still in love with you." And I said, "You've got to let go. You've just got to let go."

(Woman, mid-forties)

Solicitude and rejection may alternate with one another. Solicitude may appear if the spouse is in obvious need, and rejection of the spouse may follow anger or exasperation or fear of exploitation at the hands of the spouse. A woman had been separated from her drug-addicted husband for about three years when he appeared early one morning at her door, having been robbed and beaten while high. The woman let him stay until he felt able to return to his home. "After all," she said, "he used to be my husband." But a few days later, when he again wanted to clean up in her apartment, she called the police. It was one thing to respond to an emergency, another to let herself be used.

It might be noted that there are penalties associated with postmarital solicitude. They may be especially severe if the spouse who is the object of solicitude was initially responsible for the break, and the other spouse therefore has scores to settle. A degree of satisfaction may then accompany the other spouse's sympathy. In one case a woman in her late thirties had left her husband after years of unhappiness. Her life after separation turned out not to be much of an improvement, and when her husband came to see the children she let him know that things were going badly. His response was warm, but not unmixed with gratification at her distress.

The last couple of times I saw my husband I got crying so much that he said to me, "You know, you are really in bad shape." For the six months before this I never fell apart. I just felt I was doing the right thing, was putting an end to the seven years of shit that was going on between us. And the last couple of times I just got to crying and he got very sympathetic and he put his arm around me and all of a sudden he's the strong one. And then he said, "You know, you pushed for this divorce. I would have given you a year of freedom to do just what you want, and then we might have gone back together. But no, you didn't want it that way."

(Woman, late thirties)

*Attachment*

In Chapter 3 I noted that attachment seemed often to persist after separation. Even more than other postmarital bonds, its persistence seems to be independent of an individual's conscious desires. It can take the individual by surprise: One man believed himself furious with his wife and then discovered that he was disappointed when she was not home when he came to visit his children.

Attachment may continue though the former spouse is also disdained.

I don't like him. As a man I find him boring. If I met him at a party I'd talk with him for about two minutes and then I'd say I'll see you. But the emotional tug is still there. He is still attractive to me.

(Woman, late twenties)

A woman, exasperated by her continued attachment to her husband, said:

(96)

It is like the battered child syndrome. You never find a battered child that does not want to be back with its parents, because they are the only parents it has. I just have very much this feeling.

(Woman, mid-twenties)

Because of continued attachment the separated individual is likely to feel that home is where the spouse is; elsewhere is exile. Attachment may impel the individual to reestablish some sort of contact with the spouse, to telephone the spouse, to enter into his or her vicinity. This impulsion toward the spouse may persist despite repeated rejection.

My wife manages the bookstore where I like to go. Just this last weekend I dropped down there, with a friend of mine. I didn't expect to see her, because usually she's back in the office. But now she was on the floor and we bumped into each other, and she saw me, and then she looked the other way. It was a complete cold shoulder. And my friend looked at me and I looked at him and we laughed.

I don't go there with hopes or expectations. I have dealings with her during the week, about the children. I could say to myself, "Don't go there." I know I might run into her, and it's uncomfortable. But I say, "Well, Goddamn it, why should I alter my life because of her actions?" It is she that has the problem. We talk on the phone about the children, but when we physically meet, she won't acknowledge my presence. That's all I really ask, that she acknowledge my presence. And I get this cold shoulder.

(Man, early thirties)

Forming a new attachment elsewhere, if this proves possible, seems to diminish the force of marital attachment. The new tie assures the individual that the world is not bereft of others who may care for him or her and provides new emotional concerns with which to become engaged. But often enough a new figure, although gratifying, even exciting, fails to replace the spouse. The marriage is real; the other relationship is, by comparison, frivolous.

I wanted to be with the man I was going out with. During the time I was with him it wasn't as a substitute. But he knew and I knew that my first priority was to get the marriage back together.

(Woman, about thirty)

With time, attachment to the spouse may become dormant, but it seems not to disappear. Seeing the former spouse after the passage of years is likely to evoke not indifference but rather a resurgence of fondness and anger, of bitterness and yearning, of paler but still recognizable expressions of the emotions experienced just after the separation.

If there is no competing attachment, the attachment to the spouse can often be elicited again in full force. A woman had been separated from her husband for five years, and divorced for three, when he called, ostensibly to arrange to see the children, and invited her to have dinner with him. In the darkened restaurant they reminisced about the happy early days of their marriage. He told her how good it was to see her and led her to admit it was good to see him, too. The woman was again drawn into caring for him. She said, later, "He can always get around me." The husband had remarried, and with his new marriage in mind, the woman added, "I'd rather be the girl he dates without the wife knowing than be the wife who doesn't know."

## Hostility

In separating from someone you discover in yourself things that you had never felt before in your life. That's one of the things that really freaks you out. I've always used my mind to keep down anything I didn't like. And now I discover, wow, I can hate!

(Woman, mid-twenties)

Virtually all husbands and wives after separation feel some bitterness or anger toward the other; they have some reason for feeling disappointed or hurt, and have some justification for blaming their former spouse. Even the man who leaves his wife for someone new can be disappointed that his wife turned out not to be the woman he wanted; he may feel angry that he had been led to marry her, and angry again for the injuries she may have inflicted on him in fighting his desire for freedom.

Although both individuals are likely to feel misused, the hurt and anger of the spouse on whom the separation was imposed ordinarily appears more intense. The other spouse is seen as possessing the power to relieve the distress of separation but willfully refusing to do so. Yet sometimes the spouse who initiated the break nevertheless feels that he or she is the rejected one. One woman ended her marriage of many years because her husband, though a good provider and father, was withdrawn and unaffectionate. When she had confronted him with his remoteness, he had said simply that he did not love her. She eventually asked him to leave. The separation distress she then experienced was more painful and disorganizing than anything she had anticipated, and she almost desperately wanted her husband to return. Yet he continued to say that he could not change his feelings. Each time that the woman saw him she felt rejected anew and had new cause for anger.

**When he comes on Sunday I try to discuss with him things about the children, but he will not listen and he does not respond. He ignores me. He'll walk out of the room. I can't spend more than two minutes with him without getting terribly depressed or terribly angry.**

**(Woman, early thirties)**

A spouse's apparent absence of concern after the separation has taken place can thus be felt as a new abandonment. A somewhat older woman who had been admiring of her husband through a long married life was left by him with little warning. When he returned to discuss how they would divide their property and what level of alimony she should receive, she was almost as devastated and infuriated by his new coldness as by his earlier departure. He seemed simply not to care about her any more.

**He said, "Good evening," and I said, "Won't you come in and sit down?" and we went into the living room and he talked and said that it would be the best thing for me to have a divorce, that there was no pressure on him, and I said, well, I didn't think it was the best thing for either him or me, but this was the way the situation was, there didn't seem to be any alternative. And then he just said what he would do, period. And I asked him how I would live when I wasn't able to work any more, because the alimony**

wouldn't be enough, and he said, "Well, you can always sell the house and sell the things in it. They are worth a fortune nowadays. Or you can do what lots of other people do, go on welfare." After he left I went upstairs and passed a mirror and looked at myself and didn't recognize myself, because my face was set in a kind of rigidity.

(Woman, about fifty)

The hurt stemming from the spouse's callousness may be intensified should the spouse be critical or indicate dislike. The spouse in this way seems to suggest that it is the rejected individual's own fault that he or she was abandoned.

He just dislikes everything about me. I mean the other day I said something to him and I made a gesture and he mimicked me in a nasty way. I said, "You know, there is nothing about me that you can stand. You don't like the way I look, you don't like the way I move my hands." Well, that is going to hurt me. Until I am ninety years old, that is going to hurt me.

(Woman, early thirties)

Sometimes one spouse expresses disdain or contempt for the other in the presence of the children. The other spouse may be deeply shamed by this and fearful that the children will adopt the same attitude.

She's still vindictive. This has been very problematic for me because naturally her attitude does rub off on the kids. There's a certain disrespect I think—particularly the younger one, the ten-year-old. It's there because she observes her mother. I've had a phone call from her mother or I've had to call her for some reason and our business is generally very curt and abrupt and most of the time it'll end up with her telling me to go fuck myself. In front of the children. And this is real hard to take. The attitude thing does definitely rub off on the children.

(Man, late thirties)

A spouse's hostility can produce responsive hostility:

I have not spoken seriously with my husband in five months. This week I received a letter from him, a bitter, hateful, letter. It's so completely out of focus as to where I am, what he thinks I am, and what my ideas are, that I just want to ignore it. I'm hurt when he says I'm screwing up his child. But I just don't want to waste the time to explain it to him.

(Woman, late thirties)

Knowing that the spouse is with someone new can also fuel anger. It is easy to feel cheated: The spouse is giving to another the security that rightfully is one's own. Nor can the individual any longer identify with the spouse as a fellow sufferer. In addition there can be a sense of having been humiliated, and of being unable to do anything about it:

I had a visit from my husband. I was going to be very polite and not scream at him any more. But his girl friend was in his car waiting for my husband to take her somewhere. This I couldn't take. So I got mad and I screamed at him and then I started to cry, because he puts me down. And I said that is the last time he is coming in my house, the last time.

(Woman, late thirties)

Many among the separated, however they may feel internally, avoid expression of their anger; they try to remain friendly to the spouse, to defend the spouse to friends, and to protect the spouse's relationship with the children. Others observe no such self-discipline. An associate of mine tells of having watched a man and his wife, flanked by their respective lawyers, standing before a judge. The man's lawyer was arguing that the judge should not raise the man's support payment to the wife. Suddenly the wife, without changing expression or posture or giving any indication in the upper part of her body, which was all the judge could see, of what she was about to do, swung out with one foot and kicked her husband's shin. The husband yelped and the wife looked at him with cool curiosity. Expressions of hostility can be less amusing: In that same court later in the week armed guards were posted because a husband known to carry a gun had threatened to kill his wife and her lawyer.

Murderous fantasies in which the spouse is the victim do not seem especially rare. One well-controlled man reported reading a newspaper story of someone who had killed his wife and himself with a rifle, and then thought how easily he could do the same. A woman whose husband had left her for a younger woman talked quite seriously about killing the two of them. Her husband's refusal to respond to her needs while attending so solicitously to those of a stranger infuriated her. Some husbands and wives who do not have blatantly murderous wishes find to their discomfort that they are visited by unwelcome wishes for the spouse to succumb to accident or illness.

**In many aspects I really do hate my husband. But I don't want to think nothing but hate. You know, when I see him walking down the street, I think, "I hope when you step off the corner you get run over."**
**(Woman, mid-thirties)**

Hostility may give rise to more nearly acceptable fantasies of revenge and retaliation. "If they knew what I know about him," a wife may think, as she imagines calling her husband's boss and colleagues to expose him. Some actually carry out this fantasy by telling friends what the spouse was really like.

The shared parenting of the children provides a convenient vehicle for the expression of postmarital malice. The man may try to win the children's affections away from his wife or to obtain their custody in court. He may buy them gifts that they can use only in his home, and tell them that they would have a happier life with him. The woman, on her part, may prevent the man from seeing the children or insist that he see them only in her presence. She may tell the children directly or let them overhear her telling a friend about the man's crimes against her and the children.

The husband or wife may attack the other's property. One woman unscrewed, unsoldered, and disconnected every element in her husband's hi-fi set; she then telephoned him to say that he could move the set to his apartment. Another woman cut one of her husband's suits into small pieces and put it down the incinerator. Or there may be harassment. A man formed the practice of calling his wife in the middle of the night to berate her; among other things, he blamed her for his insomnia. Or there may be subtle or gross reminders that one now has someone new in one's life. In several cases a woman seemed to have arranged matters so that her husband would come across love letters from a new boyfriend; in one instance the woman left the letters on a bathroom table when her husband was babysitting. And men may simply announce that although their wives think them unappealing, other women are not of the same opinion.

These hostile acts are often regretted afterward. If it is unrealistic for them to hope that they will feel kindly toward a former spouse, the separated would often like at least to feel indifferent. Anger is petty and unattractive: How sad that the legacy of years of living together, of having children together, and of trying to make a marriage work should be a wish that the other step into the path of a truck. Sometimes anger, though intense, feels foreign to the separated individual, like a demon that has taken up residence in his or her body. One woman said that she felt possessed by her anger, and wanted almost desperately to be rid of it. Yet anger is likely to remain for some time despite the individual's attempts at exorcism, impeding cooperation with the spouse and so making the separation less manageable.

### Interests in Conflict

In addition to animosities stemming from experiences of abandonment, rejection, and threat at the hands of the other spouse, animosities may be produced by genuine conflicts of interest. There are four issues in relation to which such conflict is likely: property division, support, custody, and visitation. With the exception of visitation, differences in interest are almost inherent in these matters; what one gets, the other is without. And it can happen that a visitation arrangement that would most suit one is awkward for the other.

#### Property Division

Nothing can be gained through a division of property except perhaps sole use of what previously had been shared. But a good deal can be lost. The loss can then be defined either as a sacrifice made for the benefit of the other or as an injury suffered at the hands of the other.

The couple's house is often the major item of their shared property. The man on separation may relinquish his claim to it. Alternatively, he may retain title to it or permit a shared title to remain in force, while agreeing that his wife and children will continue to live in the house until the children have finished school. He may assume responsibility for mortgage payments even though he now lives elsewhere himself: One man said that under terms of his separation agreement he paid taxes and loan installments, made necessary repairs, and in fact did everything he had always done in relation to the house, except live in it. Or the man may take quite another tack and insist that the house be sold, so that he can withdraw his part of the equity; his wife and children may then be forced to seek new housing.

Men who let their wives have the house may feel they have been stripped of the one significant possession their earnings had brought them. Should their wives thereafter complain, they may react with scorn. A successful businessman, for instance, felt that, given her possession of the house and receipt of a generous support check, his wife had done well.

**My wife is really sweating over her budget. I gave her the house, which is worth eighty-five thousand dollars, and I'm giving her twelve hundred dollars a month, and she says she can't make ends meet. Isn't that ridiculous?**

**(Man, about forty)**

But wives may feel the house to be a large and not entirely welcome responsibility. They may be uncertain about their ability to keep it in repair and may worry about meeting monthly payments on it. Or, until there is an ironclad separation agreement, they may fear that somehow their husbands will change their minds about letting them have the house and they will have to move.

The stance a separated individual assumes in property negotiations can be affected by many factors. A husband or wife may drive a hard bargain over the house and other property to demonstrate that the spouse has forfeited his or her solicitude, or drive no bargain at all, to expiate his or her guilt. Malice can be expressed in the negotiations. One woman had her house furnished by her husband's mother, who earlier had moved to an apartment from a house of her own. After separation the woman's husband said that their furniture had only been lent by his mother, not given to them outright, and that his mother now wanted it back. The woman discovered when she asked her mother-in-law where to send the furniture that her mother-in-law didn't want it at all. The return had been entirely the husband's idea. And, since he lived in a room, he would have to pay storage charges on it.

Certain items of furniture may have special meaning that make one or the other spouse lay special store by them. Academic couples may have difficulty in deciding ownership of jointly purchased books. Or symbolic meaning may be associated with an item, so that one spouse may not want the other to have it. One woman refused, through her lawyer, to permit her husband to take either of the double beds they had owned: She could not endure the thought of his sleeping with another woman in one of her beds.

Sometimes one or the other member of a couple may become uncooperative just on general principles, so as to avoid feeling disregarded. One woman refused to sign a joint tax return that her husband had prepared because by not signing it she retained some negotiating leverage. But it seemed more the resulting sense of self-assertion than its realistic advantages that she found rewarding.

**My husband came and brought the kids in, and he had this envelope, and he wanted me to sign. I just couldn't bring myself to sign. I said, "Will you please give it to my attorney?" He couldn't argue. He's well-mannered enough not to push anything. But I figured that really I have gotten so little, and he hasn't agreed to any settlement in writing, and he really should be sending a copy of the income tax statement to my attorney. And I didn't really actually refuse to sign it. I just said do it through my attorney.**

(Woman, early thirties)

*Support*

Among middle- and high-income couples issues of support can

become extremely complicated and virtually demand legal help for their management. There is the designation of the husband's contribution as child support or as alimony. The symbolic meanings of the two are different, as are the tax implications and the implications for duration of contribution, since support continues only until the children are a certain age, and alimony may continue indefinitely unless the recipient remarries. There is the question of whether to consider the woman's earning power. There is the issue of tying the level of support to the cost of living, or the man's earning power, or the changing needs of the wife and children. There can be issues of responsibility for medical and educational costs. One woman's husband agreed to pay her children's medical bills. The woman thereupon entered each of the children into a protracted and costly psychoanalytic treatment. The husband refused to pay. The woman threatened suit. Finally an out-of-court settlement was made, largely in the woman's favor.

All these issues may eventually be considered in the separation agreement of middle- and high-income couples. But at first the concerns of these couples are similar to the concerns of low-income couples: How much is the man (assuming he is the primary income producer) willing and able to give to his wife (assuming she has custody of the children), and how reliably will he give it?

The case for the man owing his wife part of his income is fairly straightforward. First, the husband is responsible for support of his children, just as is his wife. That they do not live with him does not relieve him of that responsibility. Second, under some circumstances the husband may have continuing responsibility for his wife, even though he no longer lives with her. The two may have functioned as a team, in which he assumed responsibility for occupational and financial achievement and his wife assumed responsibility for maintenance of the home and care of him and the children. It would be unfair that the husband should realize all the rewards of this joint effort and the wife none. Furthermore, in conformity with her responsibilities in the joint effort, the wife may have relinquished opportunities to establish herself in the working world. The jobs she held are likely to have been chosen because they were compatible with her primary responsibilities to her husband, home, and children. When she and her husband separate, the wife may well claim that not only did she invest much of her life in her husband's occupational success, but that she did so at the cost of not now being able to earn a satisfactory livelihood.

The following may suggest the anxiety felt by some women, and their sense of helplessness, when they recognize that despite support payments, they are now essentially on their own.

**Bert went to see my lawyer, and told him what amount of money he would send, and he is sending that. He was very generous, comparatively. But for a while I was panicked, and I started looking for a job. And I couldn't get a job because I hadn't done anything for ten years except take care of two kids.**

**(Woman, early thirties)**

The man's case may be simpler. If he can support his children, he will. He might like as much as is possible to support them directly, rather than indirectly through his wife, but he will do whatever he must. He may be willing to support his wife, though she is no longer married to him, during a transitional period until she can support herself, but indefinite support may seem to him to be unlimited indenture. What obligations based on past services could conceivably justify indefinite financial responsibility?

The man is likely to be concerned about his capacity to continue to provide his wife with support for the children without absolutely impoverishing himself. A good many men comment on having little money left with which to reestablish their lives once their support payments are made. In addition, some men are concerned about no longer being able to control how the money will be spent once it is given to their wives.

**I place into my wife's hands sufficient resources to take care of her immediate needs. I take care of the medical expenses myself. But I want to control my income as much as I can. My kids want to go to camp, I want to be in a position to provide that. I don't want to put it into my wife's hands. Because I have no guarantee it will be used in that manner. I have no idea *what* my wife might do.**

**(Man, late forties)**

Early agreements regarding support may not work out. Many women complain that their husbands have reneged on their obligations; some contrast their own consequent poverty with their husbands' relative affluence. But men also have complaints about support agreements they made earlier. One man, an obstetrician, had left his wife after ten years of stormy marriage. Partly because he felt guilty, partly to gain his wife's cooperation in the divorce, he agreed to send his wife half his income after office expenses and taxes. A few years later he remarried and discovered that despite his earnings he was financially pinched. He could keep for his own living expenses only about a quarter of his gross income. He became, in consequence, furious with his former wife; once, when he came to pick up one of his children, his former wife walked the child to his car, and he rolled up his car window rather than talk with her.

## Custody

Couples usually agree that the wife should have custody of the children. If the man does not ask his lawyer to try to obtain custody, the lawyer is apt to assume that it will go to the wife. Most often, even if a man says he wants custody, his lawyer will discourage him on the grounds that custody ordinarily is given to a father only on demonstration of the mother's unfitness, not an easy thing to demonstrate, especially in courts that increasingly refuse to hear evidence of "immorality." If the mother wants to divide custody (still a novel procedure in some courts) or give custody to the father outright, because she thinks such an arrangement fairer or less burdensome or better for the children, well and good: The judge will undoubtedly approve the parents' agreement. But if the mother wants to retain custody, the man will usually be advised that there is little he can do about it.

Some men are genuinely convinced that their children would be better off with them. They believe their wives to be alcoholic, neglectful, seductive, or brutal. Or they may be about to remarry and believe they will be able to provide a more normal setting for the children. Or they may feel that the children have a better relationship with them than they have with their mothers and would prefer to be with them. These men may seek custody because they must, as responsible and loving parents. But other men seek custody for reasons other than their children's welfare. They may find the prospect of their children's loss unbearable, and be unwilling for their wives to deprive them of their children in addition to everything else. This reaction may be especially likely among those men whose wives left them, or required them to leave, with what seemed to them little cause. Or they may feel that their wives, by their actions, have relinquished any right to consideration, and that losing custody would teach their wives a lesson in responsibility; it would serve them right. And, perhaps, they also feel that loss of custody would bring their wives back to them, on their terms.

Custody battles can become intensely engaging. No matter what motivations initiated the battle, the husband and wife may begin to feel that the welfare of their children is at stake. Their children's welfare is then so important that in its defense anything goes: The children may be lobbied by both sides, psychiatrists may be called to support the husband's or wife's case, anything at all may be said in open court. Engagement in a custody battle can, in consequence, produce fear and loathing of a high order. And although some custody battles are settled once and for all in the divorce hearing, others go on and on, with the parent who lost custody almost driven to bring new evidence to new hearings.

### Visitation

If custody battles can produce a state of war between the spouses, battles over visitation tend to resemble border skirmishes. Without acknowledgment that there is any fundamental dispute, the wife may not have the children available on a day the man had hoped to see them—they are at an aunt's, or they appeared to be getting ill and it would be better if they stayed in. When the husband does arrange to see the children, the wife may insist that he clear his plans with her, thus communicating that responsibility for the children is now hers. Sometimes the wife will insist on the husband seeing the children only in her presence, because in her mind the husband cannot be trusted. Or the wife may insist that the children not meet the husband's new woman, because the encounter would upset them, or upset her. There are weapons the husband, too, can use. He may fail to show up when the wife—and the children—expect him, or insist on seeing the children at inconvenient times, or return the children at a time other than the one he had agreed to. When he does take the children out, he may do his utmost to entertain them so they can better recognize the drabness of their lives with their mother, or to treat them as responsible and mature so they can better recognize their mother's tendency toward infantilization.

Husband and wife are vulnerable to one another because of their shared parental stake. The husband, with his paternal relationship as justification, can be endlessly invasive in his wife's household, calling and showing up at odd hours. The wife can berate the husband for not being a better father even as she encourages the children to plan activities competitive with the husband's visits. Each may fear that the other is attempting to bring the children into an alliance: The husband may fear the wife is turning the children against him with garish tales of his misdeeds, and the wife may fear that the husband is playing pied piper, luring the children away from her by giving them unwholesome things to eat and allowing them to watch TV past their bedtime.

The situation encourages the husband and wife to wish that the other were out of the picture. The husband may be bitter that he can no longer simply live with the children, but must instead call his wife to arrange to see them, like someone sent by a social agency. And the wife may be bitter that she is required to prepare the children for the husband's visit, to have them washed and dressed and waiting for the time he deigns to appear, and then to be there on his return, like a servant, ready to put away the children's clothes, respond to their noisiness, and, for hours and perhaps days afterward, deal with their unsettled emotional state.

Both husband and wife may be irritated that they must share with one another the raising, guiding, and influencing of their children. This is not to say that the wife may not breathe a sigh of relief at being able to get the children off on a Sunday afternoon, or that the husband may not be grateful for the moment he can return them. But the irritations of shared parenting tend to outweigh these benefits.

## Dealing with Disputes over Support and Visitation

Disputes over issues of support and visitation seem nearly inescapable between even amicable former spouses. There are so many issues that arise. If a child goes to boarding school and the father pays the child's tuition, should the father continue to send support payments to his wife? Who pays the child's airfare so the child can visit the father if the mother moves away? If the father is responsible for paying for medical care, does he have a right to decide what treatments are appropriate for the children?

One couple's only son was sent to a boarding school at the father's urging. The father paid the school tuition and the charge for his son's maintenance. The mother wanted the father to continue to send her the regular support check even though their son was away, because she would have to continue to pay rent on the two-bedroom apartment, buy clothing for the boy, and keep up payments on his health insurance. And she would have the additional expense of paying the boy's transportation to and from school three or four times a year. The father argued that he was responsible only for his son's support, not for his former wife's expenses. And since he was now sending money to the school for his son's support, he could not be expected to send money to his wife as well. He said that he would be happy to pay for his son's transportation if his son were to come to see him on school vacations, and he thought his wife should feel the same way. The father won because he simply refused to send further checks to his wife and his wife was unwilling to take him to court. But a better way of dealing with such issues might be desirable.

A carefully drafted separation agreement does not seem to be any defense against disputes. I have seen one agreement of twenty pages, specifying, for example, exactly which day of the summer in relation to the ending of school the children would move to their father's home as well as everything else that the lawyers could think of. The couple had endless disputes about its proper interpretation.

It might be useful if separated parents could bring issues that they simply cannot solve themselves to arbitration of some sort, perhaps by a minister or social worker or other professional whom they trust. Each might be willing to agree to an arbitrator's judgment regarding the best interests of the child, whereas neither could accept the other's. Perhaps social agencies may some day provide professionals who can help separated parents over impasses that they cannot manage on their own.

Failing this, it may be useful for parents, when disputes arise between them over support or visitation, to recognize that such disputes are nearly inevitable. Their separate relationships to the children are bound to produce conflicts of interest, quite apart from either's meanness or malevolence. For the children's sake, if not for their own, it is important that they manage their differences without introducing new resentments into their postmarital relationship.

## The Postmarital Relationship

How does one cope with a relationship as intensely ambivalent as the postmarital relationship of husbands and wives? Many husbands and wives would like not to; they would like to be rid of it, to have nothing further to do with the spouse, to move away if that is the only way they can stop themselves or the spouse from picking up the phone and calling. Physically removing oneself, so there is no longer any chance of contact, does produce a solution of a sort; although the other may survive in memory, there are no new incidents to keep the relationship vivid. But, for those who have children, to leave the scene may be morally, emotionally, and perhaps legally impossible. And, the children aside, it may not be that easy to say farewell to friends, family, and job, to relinquish one's home base and seek to establish oneself elsewhere.

Most of those who separate remain in the same locale. Because of the children, out of continued concern for the other, out of loneliness, to work out the division of property and arrange for support—for all the reasons already alluded to—they continue to see one another. Their relationship does not end; instead it enters a new, postmarital phase.

Postmarital relationships tend to display a mixture of feelings. Positive and negative feelings may alternate, or be present simultaneously in a sort of amalgam, as in the husband who was both distressed and gratified that his wife found the separation hard. But some postmarital relationships are organized around the expression of only one set of feelings: sometimes around continued affection, so that the couple act toward one another like devoted friends; more often around distrust or an animosity in which almost anything goes.

As I noted earlier, the particular feelings around which the postmarital relationship is organized can matter greatly for the quality of each spouse's life. Least happy may be those whose spouse acts as an enemy. Opportunities for harming the other are too plentiful after separation. An actively hostile spouse may attempt to seize whatever had previously been jointly owned, such as the bank account, valuable objects, or the family telephone number. If there is a third person in the situation, the spouse may attempt to have adultery introduced as grounds for the divorce. A husband who wants to hurt his wife may ask his lawyer to dispossess her from the home they had shared, to fight her for custody of the children, to yield to her the lowest possible level of support. A wife who wants to hurt her husband may ask her lawyer to get title to everything he can, to keep visitation rights to the minimum, to get the highest possible level of support. If, in addition to all the other problems of separation, one has a spouse who takes every opportunity to frustrate and injure, it is easy to feel that the world has become extraordinarily threatening.

There is not really much a husband or wife can do in defense against a malevolent spouse. A court's restraining order can keep a man from banging on the front door in the middle of the night, but what can keep him from telling mutual friends that his wife is sleeping with her boss? Or prevent a wife from complaining about her ex-husband's brutality to his employer and physician and anyone else who will listen?

It may be small comfort for a spouse on the receiving end of animosity to be told that, despite the genuine injury he or she has suffered, the animosity in part expresses continued attachment. Yet a husband who wakes his wife at two in the morning to threaten that he will kill her if she does not permit him to see his children is, among other things, keeping in touch. Quarrels over property, money, custody, or visitation rights, though they express genuine conflicts of interest, can also keep a relationship alive with transfusions of hostility. Hostility, even as it seeks to damage, sustains engagement.

My husband hasn't paid my insurance bill for the car. That has not been paid. Or life insurance, he has not paid for three months and they are closing it. Twenty-seven dollars to close an account he hasn't paid and it is four months old. The medical bill he hasn't paid for six months. I put the bills in an envelope and sent them over to him and he did not do one damned thing.

I call him up about everything—if the child is sick and I want him to pay for a doctor, or I need money for a baseball glove. I haven't money for taxes, for anything. He is purposely torturing me and making me do this. He wants me to call up. So he can hang up the receiver. Because that's what he does. He curses at me; he hangs up on me.

(Woman, late thirties)

Sometimes to save themselves from having to recognize their unwillingness to lose one another, husbands and wives enter into a nearly conscious agreement to squabble. If they did not, they would have to admit their need.

I think to some extent I find friction with my wife is a way of dealing with positive feelings that I have had on occasion. You know, I've been there and we're squabbling over all kinds of petty things and I wonder if it isn't our way of keeping down positive feelings we don't want to express, kind of a defense against them.

(Man, about thirty)

Or it may be that as long as one is angry, recognition of loss can be averted.

Every time I got mad, at least I wasn't depressed. When I stopped bugging him, I really started to suffer all the feelings of loss and abandonment and all that sort of business.

(Woman, mid-thirties)

Sometimes husbands and wives feel that they can almost choose whether to express anger or affection toward the spouse. They feel both, and because they feel both, neither feeling seems entirely authentic.

He went to Alabama to get the divorce and told me that he would be back Thursday, on the nine o'clock flight. So I didn't know whether to be out of the house at nine o'clock so that if he called I wouldn't be there, or whether he would call at all. A friend called that evening and we talked until five minutes of nine. I said, "I wish I really hated him. It would be so much easier." And my friend said, "No, it wouldn't. Nothing is simple. And to live with hate is a terrible thing. You would constantly have that knot inside, that anger." And I said, "I guess you're right." And I'm glad she expressed it in that manner because I think it would be terrible to live with hate. Maybe it is better to struggle with whatever one is struggling with. We chatted until five minutes of nine and I said, "I don't know whether to run out of the house or not, whether he is going to call or not." She had barely hung up and he did call. And I did go ahead and meet him.

(Woman, mid-thirties)

The woman just quoted found it comforting for a time to see her husband. Then her anger became too great and she asked him to stop calling her. He interpreted this as a request that he call less often, which seemed about right.

Often the spouse who took the lead in the separation will also attempt to establish a friendly postmarital relationship. This spouse, perhaps, has less to be angry at and stronger feelings of continued obligation.

The first couple of nights when we were just separated I called, just to keep in contact. And she said, "We are separated, why are you doing this?" She was confused. But I like her as a person and I have been with her for five years. I don't want to be married to her. I don't want to spend the rest of my life with her. But I care about her happiness. I care about her future. I want her to be happy. Our relationship didn't end with great hatred or hostility, although there were those feelings.

(Man, late twenties)

Couples may discover that separation brings home to them their continued attachment to one another. They may not want to return to living together, but they want to see one another. The solution, strange as it may seem, may be to go out on dates.

My husband wanted to call me up and take me on dates, you know, just this ridiculous thing . . . . But it was wonderful to see him.

(Woman, early thirties)

Sometimes one member of the couple had left the marriage because of an affair, but later wanted to spend evenings with the spouse. The result can be that the spouse and the girlfriend or boyfriend exchange roles, though without the girlfriend or boyfriend knowing.

I've had four dates with my husband. It's been wonderful. When he leaves me he's going to see his girlfriend. I know that damned well. But you know, I still enjoy it. I've gone out with him four times since we separated and we've talked more than in the fourteen years we were married. Besides, I'm going out, having a pleasant evening, and it's one night I'm not staying home. I've had two years of his lying to me. Now I figure he's lying to her.

(Woman, about forty)

Occasionally a husband or wife will try to balance a continuing relationship with the spouse with a developing relationship with someone new. In that way the husband or wife can feel dependent on neither while having both.

I found that as I got more involved with someone else, that I had a tendency to see my wife. I think it was almost as a counterbalancing influence, so that I wouldn't get emotionally involved. I don't know if it's love any more. But I do try to talk to her a lot. The girl I was dating suggested that I get counseling and resolve this situation once and for all. I won't be good for anyone else until I get this thing resolved.

(Man, about thirty)

Many separated couples maintain a sporadic sexual relationship for a few weeks or months after their separation. Some couples report the occasional interruption of the separation by unanticipated sexual rejoinings. Others more deliberately establish an understanding that their sexual relationship will continue.

**Our sexual relationship was the last thing to go, and after we separated, it was on again. And that's the only thing that's left. It's convenient for both of us.**

(Woman, early thirties)

Couples may go to bed with one another despite a generally hostile relationship. The husband might appear to see the children, to give his wife money, to pick up something he had left behind, or just to talk with his wife. A quarrel might follow, ending in hysterics or in hurt silence. The husband or wife wants to make amends, and then the couple find themselves physically drawn to each other. "I come over to see the children," one man said, "and later we fight and then go to bed." More often, however, a postmarital sexual relationship seems to occur within a context of a more nearly friendly or affectionate relationship.

Both members of the couple usually view the postmarital sexual relationship as without implication for reconciliation. They agree, as one woman put it, that they can be lovers, but not husband and wife. Should one member of the couple interpret the continued sexual contact as implying movement toward reconciliation, there may be new disappointment in store for him or her.

**My expectations would get built up, after we had such a great evening, and that is what hurts, my own expectations. Because the next day he would be seeing someone else. It is my expectations that hurt me.**

(Woman, late twenties)

Some individuals report that the sexual relationship with the spouse seemed to improve after separation. There may be a special intensity in it then, as sexual gratification is heightened by the emotional relief of regaining one another. Yet in the postmarital sexual relationship there can also be an expression of the anger each individual feels and of the sense of distance each may have developed as a defense against further loss. The relief of undoing the loss may then be limited by an odd, unsettling sense of impersonality.

These postmarital arrangements may be interrupted by resurgence of anger and feelings of estrangement. Anger with the other for continuing to contribute to the individual's distress may be heightened by recognition that one has permitted oneself again to become enmeshed.

**There are some times when I sleep with Dotty at her apartment and she does something that bothers me like it did when we were married, and I feel like yelling and doing a whole big thing again.**
**(Man, about thirty)**

My impression is that most postmarital sexual relationships do not last much beyond the first few months of separation, although a few may continue indefinitely.[1] In most cases, by the time the disruptions of separation have been repaired, and the individual's life has again settled into a coherent and relatively stable pattern, postmarital sexual relationships will have ended.

Separated individuals may find ways of managing ambivalent feelings toward the former spouse other than suppressing one side or the other. They may try to avoid the spouse entirely. If they cannot move away, they may nevertheless do their utmost to avoid contact.

**I am in complete fear of seeing him. I just don't want to even pass him in the car, like on the street. When I know he's coming for the kids I'm a wreck. Even though he doesn't come in, I don't want to be in that house; I run to the neighbors. I can't explain it. If I call his mother's house, I make sure it's when he's not there, because I don't want to hear his voice. It's a very confusing feeling. Like I just**

[1] Ingmar Bergman, in his film *Scenes from a Marriage*, pictures one that continues for years.

want to forget he ever existed. Not because of hate or anything like that: I don't know how to explain it. But my reaction is so unlike myself. I'm not usually afraid of confrontation. I usually have ability with words. And yet in this particular area I'm completely a coward.

(Woman, late thirties)

Many among the separated express positive and negative feelings in abrupt alternation. This may be especially likely early in separation, when yearning for and anger at the other may both be at their strongest. A wife may ask, with affection and genuine interest, whom her husband has been dating and become enraged on hearing. Or a husband may have demanded that his wife free him from their marriage, and be flooded with affection on learning that the divorce hearing is over. Some husbands and wives manage to express positive and negative feelings simultaneously. A husband, for example, may angrily complete repairs on the house in which his wife now lives alone, in the process communicating to his wife how resentful he is at continuing to serve her, while remaining insistent that she not live in a house in disrepair.

Some separated couples allocate positive feelings to one setting and negative feelings to another. They may battle with one another through their lawyers, even testify against one another in court, yet see one another in the evening as friends or lovers.[2] One couple resumed living together after a brief separation but permitted their divorce action to continue.

Couples who behave so inconsistently toward one another often try to keep the positive aspect of their relationship secret from all but their most intimate friends. Having told her family and her lawyer how much she has suffered at the hands of her husband, a woman can hardly admit to sleeping with him. And a man may prefer that those who know of his separation not know that he now and again calls his wife in the evening and is grateful when she is willing to see him.

Some couples for a time develop a bizarre secret life, opposite to

---

[2] For an account of this see Eve Baguedor, *Separation: Journal of a Marriage* (New York: Simon and Schuster, 1972).

one they may have maintained during their marriage. During their marriage they tried to hide from friends and kin their dissatisfaction with one another. Now they are estranged in public, but affectionate in private.

A major difficulty experienced by the participants in a post-marital relationship is how to behave in an unambivalent fashion toward one another. The individual's own feelings are inconsistent. How can one both regain and repudiate the spouse? Yet this is what the separated individual may want. One man I talked with said he intended to frighten his wife into reconciliation by starting a divorce action against her. I said that if he really wanted to achieve reconciliation his best bet would be to express his fondness for his wife and try to overcome his combativeness. He replied that if he were to do that he would feel like a sap.

Ambivalence is likely to defeat any attempt at complete resolution; no matter what one achieves, some emotional striving is frustrated. Defeating the spouse in a battle over property or support or custody may result not only in a sense of triumph but also in guilt. Reconciliation may result not only in relief because separation distress has been ended but also in resentment over returning to an unsatisfactory marriage. A counselor may say to someone who has separated, "Make up your mind what you want." Better advice would be, "Accept that however you make up your mind, one set of feelings will be unsatisfied."

Maybe it is first love or whatever, but I'm still attracted to him. There is a basic something, and I can't seem to get rid of that. I do want a divorce and I don't want a divorce.

(Woman, about forty)

### Reconciliation

I was talking to my wife today and all of a sudden she said, "Do you want to sit down and talk about what went wrong?" So I said, "Why not, but why?" And she said, "Well, I just thought that we ought to talk about if we did the right thing." And I said, "Well, okay, let's talk about it," I said, "but how come this is just coming up?" And she started crying a little bit and said, "Well, I'm really lonely. I just have nobody."

(Man, thirties)

Given the many discomforts of separation, most separated couples undoubtedly give at least passing thought to reconciliation. We do not know the proportion of separations which in fact end in reconciliation, but as noted earlier, it is probably as large as or larger than the proportion that continue on to divorce. For many couples reconciliations do not work, and they separate again, perhaps for keeps; but reconciliations do work for others, and the couples thereafter maintain marriages as reliable as any others in these days of marital instability. Separation for many of the latter couples eventually will be remembered only as an incident in their lifelong marriage.

The farther along a couple is in their course toward divorce, the less likely reconciliation seems to be. In the first few days after an impulsive separation, reconciliation is more likely than not, but by the time one of the spouses has obtained a lawyer and filed for divorce, the likelihood of reconciliation has dropped precipitously. One study suggests that only about one couple in eight reconciles in the period between filing for divorce and obtaining the divorce decree.[3] But there is no point at which the possibility of reconciliation totally disappears. Not long ago a newspaper described a couple who, after obtaining a divorce, had each entered into new marriages. Many years later, upon learning that their respective spouses had died, they wrote to each other and, a year or so after that, remarried.

Some reconciliations are reached only after hours of talk in which old issues are exhaustively discussed and tentatively resolved, new pledges are made, and the problems of the reconciliation are anticipated so far as possible. Others are more nearly impulsive rejoinings that may take the couple themselves by surprise. Most reconciliations seem to fall somewhere between these ex-

[3] Data collected by Robert Rankin and reported by Irving Rosow and K. Daniel Ross, "Divorce Among Doctors," *Journal of Marriage and the Family* 34 (November 1972): 287–298.

tremes. The separation is recognized by both husband and wife as socially and personally uncomfortable; one may have wanted reconciliation for some time, and now the other can be brought to consider it seriously. A few of the issues that had been divisive in the past may be discussed, but most are not; instead each pledges to try to make the marriage work. If the marriage had been complicated by a third person, there very likely will be an understanding that he or she will be renounced. (On the basis of talks with individuals whose attempts at reconciliation failed, it seems often to have been no easier for the unfaithful spouse to relinquish attachment to a girlfriend or boyfriend than to relinquish attachment to the other spouse.)

Many among those who eventually divorce seem to have wanted at least one try at reconciliation before they admitted that their marriage could not be made viable. Afterward they may regret having subjected themselves to an additional period of marital misery, but they will be reassured that they gave their marriage every chance.

I was really in an emotional state, crying, losing weight, and I begged him to come back and see a counselor. And he went along with it. But nothing changed. It was very hard, him being gone, but it's hard now that he's back, because nothing has changed with his feelings or his emotions, anything . . . .

He wants out, it's actually what he wants. And I can't do anything about it. If he changed while we were separated, or if I could see some possibilities . . . . But I know that it's never going to happen. And I think I can accept this. I feel that I can handle it a hell of a lot better, because I know I've tried.

(Woman, about forty)

What is the likelihood of a reconciliation working? Only one study, unsystematic and out of date, offers any guidance. This study reviewed the apparent happiness of previously divorced couples after a year or slightly more of remarriage to one another. About half these marriages appeared to be happy; the other half appeared unhappy or had already given way to a new separation.[4] There is

[4] Paul Popenoe, "Remarriage of Divorcees to Each Other," *American Sociological Review* 3 (October 1938): 695–699.

no reason to believe that reconciliations that occur earlier in separation than these postdivorce reconciliations would have greater likelihood of success. Until better data are collected it may be reasonable to suppose that the chances of a reconciliation being successful are about fifty-fifty. This is inferior to the chances of a new marriage working out, but if there are children, the odds seem good enough to make reconciliation worth considering.

There may be personal risk in a reconciliation, though information on this point is slight. The risk, if it exists, is that a first separation will exhaust the individual's resources and that he or she then will be unable to cope with a second separation. One woman who had been hospitalized for depression after a first separation made a serious and nearly successful suicide attempt when a year-long reconciliation gave way to a second separation. Another woman had managed a first separation by taking her children with her to her parents' home. She was too ashamed to do this after her second separation; instead she remained in her own home, isolated and unable to shake off her despair. But these appear to be unusual instances; many of those who divorce have had at least one reconciliation along the way and seem no worse for its failure.

Certain aspects of reconciliation are easily dealt with. The reconciled partners can easily resume cooperation in household management; indeed, during the separation they may have gained new skills as well as increased recognition of the contributions the other makes. The return to shared parenting should not be difficult, although if the separation has been lengthy there may be tensions as the noncustody parent reasserts authority. The reconciled couple may briefly have to suffer the perplexity of kin and friends, and, until kin and friends accept them, tolerate being somewhat marginal to the social networks to which they had belonged. But kin and friends can be convinced rather soon that the reconciliation is reliable, and the separation thereafter will be treated as though it had never happened.

The most formidable problem in reconciliation is the reestablishment of trust in the other and in the relationship. For some time neither partner may be entirely comfortable with the other. The resentments and angers of the separation may have been only partially washed away by the reconciliation process. As one woman said, "I can forgive. The problem is to forget." Each may have to think before speaking lest lingering resentments be voiced; each may wonder what lies behind the other's silences. Awareness of the fragility of their relationship can introduce a hesitation, a kind of behavioral stammer, into the couple's interaction. It often seems to take a good deal of corrective experience before a reconciled couple can relax with one another.

**Once you separate, it's like you shoot somebody, it makes it a little easier next time. Because once this happens you have a mistrust. Rightfully or wrongfully, you always wonder, "Will this happen again?"**

**(Woman, thirties, separated for the third time)**

### Later Phases of the Postmarital Relationship

As new issues and events dominate a couple's lives, old ones recede into their past, becoming less vivid for them. Their relationship may then change in character, perhaps becoming more friendly, perhaps less. Settlement of previously divisive issues may have made husband and wife less threatened by each other and more able to be affectionate; on the other hand, continued quarrels over money or the children may turn a previously amicable separation into one marked by animosity. In general, however, as each member of the couple establishes a new life and a new identity, the other spouse becomes less important.

Some separated individuals remain so afraid of their former spouse or so angry or guilty, that they do not want to see the former spouse ever again. Some only feel reluctant to do so at the moment, but hope eventually to feel differently. Some, however, learn to establish a relationship in which anger, bitterness, and fear can be held aside; though these feelings may not have vanished, they become less intrusive, and it is then possible for the couple to be comfortable with one another.

Finally, for the first time, I was able to visit my ex-wife for an hour or so and have a reasonable conversation and get brought up to date. We'd been out of communication for two or three years, and we still have family in common, in-laws in common, that sort of thing. She didn't get over the bitterness and I didn't get over the bitterness until earlier this year. So that is a long time. You know, we lived together for over 60 percent of our lifetime, and no matter what went wrong, you still want to be able to talk.

(Man, mid-fifties)

There can be satisfactions for a long-separated individual in being able again to be with the person who was so much a part of his or her life, and who in many ways may be still.

It's rather pleasant to be able to see him and have a drink with him and not fight with him. I was married for sixteen years, and you just don't tune out that many years of your life.

(Woman, late thirties)

Some couples eventually achieve a certain steady and reliable friendliness.

I'm supposed to see him tonight. I talked with him about ten days ago, and it was very funny, we sat there talking about what happened and what went wrong. And anybody who had walked in would have thought we were friends. He said, "Oh, I was really awful to you those last two years." He went over it—it was really an admission of guilt—he went over a few things that he had done, and said that he wouldn't do that again. And it was very strange. And I know that he is there, as a distant friend. I think I got out a lot of the anger, pretty much, and now he's there. It sounds sort of weird, doesn't it?

(Woman, mid-forties)

The relationship of long-separated couples, if it becomes friendly, is nevertheless different from other friendships: the bonds underlying it are stronger; its roots are deeper. Yet at the same time each can remember being hurt by the other, and so mutual wariness may also be greater.

# 7

# Kin: The Hesitancies of Telling Them, and the Reactions They Display

My parents are rigid Catholics. The beliefs they have are very rigid. One of my cousins went and married a Protestant, and this was a terrible thing for my father. And then she got divorced and this was even worse. Well, this was only his niece. So it's not funny, how I feel about coming back to tell my parents.

(Man, thirties)

When I told my parents about all the trouble we had had it came as a shock to them. Because we had never indicated that there was anything wrong with our marriage. I would never recommend to anybody that they act that way. To have to cover it up, to live that lie, is a big strain. When I told them it just knocked them off their feet.

(Woman, about forty)

Separated individuals are generally more reluctant to report the end of their marriages to their kin than to friends, neighbors, or, indeed, anyone else, with the possible exception of their children. The anticipated discomfort of telling kin is sometimes sufficient to hold individuals in unsatisfactory marriages long after they would otherwise have abandoned them. Yet why this should be so may be perplexing, since some of these individuals see their kin only at birthdays and holidays and on an occasional Sunday, or even less often if the kin live far from them. Why anticipation of the reaction of kin should be so troublesome, and what that reaction may be, is the topic of this chapter.

## The Nature of Kin Ties and the Meaning of Separation

The kin we urban Americans feel to be of particular importance are those to whom we were close when growing up—grandparents, parents, brothers and sisters, occasionally a parent's sister or brother who was an auxiliary member of our childhood household —and in addition, for those of us who are old enough, the children we cared for in *their* growing up.

The precise quality of the relationships we and our kin maintain differs greatly from family to family. Generally, however, the relationships might be described as "close, but not too close." We are affectionate toward our kin while remaining somewhat guarded: Most of us care for our kin, perhaps love them, but ordinarily we do not take our kin into our confidence, except in limited ways or when greatly stressed. We protect our privacy. In addition to not confiding very much ourselves, we tend not to ask kin for their confidences; we try not to intrude. Should it appear that someone in the family is following a questionable course, it may perhaps become necessary to say or do something. But such circumstances aside, we prefer not to be too much aware of our kin's private life. There are many reasons for our following such a course: our awareness of the identification kin have with us and unwillingness to burden them with our troubles; our sensitivity to the possibility that kin may feel called on to advise or evaluate; differences in our values or concerns we prefer to leave unvoiced; and still others. For all these reasons most kin relationships approach the norm of "close but not too close."

Occasionally kin relationships are quite different. In some families the mother and one of her children, or two siblings, maintain an intimate, mutually sustaining relationship; they may feel themselves to be best friends as well as kin. Sometimes parents and siblings go their own ways, with hardly any contact with one another. Many families contain tensions as well as fondnesses; in some of these families past rivalries and quarrels make members cautious with one another; in others, current antagonisms sponsor distrust and estrangement.

Except under conditions of estrangement, most kin maintain a fairly regular pattern of contact with one another. Even if they live far from each other, they never entirely lose touch: They keep up with each other's major life changes; they may remember birthdays; they exchange pictures. They worry about each other's health and sometimes feel envious of each other's good fortune. They make an effort to be together—if only by telephone or mail—for the Christmas holiday, and perhaps for the Thanksgiving holiday as well. Yet their private lives remain private.

In virtually all families there is an understanding that in time of need any member of the family can seek help from any other. This understanding is qualified, sometimes abrogated, by another understanding: that it is permissible for family members to give priority to competing obligations, especially those to a new family, but also to a developing career, or to personal hopes and wishes. Nevertheless, there tends in all families to be a sense of alliance which requires family members to help each other if they can, given their other commitments. A sibling in financial difficulty, for example, may be helped by clothes being sent as a birthday gift to the sibling's children or an invitation offered the sibling's family for a holiday meal. The sibling may be lent money without requiring its return, although this might more easily be done with a parent or adult child. In families in which brothers and sisters and even parents consistently find reasons for being unable to help one another, their sense of being allied may become rather strained, but ordinarily enough survives to reassure each family member that he or she is not entirely alone in the world.

The investment of kin in each other's prosperity leads them to exchange information about the conditions of their lives. They feel it especially important to exchange information regarding changes that might imply either new needs or new resources. Therefore kin tend to be told about job promotion and job loss, illness and recovery, pregnancy, plans to move, and impending marriage or separation. They tend not to be told about more private matters, in conformity with the principle of "close but not too close," unless the private matters seem likely to lead to a change in situation. Kin tend not to learn about marital difficulties, for example, unless a separation is contemplated.[1]

### Letting the Family Know

Because kin tend not to be told about "private matters," the news of an individual's separation is apt to come as a surprise to them. If the kin were neighbors they may have been witnesses to the marriage's downhill slide. One woman, whose parents lived in the apartment beneath hers, said; "They knew as quickly as I did about the whole mess." But if kin live at any greater distance than this, they are likely to have had only the faintest awareness that marital difficulties existed. Most among the separated had said nothing at all to their parents before the actual separation that would have indicated that their marriages were in trouble.

Faced with the necessity of telling their parents, the newly separated tend to anticipate that the news will shock and sadden them; they expect questions to follow, perhaps blame, perhaps pleas to reconcile. Many feel that it is best to tell the parents in person, and so say nothing until they can see them. One woman waited to tell her parents until she and her children made their annual Christmas visit. She appeared then without her husband and, when her parents asked where he was, broke the news. A man had postponed telling his parents for several months by saying to himself that he would tell them when he next saw them: "Pretty much what I've decided to do is let it ride until I get a chance to see them in one way or another." A woman put off telling her parents, although she talked with them regularly, because she did not want to darken their happiness.

[1] There is an extensive published literature on the nature of kin ties in America which tends to corroborate the view of kin ties as alliances. See, for a recent survey, F. Ivan Nye and Felix M. Berardo, *The Family: Its Structure and Interaction* (New York: Macmillan, 1973), chap. 16, "The Family and the Kinship System," pp. 405–434.

I haven't told my parents because it would disturb them. I'm prolonging it because my father's retired and they're having a great time.

(Woman, late thirties)

In an unusual situation, a woman and her husband decided that the husband's mother, who was seriously ill, should not be told at all.

My husband's mother is in a nursing home. She's seventy-five years old. There's no reason to tell her. . . . I didn't get to see her that often, so it's not that unusual that I haven't been out there. If she calls the house I just say "He's working," or "He'll be home," or "I'll have him call you."

(Woman, early forties)

The separated usually try to tell all members of their family at about the same time, but some find it easier first to tell their siblings, who then may tell their parents. One man for a time was almost unable to tell his parents, although his sister had already passed the news along.

I didn't have the heart to call my parents. I had a lot of excuses about why I didn't call, that I wanted to call them in the evening, when my Dad is home, and I didn't have my phone installed yet. But now I've had the phone for a week and I still haven't called. I called my baby sister and she said, "You are going to get mixed reactions and you better call Mother." And I said, "Yeah, I'll call her tonight." I wrote her a letter instead. It was raining this morning when I drove by the mailbox, and I didn't want to stop and get wet. I looked at the mailbox and I said, "Gee, I'll mail it somewhere else."

(Man, late thirties)

Men sometimes leave the task of notifying their parents to their wives. In many marriages the wife is responsible for maintaining contact with the husband's family as well as with her own. Sometimes husband and wife continue this practice during the weeks immediately after separation, so that it becomes the wife's chore to inform both families. Needless to say, no matter how fair the wife might attempt to be to the husband, she tends to describe the reasons for the break from her perspective. One man reported to us that when he finally did talk with his mother she was unsympathetic, because his wife had earlier told her about the separation in a way that discredited him. One might wonder how the husband in the following report was received when he eventually got in touch with his family.

My husband has a lot of relatives in Indiana, and two or three weeks after the breakup I flew out there and told them all about it. They're very upset about the whole thing, and I can come back any time I want, but they never want to see him again.

(Woman, mid-thirties)

## Responding to the News

Some families, on learning of the separation, are immediately solicitous, immediately anxious to help. Others are gently or harshly condemning. Still others are angry, because so faulty a marriage was made in the first place, because the husband or wife is acting irresponsibly, or because the separation is in itself reprehensible. A few want not to get involved.

Immediate reactions among kin may vary as much as they do partly because we have no socially endorsed interpretation of separation to guide our response. Is it tragedy, failure, irresponsibility, the correction of a mistake, or just another change required by self-development? We know what it means if a spouse dies. But in response to separation parents and siblings are likely to be uncertain.

Some parents seem briefly unable to assimilate the news that a separation has occurred within their family. They have no prior experience to fall back on that might help them understand it.

I told my father. My mother's dead. And he was completely knocked off his wheels. He didn't have too much to say, but I was his favorite. I saw him on Thanksgiving and told him, and he couldn't even talk. . . . And he wasn't even that close to me while I was married.

(Woman, about thirty)

Parents may ask if there was another woman, or another man, or if there was drunkenness, or brutality. Incompatibility may be more difficult for them to grasp, or at any rate to accept; personal change or a desire for such change as a cause of separation sometimes seems quite beyond them.

**My mother didn't really understand our problems. If it had been one of us committed adultery, getting involved with someone else, she could have understood that. But my divorce was caused by me evolving into a different person, wanting different things out of life.**

**(Man, late twenties)**

The parents may find it bewildering that a child should give up home and marriage in pursuit of some will-o'-the-wisp happiness. They want the child to be happy, of course, but they want the child also to be mature and responsible.

**My parents were very, very, upset when we split up. They said, "You know, you have a child." And I said, "Look, I know I've got a child. But I think a child is better off with one healthy parent than two parents who are screaming at each other and throwing things all the time. And I don't want him growing up thinking that's what marriage is, people being really rotten to each other." They thought that I was acting like an infant and that I should never have left my husband. And I kept saying, "But you don't understand. You didn't see what was going on."**

**(Woman, mid-thirties)**

Kin, much more than friends, believe that their commitment to one another confers on them the right to evaluate one another's behavior. Parents, especially, assume the right to comment on the separation, to criticize it, to disapprove or approve it, perhaps going on until the separated individual is driven to exasperation.[2]

Parents may be critical of a son or daughter they believe to have ended a marriage frivolously, and they may try to argue him or her

[2] In Goode's sample, 60 percent of respondents said that their families had approved of their divorce, and 20 percent said that their families had disapproved. Respondents were much less likely to say that friends had either approved or disapproved. See William J. Goode, *After Divorce* (Glencoe, Ill.: Free Press, 1956), p. 167.

into reconciliation. One woman's father wrote her to defend her unfaithful husband. Her father said, essentially, that many men were unfaithful and that it was not fair that her husband pay so high a penalty when other men got off scot-free. If parents can feel that even infidelity might be tolerated, they are apt to have little patience with incompatibility as a reason for separation. Several sets of parents reacted to a daughter's report of incompatibility by suggesting that a baby would have been a remedy.

My parents say that because I didn't have a baby I'm not ful- filled. They mean that if you have a baby it would shield you from this Women's Lib stuff, and would also shield you from each other, and you wouldn't be so selfish because you would have some- one else to think about.

(Woman, mid-twenties)

Parents and, to a lesser extent, siblings may feel that the separa- tion is disgracing. Their identification with one another is now a source of discomfort rather than pride.

I think that deep down they think that I sort of disgraced them by not succeeding in my marriage. My parents were always proud of anything my brother or I did.

(Woman, early thirties)

Sibling rivalries may also be reawakened by separation, as by any other change in a sibling's standing. The first reactions of a brother or sister to news of a separation may include not only feelings of concern and solicitude but also a fleeting sense of triumph at this new evidence that the brother or sister was always the better child. Or a brother or sister may interpret the separation as corrob- orating a lifelong picture of the separating individual as the black sheep.

I have one sister who has had a good marriage for about six or seven years, and I really felt terrible about telling her about it. To my parents, she's the good news and I'm the bad news. I told her and she said, "Yes, I know," and she didn't say another word to me for two days.

(Woman, late twenties)

Some parents blame themselves for the separation. They worry about whether their upbringing failed to equip their child for marriage. They worry that they may have permitted or even encouraged their child to make an unwise marriage. One woman reported that her parents consulted a psychiatrist to locate the fault in themselves.

What they did after the separation was they consulted a psychiatrist to find out if they had done anything in my upbringing to make me whacked out, and if they had, they were willing to try to change so that it wouldn't happen again. Now I'm through college and I've been married, but they were perfectly willing to try to make sure that they wouldn't mess me up more. Which is an incredible response! And the shrink told them, "There's nothing wrong with you, go home."

(Woman, mid-twenties)

Siblings, too, may be concerned about what the separation indicates about them. In particular they may fear that it suggests a familial tendency toward marital instability. And, indeed, it may encourage others in the family to consider separation: One woman reported that after her separation she was called by her husband's brother's wife, who wanted to know how she'd gotten the nerve to do it, and wanted also to have the name of her lawyer.

A minority of parents and siblings totally condemn the separating individual. A few respond to news of the separation with statements like that of one woman's mother—"You're no good and you never have been"—or like that of another woman's mother— "This is the first scandal in our family, and you are the one responsible for it."

My parents were shocked. No one they knew, no relatives, had ever done such a terrible thing, you know. And they blamed the whole modern generation which questions everything and has no values.

(Woman, mid-twenties)

Or they condemn the separation as immoral, and the separating couple as sinful:

(134)

My mother is very religious and she's put some heavy stuff on the kids, telling them that their parents are going to Hell and so on.

(Man, early thirties)

The reaction of other families, in contrast, can be full sympathy and support. Some kin take the position, almost without thought, that whatever their son or daughter or sibling does, they will consider right. It can help even these kin to accept the separation, however, if they already had reservations regarding the spouse.

When we separated the first time I think my family was delighted, to say the least. But I went back and I think they felt I was doing what I had to do, and they were behind me then, too. Now that I have separated a second time, I think they're that much more pleased.

(Woman, early thirties)

The separating individual's kin may condemn the estranged wife or husband. Oddly enough, this may anger or disappoint the separated individual, who may want more understanding and less choosing up of sides.

My parents reacted like they were out of a play: "Anyone that would leave *her* has lost his mind." And that made me very uneasy, very uncomfortable, because it seemed unfair to me that they should say this.

(Woman, early thirties)

My family never liked my wife. It was sad. She's a very quiet girl, and they always ganged up on her because she was more liberal. The first thing my brother asked was, "Should I be nice to her any more?" And my mother's reaction was similar. I was disappointed in them.

(Man, late twenties)

Kin may feel saddened to realize how unhappy the marriage must have been. One woman said, "My parents feel very bad that somebody ever hurt me at all." Parents may be reassured to be told that the individual is happier now because of the separation.

I know my parents are happy if I say that I am happier now,
because I was so unhappy when I was married.

(Man, late twenties)

But more often the separation clearly has not made the separated
individual especially happy, and nothing he or she does can hide
this from the parents. In response the parents may be saddened,
a condition for which the separated individual often accepts
responsibility.

I think parents' attitudes make it a lot harder to adjust. I had a long
talk with my father and he was telling me how sad he was. I'm
sad too, and it's hard enough to deal with my own sadness, and
now I have to reassure him . . . . It's all very gratifying that they
feel for you, but all of a sudden their sadness is overwhelming, and
you're the cause of it. It makes it really difficult. In some ways I
think it's really better just to keep away from parents.

(Woman, late twenties)

Another woman commented, "Somehow having another person
living a life for you and knowing that whatever you do really
affects them so deeply is an awful burden to bear."

A recurrent complaint among younger separated individuals
was that their parents, try as they might, could not really *understand*. The separated individuals wanted to be treated as always—
with acceptance, but without intrusion. Their parents seemed to
want more; they wanted to be able to grasp what had gone wrong
in their child's marriage. And they could not.

My parents don't really know what the situation was, they don't
really know what happened. They keep trying, and no matter how
much you explain things to them, they just can't fathom what went
wrong. I find I avoid the thing. I just don't want to talk about it
with them. I actually started screaming with my mother one day
on the phone, "I just don't want to talk about it any more, because
you just don't understand!" And there was no way I could make
her understand!

(Woman, late twenties)

Parents may think they understand, but their view of what happened can seem to the separated person so distant from his or her

experience as to violate it. The separated person can feel that the parents, well-meaning though they may be, are clumsy and imperceptive in their attempts at sympathy, and may want more than anything else to be free of their intrusion.

After my parents adjusted to the fact, my mother became very supportive of me in another way that I didn't like, which was to say, "You should have left Andy. I begin to see a lot of things now that I didn't see when you two were married, and I think you were right. I've heard things from your sister about your married life . . . ." And I said, "Oh, shut up, mother. I don't want to hear. Mind your own business." Because nobody can really understand the workings of somebody else's marriage.

(Woman, about thirty)

Separation can diminish one's standing in the family. The sympathy one receives may contain within it patronization. One woman said, "I personally wish I just could avoid seeing them at all; I can't stand the thought of their 'Poor girl,' and that overly sympathetic stuff!" It may matter less to men, since they tend to see their kin infrequently, that their reputation for responsibility and maturity is diminished. But women are likely to be more involved with kin, and they may discover to their discomfort that they are newly a target for unwanted, invasive advice, or that they are now recipients of sympathy that, while well-intended, is also subtly disparaging. One woman put it simply: Since her separation she had dropped in her family's pecking order. The following story may suggest what it can be like toward the bottom of the pecking order:

We go up on Sunday to visit my mother and father and we have dinner and everything and we sit for a few hours. I think it was two weeks ago Sunday that my married sister and her husband were up and my father was fooling with Nelson. My father is very gruff and he doesn't mean it; he thinks the world of the kids, but he was fooling around. Nelson was trying to be very much a man, you know, and he didn't want to give way, but as soon as my father left the room, he came over to me and he put his head down and he started to cry. When I'm up there I'm more protective of the kids, because they don't understand the kids like I do, and I put my arm around him. My sister flew off the handle at me. She said, "Go ahead and baby him. That's why he is the way he is." And my father came back into the room and he had to get his two cents in. I told him to leave him alone. I had my arm about him and I wasn't about to take if off. I told him, "If you left him alone, he'd be all right." But as soon as they start making fun of him, he's crying, he's all tears.

(Woman, thirties)

Kin sometimes intervene in the situation of a separated individual in a way he or she may find extremely unwelcome. A parent or older sibling may call one of the spouses by long-distance phone to deliver a lecture on marital responsibility. Or without invitation, kin may attempt to negotiate a resolution of the differences between the separating spouses.

On top of everything else, I have my mother-in-law who wants to come at the end of this month. She wants to put us back together. She doesn't want me to go for a divorce. She wants me to be separated until I die; when I die I can get a divorce. I told her, "You've been running my life for ten years and it is going to stop." She's not going to come in my house.

(Woman, mid-thirties)

One woman reported that her immigrant mother had asked a priest to plead with her to give her husband another chance. She answered the doorbell one day and there was the priest, slightly embarrassed, but determined to carry out his mission. Another woman's mother attempted to engage still higher authority: She had the congregation of her church pray with her for her daughter's return to her marriage.

Friends usually accept whatever postmarital relationship individuals establish, but kin often insist on what they believe to be proper, irrespective of the wishes of the separated person. One woman's father became furious when he discovered that his daughter was permitting her estranged husband to stay overnight; in his view the man wasn't meeting the responsibilities of a husband and therefore deserved none of the privileges. In another instance a sister refused to accept a woman's definition of her relationship with her estranged husband.

I had to be away for a few days and my husband moved in to stay with the children. My sister was having a graduation party for her daughter the same day I got back. So my husband was at home when I got back and I said I was going out to my sister's for the party. And he said, "Shall I drive you out there?" And my sister called then, and she said, "I'm not inviting him. I will come out and pick you up and drop you back. Your husband is not invited. He's hurt you so much, will you cut off that relationship and let him go? Don't keep inviting him into our family and doing this."

She was saying that for my sake. Because she sees me constantly being hurt . . . . He wasn't imposing himself, but she said she just didn't even want him to come out.

(Woman, mid-forties)

Yet despite their capacity to exasperate, kin often prove helpful. Kin make their homes available as places to stay for the hectic few days immediately after the separation, offer a meal and company for the worst of the evenings, and stand ready to look after the children during the day. One mother, herself divorced, came from another city to provide her daughter with emotional support while the latter packed the dishes and the furniture. Kin may help out with money if things are tight. If the husband has dropped out entirely, a brother may do what he can to keep the car running and to lend a masculine presence to the household. There can be drawbacks and limitations to the help kin provide, but that the help is there can sometimes make all the difference.

### Going Home Again

One of the kinds of help parents offer children whose marriage has ended is the refuge of their home. Although both a son and daughter may be invited to return home, the offer seems to be made more often, and with greater insistence, to daughters.

Parental motivations for the invitation undoubtedly are more complex than a simple desire to help. The invitation may also express their lurking guilt for having permitted their child to make an unfortunate marriage, or for having failed to prepare him or her for a successful one. Having their child at home again would enable them to expiate their past failure and give them another chance to do better. They might hope to provide the grandchildren with a more normal home, and to reassure the grandchildren that although they may have lost a parent, they still have grandparents on whom they can count. Finally, having small children in the house may appear to some grandparents to be a chance to turn back the calendar and become nurturing parents again.

But from the perspective of the recipient of the invitation, there may be catches, especially if it is a daughter to whom the invitation has been made. Then it may well contain among its elements a view of the daughter as having tried adulthood and failed.

It is the separation that provokes parents to want again to nurture and protect a daughter, and again direct her life. Parents appear much less insistent that a daughter return home if she has been widowed, though widows may also have young children.[3] The parents of a young widow may well ask her to return to their home, but they are likely to respect her wishes if she declines the invitation. Sometimes parents of a separated woman do, too, but not always. The woman quoted below had already told her parents two or three times that she would not move into their home.

> I had the kids down to their house last week, and it was, "Oh, you poor thing, you can take the upstairs room for nothing, and we've already checked into the school system, and it is wonderful." I said, "Wait a minute, I'm not moving in, and that's it."
>
> (Woman, about thirty-five)

For the separated woman the parental invitation is not without attractions. Going back home can offer a brief moratorium from responsibility, a breathing space during which the woman can pull herself together without feeling guilty for neglecting her children.

---

[3] See Ira O. Glick, Robert S. Weiss, and C. Murray Parkes, *The First Year of Bereavement* (New York: Wiley-Interscience, 1974).

It can provide full-time help with the children, and reduce her financial burden. As important as anything else, it can fill the awful empty evenings with the companionship of people whom the woman loves and by whom she is loved. The cost would be reduced autonomy. The woman just quoted went on to say:

Financially it would be beautiful. I could save money and everything else. But I know I would go under. I'll be down there two months and I'll lose my grip. I know I wouldn't be able to go to the bathroom without one of them calling to me and saying, "Are you all right?"

Women who have yielded to the attractions of returning home report that reduction of autonomy does indeed occur, and that it can be distressing. One said, "My mother still treats me as a single girl; she tells me what to do, and how to do it." Some women say that their parents expect them to observe the same rules they observed as adolescents. The parents may inspect the woman's male callers and question the woman about the hours she and they keep:

It was terrible! It was really, really terrible! My father always sort of kept his mouth shut, but my mother! She'd say, "You know, there was a car outside until 2:00 A.M. last night. What are the neighbors going to think?" And I would say, "If I want to do something that the neighbors shouldn't know about I could go to a motel. I don't bother the neighbors and I don't expect them to bother me."
(Woman, early thirties)

The parents may intervene in the woman's management of her children or contest with her the right to authority over them. They may criticize the children as too noisy, without table manners, or spoiled, and thus indirectly criticize the way the woman has raised them. Or they may criticize the woman directly for being too strict or too lenient. A child may use the grandparents as allies in disputes with the mother. One little girl said to her mother, "You think you're big, but I'll tell Grandma." (The woman then lost her temper and spanked the child.)

Many women leave their parents' home feeling bruised by the clash of standards, by the need always to be deferential and considerate, by the recurrent conflict. One woman who had lived in her mother's home for three years said after leaving, "My mother and I get along much better since we separated." When this woman entered graduate school her mother urged her to give up her apartment and return home. She said, "Not again," even though returning home would have solved the problem of child care.

It seems to be unusual for parents to share their home with a separated daughter for more than a few weeks without conflict arising. An arrangement that does seem to work well, however, is one in which a separated woman makes her home in the neighborhood of her parents' home. Then there seem to be fewer opportunities for the parents to infringe on the woman's autonomy, yet the woman lives near enough to her parents to profit from their help.

Men seem to encounter fewer conflicts when they go home again. Partly this is because they become less absorbed into their parents' household; they are more likely to treat their parents' home as a rooming house in which they have special privileges. Their parents either are not concerned about their activities and hours or keep their concern to themselves. And because the men's wives have the children, there is no conflict with the parents over the children's upbringing. On the contrary, should a man's children come weekends to visit, his parents can be most helpful; they can relieve him from constant responsibility for them, provide meals, and contribute to the children's entertainment.

Nevertheless, for men as for women, returning home is likely to symbolize a return to an earlier time of life. There is a loss of status in moving from head of a household to occupant of a room in the parents' household. Yet men tend not to dwell on this. Most men who return home tend to be matter-of-fact about it: they view it as practical, convenient, and temporary.

### The Brother as New Male Figure

There are societies in which the male responsible for a child's upbringing is the mother's brother, not her husband. This is a plausible human arrangement, and some separated women whose husbands are not accessible to their children because of choice or distance, and who have brothers who potentially are available, hope that they may manage to achieve something like this themselves; that the brother will at the least provide a male presence in their children's lives.

Separated women do not seem generally to turn to their own fathers to play the role of men in their children's lives. This is not because the fathers are old and crochety, but rather because the women do not believe the fathers would adapt to the routines of their households. Fathers remain figures of some authority, and anticipation of a father's steady presence within her household would appear to make many women·uncomfortable.

Brothers often seem willing to assume the role of guiding uncle, and the arrangement frequently seems satisfactory for a time. One unmarried brother formed the practice of bringing his car to his sister's home every weekend for her children to wash. It was for them a kind of play for which they were paid. After they had washed the car he would take them for a ride. In two other instances a married brother visited his sister and her children at least weekly, and regularly invited them to his home for holidays and birthdays. However, all of these arrangements came unstuck within a year. The first ended when the woman began keeping company with someone of whom the brother disapproved; the brother stopped coming to see her. And the two married brothers each were told by their wives that they were giving too much time to their sisters' families, and too little to their own.

In general, women who used their brothers as auxiliary members of their households found that while their brothers might be helpful now and again and might occasionally provide a masculine presence in their homes and in the lives of their children, they were not to be counted on.

Sometimes my brother would hang in and help, and sometimes he would be kind of scared off. You know, if he was involved with a new chick that week, well, that was it, goodbye. But then his guilt would come out and he'd be around for maybe a day or two. He's younger than I am, and he's really not their stepfather, and that has to be kept in perspective. He's their uncle.

(Woman, late twenties)

## Relationships with In-laws

Perhaps more than elsewhere, separation forces an assessment of the assumptions underlying relationships with in-laws. With the separation, these relationships seem to be remarkably open to whatever definition the individuals involved want to place on them. There are few social prescriptions they must follow or combat.

Most important for the further course of a relationship with an in-law is the preseparation character of the relationship. Should the separating individual and an in-law have maintained only an indirect relationship, seeing one another only because of their shared relationship to the spouse, then the separation is apt to end the relationship. On the other hand, if the separating individual and the in-law like and value one another, they may remain close despite the separation.

Having children may also play a role. The children, after all, are blood kin to the in-laws. Many women feel obligated both to their children and to their in-laws to retain the in-laws as family.

Men seem generally to drop relationships with in-laws, perhaps even if they have custody. Only infrequently do men seem to have established bonds with in-laws strong enough to survive the end of the marriage. But women often maintain a relationship with parents-in-law whom they had learned to think of as family, or with a sister-in-law who was both family and friend.[4] The relationship may not be untroubled. If not immediately after separation, then eventually, the in-laws are likely to feel that their first loyalty is to their son or brother, and the former daughter-in-law or sister-in-law will have to respect this.

I think Walter's mother and I can be as close as sisters. This is a very unusual relationship. She and I are just such great friends. And his father and I—I adore his father and his father adores me, in a

---

[4] Jerry W. Spicer and Gary D. Hampe found about half their sample of divorced men, but only about a seventh of their sample of divorced women, without any contact whatsoever with parents-in-law after the divorce. See their "Kinship Interaction after Divorce," *Journal of Marriage and the Family* 37 (February 1975): 113-119.

very special way. And it always will be that way. And I think it is great for the kids, who are their only grandchildren.

His parents at first were just furious with him. I almost felt sorry for him because they were so mad. They were not even going to speak to him. Well, they made up with him. They've come to understand his point of view. In a way I'm glad that they do, because it would be wrong for a mother and father to abandon their child. But now they aren't entirely on my side.

(Woman, late thirties)

In one instance a woman and her husband had been living with her husband's parents when her husband decided he had had enough of marriage and left for a job in another state. The parents responded by displaying even greater kindness to their daughter-in-law.

I'm in an unusual position. I'm living with my in-laws. It's a strange relationship, but I think they feel kind of guilty about the way we broke up and this is their way of making up for it. We have a fantastic relationship: better than when my husband and I were married.

(Woman, late twenties)

Those in-laws who maintain contact with a separated woman and who are also in touch with their brother or son may face a conflict of loyalties. One way of managing the conflict is to avoid the issue. The in-laws may acknowledge that the woman is now alone, and may express concern for how she is managing, but avoid discussion of the husband and of the reasons for the separation. If this strategy is carried too far, the relationship can become one in which anything can be discussed except important issues.

My husband's family send me letters like everything is all right, and they call me long distance on my birthday, you know, to say, "Happy birthday." And I was just talking with them, and I didn't want to have a completely superficial conversation, and so I mentioned him. And his mother immediately said, "Oh, let's not talk about that." I don't know, its really nutty.

(Woman, mid-thirties)

Most separated women report some fading of their relationships with in-laws after separation. There may be several reasons for this: the in-laws' continued loyalty to the husband, a weakened sense of family connection, and perhaps a sense of awkwardness in a relationship that now is so undefined. Or the specific reasons may be obscure; the in-laws just aren't seen as much any more.

My husband's sister said, "You know, you and I have been friends, and will continue to be friends." And she really was a mainstay. She invited me over for bridge and for dinner. She'd say, "I'm going to be alone for dinner tonight, would you like to stop over," and I'd go like a zombie. But I haven't seen her as much recently. Partly it's my own moving away, as well as her withdrawal.

(Woman, late thirties)

Occasionally a necessary redefinition of a relationship with in-laws is severely upsetting. A woman may have felt that her husband's parents were near-substitutes for her own. She may have become accustomed to summer weekends with them or to family holidays in their home which now may have to be relinquished. And though she may be able to see her in-laws' point of view, she may be hurt.

All my holidays, every one of them, for fifteen years, has been built around my mother-in-law. I don't have a mother and father. . . . He's living there and of course that made it impossible. The first Thanksgiving and Christmas were traumatic.

(Woman, about forty)

All sorts of understandings with in-laws may have to be reconsidered after the end of the marriage. The husband may have been taken into the father-in-law's business, or one of the husband's parents may have come to live with him and his wife before the husband moved out. In one instance the husband's mother had lived with her son and his wife for years when the departure of her son left her marooned in her daughter-in-law's home. The daughter-in-law felt unable to ask her to leave: One doesn't evict an aged and infirm mother-in-law just because she has taken, during dinner, to defending her absent son. Nevertheless, the home situation became increasingly tense until one of the husband's sisters came to the rescue by inviting her mother to live with her.

Many among the separated, women as well as men, feel it perhaps regrettable, but far from a tragedy, that they lose their relationships with their in-laws along with their marriage. Some women, and a few men, do feel saddened by the loss. And some maintain relationships with a few in-laws over the years. The relationships are valued in their own right, and also serve as testimony that not every aspect of the married self was lost with the separation.

# 8

# Friends: The Changes in Relationships with Them

I remember when friends of ours separated, we were really awkward with them. We just didn't know how to talk to them. How do you talk to somebody who is so totally removed from your situation and so obviously miserable? What can you say? What can you do? You've got everything they don't have, and that is what is making them miserable.

You can't ask about the kids, you can't ask about the wife, you can't ask where they are living, you don't dare ask whether they are dating, you really don't know what to talk about. All their underpinnings have been cut out from under them. What the hell do you talk about? Do you talk about your house? Your lawn?

(Man, late twenties, separated)

## Types of Friendship and the Separated Individual

The first reaction of friends to the news that an individual's marriage has ended is likely to be solicitude, regret, and desire to help. As time goes on some of these friends remain loyal and supportive, but others withdraw from the separated individual, and he or she from them. To understand why different friendships respond so differently to separation, we must consider the bases on which friendships are formed.

We establish and maintain friendships because they better our lives. We and our friends like one another, share interests, have similar styles of life and daily routines, or similar problems in living; in consequence, we can understand each other's concerns, profit from each other's experiences, and help one another by exchanging favors.

Once bonds of friendship form, affection and mutual loyalty follow. But affection and mutual loyalty may not be fundamental to the friendship, and despite their existence, if the bases for the friendship should disappear, the friendship may be allowed to fade. Next-door neighbors, who for years saw each other frequently and thought of themselves as friends, may see much less of one another should one of the couples move a few blocks away and may, in time, realize that they have become less close. This does not mean that their friendship was simulated when they were neighbors, only that it depended heavily on proximity. To the extent that marriage provided the basis for a friendship, separation will weaken it.

Some individuals develop one or two intimate friendships which provide something like attachment in that the friendships make them feel less alone and lonely. They and the friends tend to feel intensely loyal to one another and, recognizing one another's loyalty, to be trusting of one another. They are apt to share much of their private lives with one another. Such friendships are often relatively impervious to separation. Indeed, to an individual who is separating a friend of this sort can be a godsend, a source of sustenance in what is otherwise an isolated and bleak world.

**My sister said I would never need a psychiatrist because I had my best friend, Edith.**

(Woman, mid-forties)

In order to gain some perspective on the turmoil of their lives, some men and women facing separation or already separated develop friendships that resemble intimate friendships except that there is within them more limited loyalty and trust. The friend is more nearly a confidant than an intimate: a person to whom the beset individual talks because he or she *must* talk to someone.

**There's a person who knows me, my happy days and my sad days. I hate to think that every time I see her I have something sad to tell her. I'd like to think that I could tell her some of the happy things,**

and reserve some of the sad things for someplace else. But sometimes I know I've got to talk to someone, so I have said, "Listen, I've got to spill all this garbage, so give me five minutes."

(Woman, late thirties)

Husbands and wives occasionally choose the same confidant, who may then become almost a third figure in their marriage, hearing about its stresses and strains from both. It is not unknown for the husband's buddy or the wife's best friend who has become a confidant to the other spouse as well, later to enter into an affair with the other spouse. Eventually the husband or wife may learn with dismay that he or she was betrayed not only by the spouse but also by the friend.

Friends less close than confidants are likely to be taken by surprise by the news that a couple has actually separated. Even intimate friends may not be told until the separation is very near. For example, one woman, though she relied heavily on the support of a close friend through the last months of her marriage, did not confess to her how bad things had become until the very end:

I have a close friend whom I've known about fifteen years who was widowed just five years ago and hasn't yet gotten over her husband's death. But she and I have talked very frankly. When all this was going on in my marriage I used to be so devastated I didn't know who to go to, and I used to go visit my friend and play cribbage and not talk about anything. Then just before he left I told her, because I just couldn't contain it.

(Woman, about fifty)

Most couples whose marriages are failing continue to appear to others to be still firmly linked, right up to the point of separation. Tact and good form, and a natural desire to avoid embarrassment should the separation not occur, require that couples keep their troubles to themselves. In addition, few couples have the qualities necessary for quarreling in public; it takes a good deal of extroversion to perform *Who's Afraid of Virginia Woolf*. The following is about as open as any couple is likely to be in displaying their mutual dissatisfaction:

As our situation deteriorated at home it certainly wasn't a secret to the people outside. They hear you making smart remarks that you wouldn't make normally. I would say things to her in a sarcastic tone that I would not say to somebody else.

(Man, late thirties)

But no matter how unpleasant a husband or wife might be to one another, their friends would be unlikely to anticipate their separation. If a couple are now together, friends expect them to remain together. One couple announced to close friends that in another month they intended to separate. Yet they remained considerate of one another and so their friends chose not to take them seriously. When they did separate their friends were shocked.

Just how to tell friends once a separation has occurred can be baffling. Unless the friends are intimate, a detailed account of what caused the separation may put them off. Indeed, reporting nothing more than the fact of the separation makes public a great deal of information about one's private life. But to say to a friend only, "We've broken up," without giving further information risks suggesting that the friend is someone in whom one does not wish to confide.

And what response can a friend who is not an intimate make to an admission of marital failure? A few may be able to say, "I've been through it, too." The best that most can do is, "I'm sorry" or "I hope it's for the best" or "You seemed so happy."

I've said, "Well, there is something you ought to know," and then told them. And then there is a short silence. And then they say, "Oh, I'm really sorry." And what do you say then? Thank you for being sorry?

(Man, about thirty)

Despite the awkwardness of the interchange in which the separation is reported, the separating individual may want reassurance that the separation has not altered the friendship. But since telling the news is admitting failure, the separated person may feel depressed afterward whatever the friend says.

You are communicating with all sorts of people. Some will say something awkwardly. Some will say nothing. You'll be hurt if they say something. You'll be hurt the other way.

Some people want to know why you broke up. And some of them you want to know, you want to explain. If they are not interested, you have to learn that too. Some of them are interested just for curiosity's sake, and others are really concerned.

Somebody will say, "I'm sorry." Somebody will say, "Let's play some tennis." Somebody will say something else, "I told you all along this would happen," or "You should have done it long ago." Somebody will say nothing. And you will go home with the same lousy feeling, no matter which way it is.

(Woman, late forties)

People with whom one has become friendly on the job form a special category. It is often unclear just how fully they should be informed. They are not so close that failing to inform them would be an affront. It may be inappropriate to tell them too much. Yet it may seem wrong to allow them to continue to believe that one is married when this is no longer true.

These two women I work with, they are very friendly, very nice, and I went back and I saw them today, and we were kidding back and forth. And they said, "How's the wife?" They knew her by her first name, and they know my kids. And through my mind goes, "Should I say, 'well, the last time I saw her she was fine'?" And I thought, "What is the point of going into it?" I just didn't have the courage. Or maybe I thought it was just wiser to let somebody else tell them.

(Man, about forty)

Despite well-judged reasons for hesitancy, some among the separated feel that they must report their changed marital status to their coworkers if they are to maintain reasonably comfortable relationships with them. A separation is so important an event that not acknowledging it could hardly be thought inadvertent; it would be recognized as secretiveness.

The people in my office are all very close. We do things together socially, they know my kids. When they ask how things are, I flatter myself that they really care, that they really are concerned. I don't want to make them feel, if they find out, as if they had all of a sudden uncovered some skeleton in my closet. I just want to get the damned thing out in the open. It is an unpleasant thing, but I would rather not have them whispering about it and never saying anything to me about it. I want to keep the relationships going, and the easiest way to do this is not to shock them, just tell them that we have split.

(Man, late twenties)

Work relationships and friendships based not on an individual's life situation but on his or her interests or qualities—skill at bridge or capacity for amusing conversation—should continue relatively unperturbed by separation. Women can expect to retain friendships made within their neighborhoods as members of the community of women left behind when husbands go off to work. That their particular husbands will no longer return in the evening will not especially affect these friendships, unless it becomes suspected that their new availability is a threat to neighborhood marriages. Indeed, any friendships formed by a woman acting as an individual rather than as the female member of a couple should remain available to her after separation. The same is true for men; they should be able to retain their friendships with colleagues or fellow fishermen or drinking companions.

Many of the friendships of the separated, however, turn out to have depended on their marital status as well as on their particular interests or qualities. The separated discover that, without having quite noticed, they had become a member of a social network restricted to similarly situated married couples. Separation almost devastates this sector of their social life. They may retain limited friendships with the same-sex spouses of the couples they had known: Women may see the wives for lunch or at other hours during the day, and men may also see the husbands for lunch, or as golf or tennis partners. But they no longer participate with the couples in evening sociability.

I've found that a lot of couples that we were friends with, the couples that are still together, have really rejected me. Well, the girls will visit me, but I don't go to their house because the husband doesn't want to see me.

(Woman, mid-thirties)

Times when couples act as a social unit—evenings, weekends, and holidays—can become times of social isolation.

> Many of my old girlfriends are still friendly with me, but on a weekend I feel like I'm all alone in the desert.
>
> (Woman, early thirties)

There are any number of specific reasons for the fading of relationships with married friends after separation. The very first is that the separated individual may no longer be similar enough to the married friends to fit easily into their sociable occasions.

> It was kind of an embarrassment. You know, everybody had a husband, and it's kind of an awkward thing.
>
> (Woman, mid-thirties)

The life situation of the separated person may also have changed in a way that makes getting together with friends more problematic: the woman may have begun paid employment; the man may have moved to another section of the city. The separated individual is apt to have new concerns—problems with children, difficulties with loneliness—that are foreign to the married friends. And the separated person may want something different in friendship now —more attention to current pressing problems and less small talk about minor matters.

Separation produces total loss of those friendships in which the spouse had been an essential link. The husband will quickly lose touch with the women and their husbands whom he met in connection with his wife's work or her volunteer activities, and the wife with her husband's co-workers and their spouses.

> I just haven't had any contact with married couples that we knew, except for the ones that were my friends. It's sort of like there were my wife's friends or there were my friends and my friends I still have plenty of contact with, and her friends zero contact. It's almost like it's divided down the middle.
>
> (Man, early thirties)

The loss of friends always hurts. Even when the friends were primarily the spouse's friends, rejection by them is hard to accept.

**When we moved to our new neighborhood Andy wasn't able to get home two or three nights a week. So I learned to do things on my own. And when the break came, my friends said, "Well, we never knew him anyway." So essentially those friends were my friends.**

**The ones that were his, from his work, that we saw through his business or his business associations, I never see them. In fact I saw his boss's wife and she acted almost embarrassed to see me. I didn't think she recognized me. I had cut my hair and sometimes people would say that they didn't recognize me. So I introduced myself. And she said, "Yes, I know." And she was very cold. Sort of dismissed me.**

**(Woman, early forties)**

Rejection by one's own friends hurts even more. Yet even an individual's closest friends may feel some loyalty to the spouse and, if they blame the individual for the separation, become critical or cool or openly rejecting:

**It was a traumatic experience for me. I left my wife and lost two of my closest friends. It hurt like hell. I called my buddy, my friend Carl, and he said, "I can't talk to you any more. I know you're a good person, and a good friend, but I don't want to see you that much any more." That was very threatening to me when I first left my wife. Now we see one another once every six months.**

**(Man, late twenties)**

Some among the married couples who had been friends to both husband and wife may ally themselves with one or the other after the separation. This may be more likely if the separation is accompanied by bitterness; afterward the husband or wife may feel bitter not only toward the spouse but also toward those friends who chose to side with the spouse. In more amicable separations husband and wife might each hope that both will retain their former friends. One man was irritated with those friends who wanted to side with him; in his view no true friend should have rejected either him or his wife because they couldn't live with one another.

## The Reactions of Married Friends: Three Phases

A middle-income married couple is apt to maintain friendships with a dozen or so other married couples, perhaps fewer, perhaps more, each of whom may be seen at intervals of several weeks, some more and some less frequently. These other couples together constitute a kind of married person's community for them. At the risk of overstructuring what is in reality a more fluid process, we might identify three phases likely to occur in their relationships with these other married couples should they separate.

*First Phase: Rallying Round*

Unless the separating individual assumes the role of culprit by announcing involvement with a new love or displaying callous indifference to the spouse, the immediate response of friends is likely to be to want to help. The friends may invite the newly separated person to visit, and may make their home available as a temporary refuge. They may try to respect the separated person's privacy and forbear from inquiring closely into what went wrong, although they are likely to be curious. If the separated person wants to talk, they very likely will listen sympathetically, and may offer advice. There may be some exceptions: friends who immediately become overinvolved or rejecting or judgmental. But most friends behave well.

The same generous, understanding response is apt to be extended to both spouses. Which of the couple is first invited to a friend's home may depend on the accident of which answers the telephone. Later, after this first phase of undifferentiated concern has passed, friends may decide they are more his friends or more her friends, but this seems unlikely to happen immediately.

Friends will do what they can to be helpful without being intrusive. If they are critical of the separation—and married friends are apt to have a stake in the integrity of one another's marriages—they will be cautious in their criticisms. To the one apparently responsible for the break, a friend might say, humorously, "Your marriage doesn't sound so much worse than mine." Or, going a bit further, "Isn't there an alternative to breaking up?" Generally friends try to be tactful. Whereas kin may be intrusive, friends tend to define themselves as having no right to interfere.

In this first phase friends react as much to the recognition that the separating couple's lives have been disrupted as to the recognition that they are *separating*. They would react in about the same way had the couple's home burned down. They see their friends having trouble, and they want to do what they can to help.

Both the man and the woman may be the recipient of friends' solicitude, but more may be directed toward the woman, especially if it appears that she has suffered the greater loss. The woman speaking in the following quotation had been left by her husband:

When your marriage ends you find out who your friends are. People had always said everyone deserts you, except for one or two really close friends. Well, the whole world has been so good to me this past three weeks. I just can't get over people's reactions. And the love that has been given to me, and the consideration. My social life if anything has improved. I get two calls a day, do you want to go to the movies, do you want to do this or that? People are really responding to me in this trouble. And it's the most beautiful thing I've ever experienced.

(Woman, about forty)

Even during this first phase, as friends rally round, a false note may be struck. The friends may be too determined to be understanding; their solicitude may be too insistent. The separated person may feel treated by friends as though he or she were an invalid, but this is different from being treated like a friend. The friendship is changing.

This happened to me last week. I went over to see a good friend of mine. He got divorced, oh, two years ahead of me. He's remarried now. Well, I went over to see him, and we had dinner together, had a nice evening. And toward the end he walked me out to my car and said, "Listen, I just wanted to tell you, it's great seeing you. And any time you want to see me, give me a call, because I really know all the pain you are going through." This was after I really had this great evening. And I was driving home and all of a sudden I said, "I really feel awful now." I don't want to have somebody come in and say, "Hey, I know you are having a rough time." I'd rather just say, "Maybe I am going through a rough time and maybe I'm not. But let's just keep it like it was."

(Man, early thirties)

## Second Phase: Idiosyncratic Reactions

Rather soon after the separation married friends begin to recognize that the separated individual is moving to a new way of life, in which he or she will be confronted with the freedom and anxieties of being alone. And now friends react in a wide variety of ways. Some continue to be welcoming, but others appear to feel burdened by the separated individual, as they might by anyone making too heavy a claim on their sympathies. Some seem frightened of him or her, as though the separation were a communicable disease. Some are both appalled and intrigued, as one might be with someone who had undergone a procedure so reckless as to be nearly unthinkable, like a sex-change operation. And still others react with envy, admiration, or curiosity about the separated person's assumed new freedom.[1]

The reaction of the friends, and whether they continue to be accessible or instead withdraw, seems to depend as much on their adaptability, their reaction to the separated individual as an individual and to the separation itself, as on the history of the friendship. The closest of the individual's friends when he or she was married may be unable to tolerate the separation, while friends who were somewhat more distant may continue to be warm and understanding.

In this second phase the separated individual is recognized as separated, and thereby different. He or she is no longer the married friend in trouble; instead he or she has become someone new, a separated man or woman. Because the implications of this change are mysterious, they can become fantasy-laden, and the separated individual can become a target for friends' projections and identifications. Friends may imagine that the separated person is having a marvelous time or a terrible time, on the basis of their fantasies

[1] For a listing of friends' reactions to separation see Arthur A. Miller, "Reactions of Friends to Divorce," in *Divorce and After*, ed. Paul Bohannon (Garden City, N.Y.: Doubleday, 1970), pp. 56–76.

of what *their* life would be like if they were single again. Or they may decide that the separated person is sexually attractive, or needful, or self-centered, or wounded, or reprehensible, or bereft, all on the basis of their unconscious reactions to the idea of separation.

There are still other ways in which friends find personal relevance in a man's or woman's separation. They may see it as a warning to themselves if they let their marriage go on as it has. Or they may see it as a realization of something they had themselves considered; they may want to know what separation is like, to judge whether their decision not to separate was correct. And so the friends may arrange a lunch with the separated person, or ask him or her over for coffee, and then ask, "Are you happier since the separation?" and "How do you manage?"

Some friends become oppressively nurturant; they hover about, as though the separated person had become critically ill and they were the only medical personnel in miles. One can only speculate about their motives. They may have some need to rescue any figure that appears to have been abandoned; perhaps they hope in this way to defeat their own fears of abandonment. Or they may need to deny some secret gratification stemming from the separated person's troubles.

A friend gripped by identification or reparative commitment can be more condemning, rude, or hostile to the other spouse than is the spouse who is nominally being championed. In one instance a man had left his wife for another woman, yet continued to see his wife from time to time. A woman who before the separation had been a friend to both came to bring the wife a present of good brandy and found the husband in the front room, visiting with the children. The woman marched past the husband without a word, handed the brandy to his wife, and said in a voice that carried through the house, "Don't let *him* have any of it." The wife, though she was delighted by the friend's loyalty, regretted the hurt to her husband.

Friends of the other sex can see the separated person as having become newly available. Separated women sometimes complain that, quite without encouragement, one or more of the husbands among their friends has proposed a discreet affair. Sometimes the proposal is made behaviorally, without anything being said; one man began stopping after work at the home of a newly separated woman "to see if everything was all right." But often enough at least one friend's husband, perhaps emboldened by a sense that the separated woman is of diminished standing, makes a proposal that is startling both for bluntness and for insensitivity. The following story is unusual for its dramatic value, but not for the nature of the incident; other separated women also report being pawed or chased around tables by male friends anxious to help them deal with their deprivations.

I've been very close to a girl that lives three blocks over from me for a couple of years now. And I was over their house this week and had a couple of drinks. And her husband offered to walk me home. He and I had a brother-sister relationship. You know, "Hello, how are you?" Or sitting around talking about nothing. So he offered to walk me home. Maybe I should have known what was going to happen. I turned around at my door to say, "Thank you for walking me home," and it was pawing and grabbing and, "You poor thing, what are you doing for sex? You really must be hurting." And I said, "You goddamn bastard. I'm friends with your wife. Don't you ever, ever, put your hands on me again." And he said, "I know what it is like to be a divorced woman. You really must be hurting." And I shoved him so hard he fell off the steps. And I went in and shut the door and I threw up, I felt so degraded.

(Woman, mid-thirties)

Men, too, may be identified by their married friends as available. A separated man reported an incident in which a woman who had become his confidant, and who was married to a man with whom he had been friendly for years, called at his apartment late one evening to discuss her own shaky marriage. The man had no desire for an affair that would propel him into his friends' lives, and though he recognized that it would cost him their relationship, he sent the woman home.

### Third Phase: Mutual Withdrawal

The third phase in the relationship between the separated and couples who had been their friends when they were married is mutual withdrawal. The idiosyncratic reactions of the second phase gives way on both sides upon recognition that the separated person's life is now different and that the friendship is less rewarding than it once was. There is no explicit ending of the friendship, although once in a while a separated person or a member of a married couple may express disapproval of or disappointment in the other. Rather, the friendship is allowed to fade. Neither the separated individual nor the married friends call to arrange a visit.

Sometimes the separated blame the married friends for this. They imagine themselves to have been rejected unfairly by friends who condemn them because of their separation. Or they suppose that their friends avoid them because of their unhappiness, in the belief that they are self-pitying and that when they complain of their sorrows they are hoping to elicit sympathy. Or they imagine they are seen as a threat because they are now single, and that same-sex friends fear the loss of their spouses and friends of the other sex fear their own impulses.

But there is discomfort for the separating as well as for the married in remaining within the same social network. One man asked, "How can I go to a party there as a single, knowing that they know my wife?" Nor is there that much profit in seeing the former friends; no longer does a similar life situation produce the conversational currency of similar interests. And while spending an evening with married friends can sometimes reassure a separated individual of his or her continued social validity, it can also force the separated individual to recognize how much has changed and how different he or she has become. The happy home of married friends can provide a warming hearth, but it can also make loneliness more vivid. Some separated individuals reported that seeing married friends filled them with desperate envy and almost unbearable self-pity. Rather than feel emotions so ugly they preferred to withdraw from the relationships.

Many separated individuals remain in touch with one or two couples, and may even become more friendly with them than they had been when they were married. These couples become the "married friends" of their postmarital life. Other friendships lapse, although a sense of failed obligations remains as a reminder of their former existence. An accidental meeting between the separated individual and lapsed friends may produce mutual embarrassment and hollow declarations of intent to get together in the near future.

Having access to at least a few married friends can be valuable for the separated. One woman described a couple as having provided her with an oasis in an otherwise barren life. But why the earlier friendship of a separated person with some couples is sustained while friendships with other couples fade is often unclear. Their social standing may be a bit less formidable than that of most members of the social network, and the separated person may therefore feel more comfortable with them. Or they may simply be warmer and more accessible than others.

### Social Isolation and Its Symptoms

Despite continued friendship with one or two married couples, most among the separated lose access to the network of married friends to which they had formerly belonged, and to the dinners, parties, or get-togethers based on this network. (An exception may be those gatherings held in the separated person's immediate neighborhood; then it would be insulting for the separated person not to be invited.) With loss of the network comes loss of a sense of membership in a community of friends, and with this come the discomforts of social isolation.

Many among the provisions we think of as coming from friendships are in truth the work of a social network; that is, a set of one's friends, may of whom are in turn friendly with one another. Such a network provides the occasions that enliven our routine, and bring us into sociable contact with friends we might not ourselves arrange to see. Through it we hear news of still other friends (sometimes in the form of gossip), as well as information about movies and pediatricians and the housing market and whatever else might concern us.

It is the *network* of married friends, more than specific friendships, which is the casualty of marital separation. Those among the separated who are employed sometimes establish functioning networks with coworkers or colleagues, and some women who are home can find community among kin. But for most, social integration requires a network of friends, and the separated may for a time be as bereft of community as they would have been if they had picked up stakes and moved to a new part of the country.

Social isolation gives rise to a form of loneliness that is almost as painful as the loneliness of emotional isolation, although its symptoms are different. The symptoms include feelings of exclusion, of marginality produced by rejection. Because there is no one to share one's concerns, daily tasks may lose their meaning; one may become slothful because there seems so little to justify effort. One becomes subject to leaden, almost intolerable boredom. Sleep difficulties may develop just as in emotional isolation, but here less as a consequence of tension and vigilance and more as a result of difficulty in imposing a pattern on one's time. Social isolation sometimes leads to napping through the afternoon and wakefulness at night.[2]

New problems arise constantly in separation: Who might be a good lawyer? How does one go about selling a house? Is there a good summer camp for the children? It is difficult for the separated individual who is socially isolated to get information, or even to learn where such information is obtainable. And without access to a social network it is also difficult for the separated individual to learn how others respond to his or her ideas on how to manage. He or she does not have the opportunity to discuss the same issue with several friends, or within a group context, so that responses made by one friend can be compared with responses made by another. In consequence the separated individual's judgment suffers.

Social isolation can complicate the condition of those among the separated who are already beset by emotional isolation. Now it may become difficult for them to specify the relationships that would end their loneliness. A new attachment will leave them still

[2] For additional material, see Robert S. Weiss, *Loneliness: The Experience of Emotional and Social Isolation* (Cambridge, Mass.: M.I.T. Press, 1973).

feeling without community, just as new friends will fail to meet their need for attachment. Unless the separated recognize that their deficits are multiple, they may wonder, when they reduce one of them, why they remain dissatisfied.

## New Alignments

Eventually the separated person is likely to establish a new community, perhaps less interconnected than the now-lost network of married couples, but nevertheless reasonably satisfactory.[3] The new set of friends may include one or two married couples with whom an active relationship remains, the same-sex member of others among the married couples that had formerly been friends, an intimate friend, and a number of less close friends also without marriages, with whom the separated individual can share the concerns of those living a single person's life. Some among the separated eventually believe themselves to have a richer social life than they had when they were married: Their new friends are likely to be more varied than were the friends of their married days, and the latter, though most of them may be seen hardly at all, may still be thought of as potentially accessible.

As time goes on the separated individual is apt to give increasing time to friendships with others who are separated or divorced.

[3] Goode found that among those of his respondents who had been separated less than a year, 29 percent said they had no friends or were just finding friends. Among those who had been separated between one and two years, the percentage was 26 percent. But among those who had been separated as long as three years, the percentage dropped to 14 percent, of whom 4 percent said they were just finding friends and only 10 percent said they still had no friends at all. These findings suggest that loss of former friends might be nearly complete for about a third of separated women with children (the group with whom Goode worked), and that about two-thirds of *these* would find new friends within three years after the separation. See William J. Goode, *After Divorce* (Glencoe, Ill.: Free Press, 1956), p. 248.

However, as I note later (see p. 323), survey techniques undoubtedly lead to an underestimate of social disruption. In addition, Goode's figures provide an estimate only for a single point in time. The proportion experiencing social isolation sooner or later during their separation would be greater, perhaps much greater.

These friendships may be no closer than were the now-faded friendships with married couples, but they provide people whose situation matches the separated individual's own. Some eventually find the shared concerns so predictable as to be tiresome: conflicts with the former spouse, problems with the children, despair at the unremitting loneliness. Nevertheless, the separated individual is able to feel membership in a community, and it can be surprising to the separated individual, when he or she finally enters into the community of the unmarried, how many others are there.

**Maybe it's because of my status now and because I feel more comfortable with it I'm now aware of more people who are separated, single, divorced. I think it's half the street.**

**(Woman, mid-thirties)**

Some among the separated form friendships with someone of the other sex in which there is no romantic interest—they are "just friends"—but in which each becomes confidant to the other. There would seem to be no analogue to this sort of relationship in the lives of most married persons. The relationships tend to be stable—more stable than most dating relationships—and valuable: They make it possible for both man and woman to talk frankly to someone of the other sex; they provide a measure of companionship; and they are emotionally safe. Here is a man's description of such a relationship:

**There is this one girl who was in this real bad marriage. They split, but she is having a real bad time of it. Sometimes we get together and I talk to her and I feel, gee, I'm being a little useful, I'm helping her along, you know. And it feels good. Sometimes some of the things that she is talking about strike responsive chords in me.**

**(Man, about thirty)**

And here is a woman's description of the same sort of relationship. The image of playing psychiatrist is one that comes easily to mind as individuals try to communicate what the relationship is like:

**I have become very friendly with a fellow in our office. There's no romantic interest; it's just he's somebody nice to talk to. He comes**

over the house, and I tell him all the terrible things that happen to me. He's my psychiatrist. He tells me how good I am. And how rotten he is . . . . He spends a couple of hours and then he goes home.

(Woman, late twenties)

Utilizing some or all of these kinds of relationships, the separated person can construct a social life different from, but not necessarily inferior to, the social life he or she had maintained before the separation. The difficult time is the long period of transition, when the individual's earlier social life has been disrupted, and no new one has yet been formed.

# 9

# Effects of Separation on Relationships with One's Children

One of the things I'm still a little bitter about, right now, is missing the little things that happen. The little things that make the kid's life.

(Man, early forties, one child)

I'd love to go to the Holiday Inn overnight, just to go there and sleep and not be responsible for anybody.

(Woman, thirties, three children)

More than 60 percent of divorcing couples have children at home. About two-thirds of those with children have only one or two. A typical postmarital family is a mother with one or two children in one household, and a father alone in another.[1]

At one time it may have been conventional wisdom that couples, no matter how unhappy with one another, should stay together for the sake of the children. More often today, couples appear to believe that a stressful two-parent home provides a less satisfactory setting for a child's development than a tranquil one-parent home. Indeed, a reason sometimes given for separation is that the tension-filled marriage had begun to upset the children.

In support of this view, some parents report that the separation

[1] U.S., Department of Health, Education, and Welfare, *Summary Report: Final Divorce Statistics, 1971, Vital Statistics of the United States* (Washington, D.C.: Government Printing Office, 1974), Table 5.

seemed to have helped their children, that they should have separated earlier than they did.

I did not believe in separation. I waited too long before leaving. My husband was alcoholic and abusive. We had some very bad fights, that last year. After one I wound up in the hospital. Well, my two younger children are all right, but the older one still hasn't got it together. I think he had too much happening around him.

(Woman, late thirties)

But many parents are deeply concerned at the time of the separation that the children may suffer because of it; that the children will doubt the love of the noncustody parent or blame the custody-retaining parent for sending the other away; and that they will be harmed by growing up in a one-parent home. Parents may also worry about their relationships with the children. Noncustody parents especially may be concerned lest their contact with the children be lost, or the children learn to reject them.

What I'm really worried about is that I want to maintain a relationship with my children. Not necessarily one of being an authority figure or anything like this; I'm worried about maintaining a *relationship*. Suppose that the children have the freedom, as they get into teenage, to come and go in two households, mine and hers. Are they going to have problems of loyalty? Or can they feel just sort of comfortable both places?

(Man, late thirties, two children aged eleven and nine)

In this chapter and the next I present materials bearing on these parental concerns. In this chapter I review the changes that separation introduces into the relationships of parents and children. I describe the changed structure of the one-parent home, which results in modification in the relationships of custody-retaining parents and their children, and I also describe the fundamental changes in the relationships of the noncustody parents and their children. In the next chapter I consider the effects parental separation appears to have on children. At the close of the next chapter I suggest some principles that may help parents help their children to deal with their separation.

### Custody

For the past fifty to one hundred years it has been customary for mothers to be given custody of the children by our courts, except in those cases in which the mothers could be demonstrated to be incompetent or immoral. In many courts matters of morals are now being deemed virtually irrelevant to issues of children's well-being, and fewer men are now attempting to gain custody by showing that their wives committed adultery when they were married, or since the separation permitted boyfriends to stay overnight.[2] This development has been paralleled by another, however, in which mothers increasingly have chosen to relinquish custody to their husbands, either indefinitely or for a limited period, for a variety of reasons. The increase in men gaining custody because the children's mothers wanted a year to pull themselves together, or believed the men to be the better parents, may be just about offset by the decrease in men gaining custody by proving in court that their wives are morally unfit.[3]

Many separating couples, and many divorce lawyers along with them, simply assume that the woman will take custody of the children. For some men this is a relief; for others it is an additional insult, still another demonstration, along with support orders and unfair divisions of property, that society is tilted in the woman's direction. And some women, while they are pleased to have the children, also feel it unfair that they must now manage the bulk of child care alone.

It may be a bit more difficult for a father to assume custody than for a mother in that a man is less likely to have the skills required for homemaking and child care. He is also less likely to have made

2 See Michael Wheeler, *No-Fault Divorce* (Boston: Beacon Press, 1974), pp. 75–80, for similar observations.

3 No statistics are available regarding the proportion of custody awards given to men. However, the Census Bureau has found in the most recent of its yearly Current Population Surveys that about 8 percent of children of divorced parents live with their fathers. The proportion may be increasing: It was 6.7 percent in 1970, 5.7 percent in 1971, 7.2 percent in 1972, 8.1 percent in 1973, and 8.4 percent in 1975.

the connections with a community of mothers that can lighten the task of raising preadolescents through exchange of child surveillance chores. Nurturant behavior may just possibly come a bit less easily to him. And a single father may give greater weight than a single mother to the demands of career or work, and so may be more resentful of the competing demands of family. Employed single mothers, while they also have all they can do to meet the demands of both home and job, seem less inclined to judge themselves by their job success.

A father with custody appears more likely than a mother to bring a housekeeper into the home as an employee or to prevail on a relative to serve unpaid. Fathers unable to obtain a housekeeper sometimes complain that job and family together constitute a heavy burden. A man deserted by his wife said:

> It is kind of hectic for a man to work and take care of a child and to do the laundry and iron, which I can't. And I can't cook. I have many things going against me. You know, your head is spinning when you come home, because you have the job besides.
>
> (Man, about thirty-five)

But we have encountered fathers who have been able to maintain for months routines in which they get the children off in the morning before getting themselves to work and return from their jobs in the evening to prepare the evening meal, in the same fashion as employed separated mothers.

Some innovative couples have tried to work out what seemed to them more desirable custody arrangements than the usual allocation of full custody to one parent and reasonable visitation rights to the other. I have known couples who split custody within the week: Each week the man might have the children Sunday through Tuesday, and the woman Thursday through Saturday. Wednesday would be the woman's day one week, the man's day the next. For one couple who had older children, the system broke down almost immediately. It required too much coordination and too much transportation. Another couple, who had one preschool child, had already maintained the system a year, and were continuing it when I last saw them. My impression, though, is that just the mechanics of transferring the child from home to home, quite apart from the demands of child care, absorbed a good deal of their energy.

Couples have hit on still other ways of sharing custody. Some couples arrange for the father to have the children one or more months in the summer, his only contact with them the rest of the year being by mail or phone. One couple, in an elaboration of this, alternated years with the children: the father had the children one year, the mother the next. They claimed, after three years, that the system worked well, and that the children rather liked alternating schools and sets of friends. Still another couple every three months changed places as parent in the home with the children. They too claimed that their system worked well. It permitted the children to remain within the same school district and same network of friends while living part of the time with their father. And it avoided the many problems of the more usual Sunday visitations, including their artificiality and their requirement that the children relinquish seeing friends on Sundays.

There is urgent need for research on the implications for the children of different custody and visitation arrangements. At this point we simply do not know what difference it makes to children of different ages to be subjected to any of the wide variety of possible arrangements.

In the following sections I shall, for the most part, assume that the mother has custody, since this is usually the case. But it is my impression that, for the most part, the parent with custody will have similar problems of overload, whatever that parent's sex, and similarly that the other parent, whether mother or father, will have to come to terms with a drastically changed relationship to the children.

### The Separated Woman as Head of a One-Parent Family [4]

Many women in the days and weeks just after their separation are thankful that they have children. The children provide structure

[4] This section is based heavily on as yet unpublished materials from my study of primary ties among single parents. This study was supported by the Department of Health, Education, and Welfare, Grant No. CRD 294(2)-7-245.

and meaning to their lives, living assurance that they are needed. More than one woman has commented that her children kept her going through her worst days. One noted, only half in jest, that she could not commit suicide because she had to get the kids' dinner.

The children's need for them provides recently separated women with a sense of themselves as still in some degree valuable. The mothers may pledge to themselves that although other areas of their lives are in a mess, this one area, their relationships with their children, will be protected; that they will make their relationships with their children good ones; and that so far as they have anything to do with it, their children will not suffer because of their separation. They may even formulate the separation as providing opportunity for unhampered attention to their children's needs.

This program, so attractive and with such promise for sustaining a mother's morale, generally proves unrealistic. Although the children are apt to continue to come first in the mother's order of priorities, the relationships with them are likely to be insufficiently gratifying to permit her to devote herself to them without regret; indeed, it is easy for the children to get on their mother's nerves. But just because success in child care matters so much to many mothers on their own, the inescapable disappointments and failures in their relationships with their children can be deeply distressing to them.

One disappointment the single-parent mother is likely to experience is that living with the children does not prevent her from being lonely. Children by their demands and their chatter can keep the mother busy, reassure her of her importance, and to some extent prevent her from becoming mired in obsessive rumination; but children do not ordinarily function as attachment figures. During the days, the tasks of child care may fill the mother's time and to an extent her thoughts, but in the late evenings, after the children are in bed, unabated loneliness is apt to appear. And since the mother may then feel that it is her commitment to the children that prevents her from leaving the house—that her devotion to her children has turned her into her own prison guard—she may become intensely resentful of her commitment to mothering. She may feel herself to be society's fool. One mother said bitterly, "At what age do they start teaching you that a mother's life revolves around her children?" But those few young mothers who seek to escape loneliness by entrance into a hectic dating life are liable to feel intense guilt as they recognize their children's unmet need for care.

There are still other problems in being a single parent in addition to the failure of the children to function as attachment figures. Indeed, whatever the problems of the parent in a two-parent household, they are apt to be present in increased magnitude in the single-parent household. Problems of task overload, emotional overload, and unending responsibility, and problems having to do with just being restricted in one's freedom to move, to get out of the house, also occur in the two-parent household; but in the one-parent household they are more severe. In addition, there are certain problems peculiar to the one-parent household that have to do with the absence of another adult with whom to talk, to share responsibility, and to compare one's perceptions.

In only one respect does being a single parent seem easier. In the single-parent household there is no other adult to undercut one's authority by permitting the children to break rules one has set. Or, more accurately, that other adult who might undercut one's authority is now outside the home, and so less effective—though also more difficult to control.

Despite all this, their children are the central figures in the lives of most single-parent mothers. Their children's well-being is more important to them than anything else within their control. We do not know how to account for the force of this maternal commitment to children: to what extent it has biological bases, and to what extent it is societally imposed. But that it is there gives rise to a paradox in the situation of single-parent mothers: The relationships of single-parent mothers with their children, although they may be gratifying in their own way, fail to provide certain important relational elements and are almost always burdensome and restrictive; and yet they are the relationships of highest priority in the women's lives.

In what follows I do not intend to paint a dismal picture of the single parent locked away with her children and her commitment to them, sentenced to emotional hard labor until the children become adult. There are joys and fulfillments in parenting alone as well as in parenting in partnership. I do want to outline the realities of the situation that make it unlikely that a single parent will realize the aspirations she may have to be the perfect parent for her children. Just because the relationship with the children is so important to single parents, its failures may be the more depressing. I want to point out how demanding is the single-parent situation, as a way of suggesting that some measure of failure within it should be expected and tolerated. The same might be said for the two-parent situation, of course, except there a downhearted parent at least has another parent to turn to for commiseration.

### A Changed Family Structure

The single-parent family is not quite the same as a two-parent family with one parent gone. Rather, the departure of one parent leads to a change in the way in which the remaining parent and the children relate to one another. Usually the mother becomes closer and more responsive to the children, so that even though she remains clearly their mother, she is more nearly on their level than she had been when the husband was in the home. Occasionally the mother may feel that with no husband to back her up she must become more authoritarian herself, or everything will fall apart. Even a mother who takes this tack may find that although she does more directing of the children after the departure of her husband, she also feels closer to them.

Most two-parent homes have a fairly distinct division between the level of adults and the level of the children. The father and mother together develop rules and standards. For either parent to allow the children to ignore these would mean breaking his or her implicit or explicit agreement with the other parent. Although parents do occasionally fail to back one another up, they ordinarily are aware that they should, that they have an obligation to defend one another's position as parent in relation to the children.

In the single-parent household the level of the adult and the level of the children are far less distinct. The children may negotiate rules and standards or even help formulate them—and the adult has no ally to support her feeling that these are only children and not to be taken seriously. Indeed, the children may enter into negotiations over virtually everything. Some mothers react by dictatorial firmness—"You do what I said because I said it!"—but more usual seems a tendency for mothers to be drawn into the negotiations, and to find themselves constantly bargaining—"All right, watch to the end of that TV show, but then come to dinner and no more delays." When the husband was at home they would not have had so much freedom to compromise; the husband would have been irritated at waiting for dinner until his children's TV show finished. But now it is possible and, more, seems easier. Eventually it may seem still easier to consult the children before making decisions about meals or other items of home management. Yet the consequence of systematic negotiation and parental accommodation can be what appears to an outsider as a nearly child-dominated situation:

My son and I have been alone since he was a year old. I can tolerate a lot from children and I did. Until this summer, when we lived with my uncle and aunt. And it just became obvious to me that he was unbearable in lots of different things. He was just eating whenever he wanted to. We had meals, but they were built around whenever he was hungry. There were the two of us, and it was just as easy that way.

When we lived with my uncle and aunt, he couldn't go into the refrigerator whenever he wanted to, because it wasn't my food. I think it was really great for him, because I had to make him, you know, eat at six. I'd give him a snack in the afternoon so he wouldn't be starving, and he just had to make that do, he had to live in the house. People did tell me that he was a nice little kid, but he shouldn't have the feeling that he ruled the world.

I was really delighted. It wasn't all that difficult to teach him. But if I was by myself, I wouldn't have stuck with it.

(Woman, four-year-old son)

In the absence of the second parent one or another child may try to assume part of that parent's relinquished authority. In one family the older daughter began competing with the mother for authority over the two younger children, although the mother told her repeatedly, "I'm the mother. When I need an assistant, I'll hire one." But the mother may also value a child's capacity for responsibility, and she may rely on it so heavily that the child will be not only relieved, but also awash with rivalry, should a new man appear on the scene.

There are, to be sure, benefits in this new family arrangement. It may be a relief not to have to argue principles of child raising with one's husband every time a child wants to stay up late. And there may be a new cooperative spirit in the home. One mother who was planning to have a party told her three children, the oldest aged ten, "I'm going to have a party here, and I'm going to need your help. Let's work out what you can do." The children were excited to be part of things, and helped out happily. In a two-parent household they might well not have been included at all. The single-parent family form may also foster a certain maturity in the children, as the children come to recognize their mother's efforts and recognize also her reliance on their cooperation.

The following is a mother's description of a well-functioning single-parent family:

I've built a relationship, I think, with my children of explaining to them, so they know it's difficult for me. But they're aware that I'm hanging in there and trying. And a kind of mutual respect has grown, me for them and them for me. And mutual gratitude, like when they help me out. I've needed their help. And I thank them and appreciate it. And it also works the other way; they are considerate of me in ways they weren't before. And I don't think it's an instability kind of thing; I think it is something that has grown and will continue to grow.

(Woman, two children, eight and ten)

## The Problems of the Single-Parent Mother

### Overburden

No matter how well-functioning her family, the single parent who has custody is likely to be overburdened. There are too many decisions to make, too many tasks to complete, too many tensions to bear, too little time she can call her own. Two parents would seem hardly enough to deal with all the demands of child care. One parent seems clearly to be insufficient. This is especially true if the mother must work. Yet work may be a near necessity, both as a source of income and as support for the mother's morale.

A working mother may have days in which task follows task without intermission. Such days might begin with her getting the children up, dressed, and off to school, and then, after quickly cleaning up the breakfast dishes, getting herself dressed and off to the job. Then there is the day on the job, after which she may hurriedly shop for a few extra items needed for the evening meal and then rush home to join the children or to pick them up from the neighbor or sister or whoever had taken care of them during the afterschool hours while she was still at work. The evening meal must then be fixed and served and afterward the dishes done. Then the children have to be settled in to an evening activity. There may be homework to supervise, their play to be aware of, and, too often, their fights to referee. Meanwhile the mother must prepare clothes for the next day. At eight-thirty or nine, after a bedtime story, or, if she is too near exhaustion, a final television program, and perhaps a final battle over getting a drink or staying up to see another show, she will have gotten the children to bed. She can then sit down to a cup of tea and wonder where the day went. This would be an ordinary day. If one of the children became ill there would be more to do.

For both working and nonworking mothers, the absence of another adult in the house means that there is no one to take over at any point. It means that if a child has a question, or feels anxious or misused by a sibling, the child comes to the mother. There is no point at which she can say, "I have a headache, I want to lie down and not be bothered," and know that she won't be bothered. The only way she can go to the store is to say to the children that the oldest is now in charge. She may dislike doing this because it gives the oldest too much authority and too much responsibility; yet it is the only way she can get out even for a moment.

*Sole Responsibility*

As the parent with custody, and as the only adult in the household, the mother after separation is apt to think of herself as having sole responsibility for her children, and to be seen in this way by others as well. The father may play a consultative role, as an interested outsider who has a right to voice his opinion, but the authority and final responsibility for decision rests with the mother. It is entirely her responsibility to decide whether the children can eat before a meal, whether they can go out on a school night, what time they have to be in bed. There are, of course, attractions to women in this, particularly to those who had for some time been dubious of their husband's child-care philosophy. But there are problems as well.

One problem is having no one with whom she can discuss issues about whose resolution she is uncertain. Some mothers ask their husband's opinion, or a friend's, or their own mother's. Where it is possible to do so, mothers may try to take cues from the neighbors, and may go farther than most other parents in adapting their standards to those of their milieu.

If I see that all first-graders walk to school by themselves, then I will really put my back up and insist that he go by himself. If all the kids in his age group more or less draw back, then he can't do it. ... That is how I keep my anxiety down.

(Woman, early thirties)

When larger issues arise, the fact of sole responsibility may weigh heavily on the woman. In one instance a child was stricken with paralysis and the mother's doctor advised an operation that might provide the child somewhat greater mobility, though at the cost of inflicting minor permanent damage. The woman consulted her husband, and talked at length with a friend, but ultimate responsibility for the decision was hers alone.

Some mothers share responsibility with their children, or delegate responsibility to the children, even when the children are quite young. One woman received a note from her ten-year-old son's school, after all the children in his class had been examined by a dentist, saying that the boy needed orthodontia. The woman was told by her own dentist that the boy's teeth should be straightened, but that the work would be expensive. The woman was skeptical; she suspected that the gain would be only cosmetic. Still, the procedure had been recommended by both the school dentist and her own dentist. In a quandary, she asked her son whether he wanted to have braces on his teeth. He said that he did not. If he had said that he did (perhaps unlikely, given her phrasing of the question), she would have had the work done.

Sole responsibility can overburden a woman as surely as can a succession of days filled with too much to do. The overburden is of a different nature; it is a moral overload rather than a physical one. Often recognition of their sole responsibility seems to make women who are single parents even more vulnerable than other parents to anxiety lest they somehow fail their children, and even more vulnerable to guilt for any shortcomings in the way things turn out.

### Getting the Children to Mind

Many women who are single parents complain that their children became less respectful after their husbands left the home. They say that since the separation the children have become more willful and harder to control. They are more likely to balk at cleaning their rooms, more likely to squabble with their siblings, more likely to break rules regarding television and bedtimes. Told that they cannot go out after the evening meal, they are more likely to object and more willing to display their resentment. Told that they must return home at a certain time, they are more likely to be late, and then to offer only the lamest of excuses. They argue back more than they would have dared if their father were still at home.

When the children's father was home, he may not in fact have done very much disciplining. The mother may have threatened the children with the father's wrath to intimidate them into good behavior, but she might have been reluctant actually to involve the father in a dispute with the children: To have done so would have admitted her incapacity to deal with the children alone; the father might have objected to being burdened with the mother's difficulties; and the father's response might have been unpredictable, but conceivably drastically punitive. Having the father in the home seemed to be important not for his active participation in rule setting, but rather for his presence as an allied adult; just by being there, he backed the mother up. Now, as a single-parent mother, the woman is apt to feel beleaguered in her confrontations with her children.

In addition, single-parent mothers may be made more anxious than are mothers in two-parent families by children's balkiness. Many parents, in two-parent families as well as in one-parent families, worry lest their children become resistive to adult direction and insist on moving down a road that appears to lead away from a respectable and potentially happy adult life. Single-parent mothers, as sole responsible adults, have only their own resources, already stretched, with which to protect their children from being misled by the children's own impulses. Even more than other parents they are likely to be made anxious by indications that the children may be getting out of control.

### The Aggravation Cycle

*First woman:* That one big explosion is not going to affect them in time to come. If you have that one big explosion and then are sorry, but show them daily love, it won't hurt them.
*Second woman:* But what if you have daily explosions?

All parents are now and again made tense by their children. But the commitments and the situation of the single-parent mother seem calculated to put her on a short fuse.

The very commitment of single-parent mothers to be good mothers, to see to it that their children are adequately loved and nurtured and cared for, sets the stage. If children find a reasonable objection to a mother's request, the mother may feel obligated to consider it. If the children want to change a household routine, postpone a chore, escape, just this one time, a rule of the household, the mother may try to accommodate them as far as she can. If the children are clinging or provocative or insistent on being attended to, the mother may do her utmost to indulge them. But the negotiations, accommodations, and indulgences take their toll on the mother's nerves.

Many single-parent mothers report a sequence of events which begins with cumulative irritation. One mother wanted her six-year-old to play outside, but he wanted to stay in the kitchen, where she was preparing lunch for friends. She shrugged and said, "All right." Then the six-year-old wanted to sit on the kitchen table. She told him he couldn't sit on the table, but he could play at the table with his coloring book. While coloring, the six-year-old accidentally tipped the sugar bowl. The mother noticed this and sighed deeply. The six-year-old began making designs in the sugar. Then, to have more sugar to work with, he spilled some more. Now the mother said he absolutely had to go outside. But the six-year-old said again that he didn't want to go outside. "You must," the mother said, starting reasonably enough. But suddenly she was unable to control her anger at the boy's willful opposition and her rising panic lest she be unable to manage him. She began shouting at him, "I told you to play outside. Now you get right outside, right this minute!" Shaken, the six-year-old left the kitchen, while the mother, equally shaken, remained behind, aghast at her own fury. Later that morning, before her friends arrived, the mother called her son in and explained that all parents sometimes lose their temper and her losing her temper didn't mean that she didn't love him.

This is the aggravation cycle: cumulative irritation which the parent attempts to tolerate, indeed may hardly be aware of, until there is a sudden breakthrough of anger, perhaps heightened by panic, after which the parent is remorseful. The fury may be triggered by a particular incident—a child in his Sunday best jumping in a puddle, or a child cheekily telling a parent "You're not so big." But ordinarily there has been a preceding series of irritations, not all of them necessarily produced by the child.

Depending on the level of frustration I have had for the day, I tend to get angry with the children for not doing their share . . . as far as their responsibility. . . . I mean if there are rubbers and jackets and lunch boxes and papers on the floor, they haven't really done their share. . . . And they know that it adds to my frustration.

(Woman, mid-thirties, three children)

Some children are more provocative than others. A truly provocative child could drive anyone wild; it is no trick for such a child to torment a mother whose hands are already full without his contributions.

Every morning, trying to get my son dressed—by the time I get him to that school bus I am all knotted up. He sits there and he looks at the ceiling and I'm saying, "Come on, Nicky, or you'll miss the bus." And a few minutes later one sock is on. And then for fifteen minutes he is dreaming.

(Woman, three children, oldest a boy, five)

Most single parent mothers I have talked with indicate that their reserve of tolerance seems to have been reduced since they got on their own. At times, when their energy is absorbed by their own concerns, or just by the tasks of the day, the children's demands seem like a raid on badly depleted supplies; they must either fight off the demands or give up totally. At other times when they are more accommodating of their children than they would have been before their separation, their accommodation has in it a measure of defeat, as though they are admitting that they cannot fight endlessly.

A temporary reverse may lessen a mother's resilience. One mother who had been on her own for some time became involved with a man she hoped to marry. When the man ended their relationship she suffered the usual painful separation distress. Her twelve-year-old daughter, who had also hoped that the boyfriend might become a permanent addition to their family, was especially irritating one evening. Her mother asked her to behave herself and the daughter flung out, in return, that maybe the mother should learn to behave *herself* so that men wouldn't be forever leaving her. The mother slapped the daughter with all her strength.

Later that evening, long after the daughter had gone to bed in tears, the mother taped on the refrigerator a note in which she asked her daughter's forgiveness.

Some mothers, when the level of aggravation to which they have been subjected reaches their flash point, react by yelling at their children. Others report slapping their children or shaking them. At least one mother who reported hitting her children when she lost her temper had prided herself, before her separation, on never having spanked them.

Some mothers have developed strategies for dealing with their own mood on days when they can sense themselves becoming unbearably tense. One such strategy is to be nice to oneself; perhaps to visit a friend, if possible without the children; or perhaps to arrange to see a movie.

**If I'm in a bad mood, things have gone wrong that day, I have a headache, when I pick up my son I'll say, "Let's go get an ice cream cone." Something to break the routine. Or we go over to see my friend.**
**(Woman, early thirties, one child about eight)**

Talking with an understanding friend can help to restore one's sanity; being nice to oneself is a way of augmenting one's emotional supplies. But there probably is no strategy by which a single-parent mother, solely responsible for her children and her household, can avoid intervals of stress. It might be useful if single-parent mothers could learn to display the same understanding indulgence toward themselves that they often feel called on to display toward their children.

*Problems of Unchallenged Perceptions*

It is easier for the single-parent mother than for the mother in a two-parent household both to be despairing of her children and to be unrealistically enthusiastic about their development. The absence of another adult means that the mother will rarely have occasion to formulate her view of a child and then to examine that formulation in the light of evidence. Perhaps even more important, the absence of another adult in the household permits a mother's misperceptions to flourish unchecked by confrontation with another view, which might be equally inaccurate, but would at least be different. In consequence, single-parent mothers are liable to feel that children are hopeless when they are not or to overlook gross disturbance in a child which other adults see only too plainly.

Undoubtedly all parents bring to their perceptions of their children memories of earlier relationships in which they participated during their own childhood. They may identify with a child and want him or her both to master and to escape the events of their own childhood. Or they may see in a child a younger sister or brother whose arrival they deeply resented or an older sister or brother whose bullying blighted their early life.

A mother may be indulgent with one child and furious with another, without being able to justify either feeling. One mother identified her older son with her own older brother who had, in her mind, gotten away with murder throughout her childhood. She saw her younger son as like herself, essentially good but insufficiently valued. When she discovered the younger son lighting matches, she scolded not him, but his brother, for not having cared enough for the younger son to stop him.

Single-parent mothers sometimes see the children's father, or some of his traits, in their children, and respond to the children partially in terms of their feelings about the father. And, like all other parents, they now and again see in their children some regrettable aspect of themselves, such as insecurity or timidity or selfishness, traits they would prefer to disown. Especially if they are determined to combat these traits in themselves, they may be overly alert to them in their children and exaggerate the extent of their occurrence.

Here, as elsewhere, it can be useful for single parents to have someone with whom they can discuss their children. In separations that permit it, the other parent might do. But it is my impression that most separated couples are too defensive with one another to be able to talk frankly, especially in the area of parenting. Perhaps we need new social forms, or increasing use of existent forms such as agency-sponsored single parents' groups, that will permit single parents to review their appraisals of their home situations with one another.

*Getting Away*

The single-parent mother, like the mother in the two-parent family, is apt to find that her children restrict her mobility. But the single parent, because her responsibility is so unrelenting, has even more need to get away for an evening, or a weekend, or a brief vacation. And it is even more difficult for her to do so.

The possibility of a future vacation, or the memory of a past one, may be like a vision of paradise: to be away; to be free of the uninterrupted demands of child care; to be able to relax and enjoy oneself. It would be necessary to be assured that the children were well looked after, but if the single-parent mother were able to trust her child-care arrangements, the freedom would be heady.

**Going on vacation from my children was the most glorious experience of my life. The children were fine; they survived. They were with my married daughter. . . . I think with teenagers you have to put a little space between you now and then.**

**(Woman, late forties, two children at home aged fourteen and seventeen)**

Making reliable child-care arrangements can be troublesome. Family members are not always cooperative, and it may be imposing on their good nature to leave children with them for an extended period. Babysitters are expensive and not always obtainable. Leaving the children in the care of the oldest is possible if the oldest is a teenager, but may impose too much responsibility on him or her. Yet the difficulty of arranging child care is not the most serious barrier to the mother's getting away. The most serious barrier is the mother's guilt. The mother may feel that her children have already experienced the loss from their homes of one parent and that they will be desolate by seeing the other leave, despite her assurance that she will return. And the children may indeed be distressed by their mother's absence.

I was gone four days this spring, and the younger boy didn't seem to mind my going, but the older boy was just terrible. His teacher in school knew something had happened at home. She finally asked him what was wrong. He had a terrible week in school—cried the whole time.

(Woman, two sons, eight and six)

The mother in the above story, needless to say, responded with guilt and remorse. Yet she needed the time away. The conflict between desire for time away and concern for the children repeatedly puts single parents in an excruciating dilemma; they are made to feel by their children that the time away they need for their own emotional well-being is obtained at the cost of the children's despair.

I took a vacation three years ago. I want to go on a vacation now. I just casually mentioned it the other day and all their eyes filled up. And so I feel trapped. I feel I deserve it. But I feel guilty about it, because they just looked so lost. And when I went away three years ago they were in their own home. My parents came to stay with them.

(Woman, three preteen children)

It is not only maternal vacations that distress children. Just the mother's going out for an evening may be protested.

I'm going out the door and I hear them call, "Ma." Well, I keep going. But then the older one says, "How come you go out so much and leave us all alone all the time?" And I've been out maybe two nights in this week. So I feel guilty going out at all.

(Woman, two preteen children)

One approach to resolution of this dilemma, so natural to the single parent, is negotiation with the children. The mother may hammer out an agreement with the children: She can be out two or three evenings in the week if she is home the remaining evenings. Those mothers I have talked with who established this sort of bargain say that it worked well. One who had decided with her children that she could have two evenings a week said that at the end of a week during which she had been out only once the children reminded her that the next week she would have an extra evening coming.

I would support single-parent mothers who want to take time for themselves. The children may themselves profit from a mother who is not suffocating in child-care responsibilities. Yet the children's well-being must be considered as well. If the children are school age and have siblings to keep them company, the mother may feel somewhat freer. If the children can be left with their father or, failing this, with their family—grandparents or an aunt —so much the better. If they are able to remain in their own home so that they can continue to see their friends, better still. But a young only child who would have to be moved to a strange home with people he did not know presents a situation that should give the mother pause. Perhaps under these circumstances the mother might postpone her vacation from child care until a better plan can be devised.

## The Father as Parent Without Custody

After separation, despite the modifications I have described, the mother's relationship to her children remains fundamentally the same: The mother is still the guiding, nurturing, parental figure within the home responsible for the children's care. In contrast, the father's relationship to his children is likely to change fundamentally after separation: The conditions under which he and the children are together change; the assumptions regarding his role in the children's lives are different; he is a quite different sort of parent.

The most important source of difference after separation is that the father no longer is a fellow member of the children's household. A number of consequences follow from this, one of which is that he is likely to feel out of touch with the events of their daily lives. Contact weekly or every other week, of several hours together, does not provide the same continuity of awareness as living within the same household. By the time the father meets with his children, the events and crises that occurred in the interval since the last meeting will have been nearly forgotten. And even if the children do remember to say that they were kept after school one day, or were on the honor roll, being reported to is not the same as being present when an event was emotionally real.

**I'm bitter about missing the little things that happen, the little things that make the kid's life.**

(Man, about forty)

The father's awareness that there will be an interval during which he will not see his children makes every departure from them another separation. Many fathers report feeling bereft and depressed at the end of a visit.

**When I'd come to see them, that was a joyful experience. They'd be running, jumping, over me, and really make me feel welcome. Then, when I was going, I would be very sad to be leaving them. I'd be depressed and very lonely. And that night and the next morning were terrible times.**

(Man, late thirties)

The children, too, might be sad at the father's departure, increasing his own sadness and also making him guilty for his role in the separation. Sometimes the children show by withdrawal or by open anger that they blame the father for the break.

**I drive away and see my daughter standing on the doorstep and she's got tears in her eyes and that hurts me. And I find that when I go to talk with her now she acts difficult, because she's hurt.**

(Man, about thirty)

Not being a fellow member of the children's household may have other implications for the father's relationship to his children in addition to loss of continuous contact. It may weaken, or end, those aspects of the father's relationship that depended on his role in the household as head of the family, protector, and provider. These are, of course, traditional definitions of the father's role and have come under attack from those who would rather have marriages more nearly symmetrical in the ways in which husband and wife participate. But they continue to be recognized in most households of the married; to the extent that they structured a particular father's household, his losses after separation are likely to include the underlying assumptions of his relationships to his children.

The father after separation is no longer head of the household. No longer is he even symbolically final authority, court of last resort, in household matters. Indeed, his voice after separation carries only as much weight as his wife permits. Whereas formerly he might have been able to contribute to family debates with assurance that his viewpoint would be seriously considered, and might well be determinative, now he is an outsider. His opinion might or might not be solicited; he may be able to voice it only as criticism of the way the mother does things. In any event, the final decision is the mother's.

Secondly, before his separation, the father is likely to have been seen by everyone in the family as at least symbolically a guarantor of family safety and of the integrity of the family's boundaries. If he was at home, he would be the one who would send away a persistent salesman, and even when he was not at home his role might be invoked by his wife: "I'll have to ask my husband." Should he be away overnight, his wife might become anxious about noises in the home. And if his wife's sense of security depended partly on his presence, so did his children's. And the father might himself recognize and value this role.

Fathers after separation may be dismayed that they can no longer protect their children against danger. They may feel helplessly aware of the many sources of threat: predatory adults, bad companions, and the children's own naïveté and recklessness.

One of the fears I always had, and I can't do anything, I have no control over it, but my daughter's going to start going out, and I'm not there to ask the guy, you know, "Are you a safe driver?" I don't know what she's doing really. . . . I have no control. I have to rely on my wife and my kid's judgment.

(Man, about forty)

Finally, fathers may be chagrined to discover that separation has reduced the extent to which they are seen as their children's source of support. Though they may faithfully send support payments to their wives, the role of family provider is largely a household role, and with separation the father is no longer that member of the household responsible for its income. The mother becomes family provider in his stead, and the father becomes merely an income source, like an employer or Social Security. It may be recognized in the family that the father provides the money because of his continued commitment to his children and concern for their well-being, but it is up to the mother to insure that the money is received. Often the mother seems to define the father's support payments not as an expression of the man's continued responsibility for her household but rather as her payment for caring for his children, or as a return on her past investment in the father, or as reparations for injury.

Fathers often search for other means by which to let their children know they remain providers. They may treat the children to an expensive outing, or send their children expensive presents. They may do this at the same time that they reduce their support payments or skip them entirely, in part because of resentment of their wives' exploitation of them as income sources. One father planned to take the children on an expensive vacation though he had skipped at least one support payment and would not now help their mother with her rent. (The mother finally refused to permit the children to go.) Should a father who takes such a course be out of touch with his child, he may add to the mother's consternation by planning an outing or sending a gift that is inappropriate to the child's age level; one man, for example, sent his wife a full-size bicycle (unassembled) for their six-year-old. In another instance a father who had skipped several support payments sent an expensive portable typewriter to his six-year-old son who was, as it happened, not yet able to read. And yet one can sympathize with the father who wants to communicate to his child that, despite his removal from the child's household, he will continue to provide the equipment the child will need in life.

Mothers may fail to recognize how much the relationship of father and children is affected by the father leaving the home. The following comment represents a view many mothers hold:

**My husband wasn't really that available to the kids when he was home. So he is probably giving them more now.**
( Woman, mid-thirties )

In response, men are apt to point out how unnatural their relationship to their children becomes after they have left the home, how much energy they must give to its maintenance, and how worried they are that, despite everything they do, they may fail their children by living away from them, or, indeed, may have already failed them by leaving their home.

The relationship of fathers with very young children may indeed improve after separation. The sort of concentrated attention provided by the father described below may work well with them. But the relationship of fathers with children of school age seems more often to be stressed by separation.[5] Older children may do better with a father who is regularly available than with one who, when available, concentrates his attention on them, even though the latter is very much to be preferred to the father who maintains no relationship at all.

---

[5] Judith S. Wallerstein reported this as her impression, based on preliminary analysis of data she and Joan B. Kelly had gathered. She believed that in their sample of approximately sixty families in which there had been a separation, father-child relationships with preschool children had tended to improve, but that relationships of fathers with older children generally had not, and in a significant number of instances had gone downhill. She also noted that the state of the pre-separation relationship did not seem to have been a good predictor of what would happen after separation. Her remarks were made in discussion of the following papers: Joan B. Kelly and Judith S. Wallerstein, "The Effects of Parental Divorce: The Experience of the Child in Early Latency," and Judith S. Wallerstein, and Joan B. Kelly, "The Effects of Parental Divorce: The Experience of the Child in Late Latency," both read to the meetings of The American Orthopsychiatric Association, Washington D.C., March, 1975.

Here is a passage of dialogue between a single-parent mother and a man whose daughter is barely two:

*Woman:* It seems to me that the divorced father who really cares about his kids thinks more about them after a divorce than he does in the family situation. He has less time but then the quality of that time is higher than it was perhaps even in the family. When I think of the relationship that my kids had with their father at the stage that yours is at—they got so little from their father. . . .

*Man:* Well, she's at a very delicate age where almost daily accomplishments take place and I'm really scared I'm going to miss something. Mercifully this separation happened when it did and not three months earlier, because she is just learning to talk, and even already she can express herself. But things that she says, if I hadn't been around to interpret what she was saying, would totally escape me. I have to work . . . to see her and follow her and maintain a continual relationship. I find myself being much more concerned when I'm with her than I would have been before.

The man who was speaking had just separated from his wife and was maintaining the sort of frequent contact with her and their child that is possible in very early separation. He returned to his former home for a visit two or three times in the week, and in addition babysat one evening in the week. Later he reduced these contacts to a more usual spacing, as the earlier arrangement proved too uncomfortable for both his wife and himself.

During the first weeks after separation a good many men try to see their children several times a week, in an attempt to continue the relationship established when they were still in the children's home. One man spent several evenings each week in what was now his wife's home, talking with the children, or just being there, reading the paper and watching TV. Another man drove his children to school every morning; another met them after school.

I see them regularly now. I see them about every day, after work. I don't go in the house because I can't stand going in any more. I tell them where I'm going to be and they meet me and we go some place, on a regular basis.

(Man, about forty, recently separated)

However, it soon becomes apparent to these men that they cannot sustain this program of daily or near-daily contact; neither their own schedules nor, often, their children's schedules permit it. A more sensible arrangement must be developed.

Some men at this point wonder if it is not hopeless to attempt to maintain any relationship at all with their children. Visiting weekly or every two weeks may strike them as harrowing and pointless. The idea of ending their contact with their former family is likely to occur to them.

**I can always walk away from it. I think society is designed for the man copping out. I got so many friends telling me, "Make another life for yourself!"**

**(Man, mid-thirties)**

But most men seem to attempt to retain whatever they can of their former paternal relationship, so long as they live in the same region as their children. If they or the children move to another region of the country, it is my impression that the father's income level largely determines his relationship with his children. At lower income levels the father may not see his children at all. At middle and upper incomes the father is likely to visit the children once or twice in the year when they are small, and when they become older to have them stay with him during the summer, for anywhere from a week to the entire summer.

Fathers who remain in the children's locality and who seek to maintain a regular schedule of visits may encounter a number of problems. The first may be finding a satisfactory structure for the visit. With very young children the father might play with them, read to them, or simply be with them, in his wife's home or in his own. He would tolerate the awkwardness and artificiality of regular returns to the home he had left in order to maintain his contact with the children. With slightly older children the father may organize visits around activities outside the home: visits to a museum, zoo, amusement park; attendance at a children's theatre, a ball game, the circus. But provision of a steady sequence of these outings can turn into a chore; fathers who can find no alternative may feel that they have become tour guides for their children. Some increased use of museums and other public entertainments seems almost inescapable for many fathers, but fathers who also have a place of their own where their children can come and be comfortable seem to be more nearly satisfied with their visiting. Also helpful, it seems, is the occasional presence of other children, although not if it means that the father is then unable to give attention to his own.

Fathers of preadolescent children who have their children with them for two consecutive days or longer will have some of the problems of the custodial parent. The father will have to provide meals and set bedtimes, and decide what clothing must be worn for the outdoors. Should the child become too ill to go out (itself something he will have to judge), he must decide whether to call the doctor—and which doctor to call—and devise ways of amusing the child indoors. He has to learn to play the role his wife had assumed before the separation. There are both gratifications and annoyances in doing so.

**The man feels closer to the child than he did before. He's not being kept from the child by the mother. But he doesn't know what to do with the child. He doesn't know how to be nurturant. He knows how to be a father all right: how to advise, how to be a model, how to correct. But he doesn't know how to comfort, how to nurse, how to arrange for playmates. He makes mistakes and feels a fool.**

**(Man, about thirty, six-year-old son)**

Visits with adolescent children pose a special problem. Preadolescent children are ordinarily delighted to accompany Dad on outings. And even if they now and again have mixed feelings about leaving home and friends, they ordinarily are too much in awe of adult plans to become balky. But adolescents are likely to have their own plans; in addition, instead of wanting, so far as is possible, to cement a relationship with both parents, as is true of most preadolescents, they may want to establish their independence. The relationship with their father may mean as much to them as it ever did, but they may be resistant to accompanying him on outings or, indeed, to spending much time with him when he comes to visit. Their resistance may be only half-hearted protest, primarily for the record, or it may be genuine preference, after a few minutes of conversation, for activities elsewhere.

My boy says, "When are you going to see me?" So I say, this time, or that time. So I get there and it's half an hour and then, "I got to go play ball." Well, he did that when I was home. I guess with teenage boys you see them at breakfast and supper and that's about it.

(Man, early forties)

Some men react to the apparent indifference of their adolescent children by requiring the children to initiate contact: "If they want to see me they can arrange it." One mother whose husband had adopted this strategy said her children were hurt by it; they thought it expressed their father's coolness toward them. But a father who had used the technique claimed it worked well:

I think if your children are adolescents you should shift part of the responsibility for the contact to them. They know where you are, where you can be reached. I tie this to the idea that they are trying to establish their independence, and this is a means of doing it. This is the route that I have taken. It works out pretty well. I just said, "Why not make this a two-way thing. Why make it wholly one-way?"

(Man, late forties)

Fathers who have children of different ages have further problems to solve. The children are at different points of development; they behave differently; they have different interests. Taking them out together does not work.

For all five of us to go out at one time, its ridiculous. Because the two younger ones, they fight about who's going to sit in the front seat and that sort of thing. And it's "Let's go get some ice cream." The other two are getting to the point where I am getting embarrassed about going with them for ice cream.

(Man, forties)

Fathers who were members of their children's household would see all the children together at the evening meal and might talk or play with each separately during the week. But fathers who are no longer members of their children's household must plan occasions for interchange. If the fathers structure their relationships with their children around activities and outings, this may mean separate plans for different children, and less time available for each.

**Ruthie, who is six, still wants to be with me all the time, to go with me to the zoo, to the playground, and the older kids don't want that any more. Larry is more interested in being with kids his age. He and I are going out to a restaurant and he is real pleased with that. And Vinnie likes to play ball and go to basketball games and football games. So we're moving in the direction of my spending less time with each of the kids, but there are still lots of times when I spend time with the three of them. Part of that is because if I wanted to see each of them separately, there is just that much more time that I need.**

(**Man, late thirties**)

The relationship with his children is in many ways a source of pain and frustration for the separated father. He must tolerate the loss of many of the ways of relating to the children that may have once been important to him, including being accessible to them during the evening; he must accept that he no longer has genuine authority in relation to the children; he cannot give the children the time he would like to; the occasions for being together sometimes seem stilted and artificial; when the children reach adolescence, they may become elusive, though they will want to retain contact with him. The structure that once supported the father's relationship with his children is no more, and the father must fashion his own structure as best he can.

My impression is that those fathers have managed best who were steadiest and most assured in communicating to their children their continued caring. Among the most successful may have been those occasional fathers who were able regularly to replace the children's mothers as parent within the children's home. In this way they could relate to their children as custodial parent while not removing the children from the children's neighborhood world —and, incidentally, while giving the children's mothers a bit of vacation. Other fathers found it useful to provide their children with a place that was the children's within the father's home; in effect they provided their children with a second home additional to the children's real home.

All fathers, despite the frustrations they may experience in maintaining their relationship with their children, and despite the loss of many of the bases for that relationship, remain valuable to their children. They remain, to begin with, figures whom the children respect. Although they are no longer heads of the children's household, they retain a measure of their former authority, like a chief of state in exile. They are in addition a kind of reserve parent, a guarantor of the children's security should anything happen to the children's mother. Despite the spacing of their visits, they can establish relationships in which they support and offer direction to the children's interests and strivings. Although the children cannot bring them their problems as they occur, the children can continue to consult them on issues that are for the children persistent worries.

Tuesday night I had dinner with the kids. I took them out to dinner and we came home and we had this big discussion about, "Daddy, when do I have to get drafted in the war?" You know, this is a recurrent fear they have, with this invasion of North Vietnam [6] getting a lot of talk. And we started discussing it and all the alternatives. And I was amazed. Because I had figured they'll come out with things and I won't be there. But it doesn't seem to be happening that way.

(Man, mid-thirties)

Fathers can be confident that no matter how much time passes after they leave their children's homes, they will neither be forgotten nor become figures to whom the children are indifferent. There may be resentments; children of separated parents often feel cheated of the happy intact home in which they imagine other children grow up. Occasionally children are actively hostile toward their father, because he has left them, because he seems an embarrassment to the mother or themselves (as in the case of

[6] This was during the last days of American participation in the Vietnam war.

one father who was alcoholic), or because he has been brutal to the mother or them. Their hostility may also be an expression of identification with a hostile and vengeful mother. But most often father continues to be a loved and important figure; a different kind of father, to be sure, but father nevertheless.

## Separated Parents

Whom children have joined together no mere decision to separate can put asunder. Only if the man drops out entirely will the couple not have to acknowledge one another throughout their children's lives. Early in separation the other spouse may seem to hover constantly in the background of each one's relationship with the children. Later in separation the other may simply be a factor always to be taken into consideration.

Early in separation the father may seem to his wife almost everpresent, if not in person, then on the phone. One reason for this is likely to be the father's continued attachment to her. But another may be the father's desire to retain his previous closeness to his children despite his departure from the home and his unwillingness that his children be lost to him along with everything else.

The hovering father of the first weeks of separation can be a pain in the neck to his wife. In addition to making it more difficult for his wife to get her bearings, he may be critical of her mothering or insistent on certain ways of dealing with the children. One man, for example, insisted that his wife tell the children that they were to be divorced, although his wife was far from convinced that telling them was a good idea.

Some women eventually accept their husbands' visiting the children in their home. It has its awkward moments, but it also has its advantages.

At first my wife was up tight about my coming over, but then I got the feeling that she was going to make the best of the opportunity to get out without the kids. I'm not really sure at this point.
(Man, late thirties, three children, two of them preschool)

For the man, as I have noted, being able to visit his children in their own home has great advantages, especially if his children are small or of different ages. The children, too, may like it. The man just quoted went on to say:

They want me to come up there and to cook for them. Previously I would say they were always delighted to go out to eat; now they prefer that I cook for them. They seem comfortable when I come over to the house. Generally my wife leaves or stays and goes to another part of the house. Sometimes I play with them there, or not get in their way, just be around. It's easier for me to go over there than to find some place to take them all the time.

The wife may want her children to recognize that their parents are able still to accept one another.

I want the children to be comfortable with him in their own home. I also feel they shouldn't feel that we are from separate camps: "When you come, Mommy has to go; you come in the back door, and Mommy goes out the front door."

(Woman, mid-thirties)

Many wives, however, do not want to foster their husbands' relationships with their children. They feel that the husband has behaved so badly that he has forfeited his right to his children's love as well as theirs. And they may feel hurt if their children do not seem to agree with them.

I felt quite hostile towards my husband for a long, long time after we broke up. And I found it very hard to understand why the kids didn't see how he was treating me, and all. And I find it difficult to accept the fact that they still love him and want to be with him. I really do.

(Woman, mid-thirties)

Wives who feel this way may not only discourage their husbands from seeing their children within their home but resent cooperating with them in any other visiting arrangement. They may support or even elicit the children's anger with the husband, and then use that anger as justification for refusing visitation. But most wives accept that their children's relationships with their husbands are separate from theirs; while they need not go so far as to offer the husband a drink when he comes to call for the children (though some wives do), they may try to keep their animosity to themselves.

Many wives who do not want to interfere with their husbands' visiting are made anxious by the prospect of the children going off with their fathers. If the father appears to have tendencies toward irresponsibility, the mother may wonder about her own responsibility to the children. Should she not insist on being present during the father's visit?

The mother may be in a quandary. A child has a right to two parents. Suppose the father is sometimes drunk, and might possibly drive while drinking. Does that justify preventing him from taking the children with him? What if he pledges not to drink while he has the children? What if he has never yet had an auto accident? Can he be trusted? Is distrust alone sufficient grounds for keeping the children home? Suppose the father has in the past left the children unattended for hours on end, once taking them to a restaurant and leaving them there for an hour or so. Does that justify telling the children that they cannot again go places with their father?

Yet it is easy for the wife to be punitive toward the husband under the guise of being protective toward the children. One woman believed her husband, a pleasant, entirely harmless man, to be homosexual. She insisted on accompanying him whenever he took the children out. He felt shamed by this, but helpless to change it.

Many women are made uncomfortable by the idea that the children may see their husband's girlfriend, especially if the girlfriend was instrumental in breaking up their marriage. They feel threatened by the new woman, but also sometimes feel the new woman is somehow unclean, and that her uncleanliness can be contaminating. They do not want their children touched by her.

Well, this is what I said to my thirteen-year-old daughter. I said, "Alice, I really feel that your relationship with your father is one thing, but if I am to maintain my sanity and run this home and work, I am going to have to be considered, and I don't want you to have that association, I don't want that woman's hands on you, I don't want her to be around you." I just feel like I'm going to lose my kids to her too. And this is the first time I've ever been this violent on any subject. I'm usually very docile emotionally.

(Woman, late thirties)

If the father marries the other woman, the mother may have to adjust to the children's acceptance of her. But it can feel like one more bitter imposition. So long as that has not yet happened, some mothers insist that their children's fathers not bring the children in contact with the other woman.

In Chapter 6 I discussed some of the ways in which the mother or father may use their relationships with the children as a vehicle for hostility toward each other. Mothers may sabotage the father's visiting by scheduling competitive activities for the children, or deciding that the children are too ill to go out, or encouraging the children to reject the father. And fathers may be vague about when they will fetch the children, or make plans and then break them, or fail to return the children when they said they would, causing the mothers anxiety and disrupting the children's bedtimes. Or fathers may be unreliable with support and, if the mothers are then uncooperative in relation to their visiting, they may claim that the mothers are holding their children for ransom.

Fathers sometimes complain that their wives attempt to alienate the children from them, and mothers sometimes complain that their husbands attempt to seduce the children with candy, movies, and excitement. Fathers resent the smidgens of time that are all they have with the children, and mothers resent having all the chores and drudgery of child care while the fathers become specialists in outings and happenings. And while the fathers may envy the mothers' being with the children when all the little things are happening, the mothers may feel chagrined that the children are flushed with excitement when they return from being with their fathers. As one mother said, "He's a tough act to follow."

The fathers are apt to be even more permissive with the children than they were when they were at home. If one is with one's children for only four hours on the weekend, there's not much attraction in devoting that time to being the heavy-handed father. And it is easy to want to indulge the children, out of guilt and desire to make up to the children for their deprivations, and because of just plain ineptitude as a parent.

**Initially there was a tendency, when I took the children out, they'd see things that they'd like, and I was kind of inclined to buy it for them. But I decided after a while that I didn't want to become a Santa Claus figure.**

**(Man, early thirties, two boys in primary grades)**

Mothers are apt to be irritated by this indulgence. The fathers, they feel, obtain the children's gratitude for permitting them to do what they want, eat what they want, stay up as late as they want; but it is they, the mothers, who must suffer with the children when they are tired and grumpy the next day, or must nurse them if they come down with a cold.

The children themselves, though they may fervently want their parents to reconcile, often contribute to the parents' irritation with one another. They may return from a visitation afternoon or weekend with the father out of sorts or belligerent toward the mother. In this way they are expressing their distress at having again lost their father, and their anger with the mother for her role in the situation. But this does not make it easier for the mother to accept.

Children of separated parents, like children of parents living together, may report that they have the support of one parent in opposing the rules or directives of the other. If the parents are separated, however, there is no chance for them to check with one another regarding the accuracy of the children's reporting. So if a child responds to his mother's admonition to turn off the TV with the assertion that "Dad lets me watch the late show," the mother may simply accept that her husband lets the children do what they want, and may become grimly determined that if he refuses to follow her bedtime rules he cannot take the children overnight. And there may be a new tension in her greeting to her husband when he next comes to pick up the children.

Occasionally children of separated parents threaten that they will leave one parent to go to live with the other. Some mothers become upset by this, or resentful at this new betrayal. But more than one mother confronted by an adolescent with whom she felt helpless to deal has finally said, "Well, perhaps you *should* live with your father. Maybe it would work out better all around." This can happen even among mothers who had earlier pledged to themselves that they would always protect their children from the harm their fathers might visit on them.

Though mothers may later feel guilty for having told the child in so many words that he is not wanted, it may be useful for a child to be able to think of the father's home as a resource, an alternative place to stay should life with mother get too hot or too enclosing. And there may be nothing wrong with an adolescent actually moving from one parental setting to the other. Indeed, having another home to go to may be one of the few valuable by-products for a child in a parental separation, and perhaps parents should encourage its use.

### Ceremonial Occasions and Family Holidays

At least in the early years of separation, before the couple have established a pattern, they may be uncertain regarding how to manage holidays and ceremonial occasions which both would have attended had they remained together.

Public ceremonials present one set of problems. Each parent may want to attend a PTA meeting or a school graduation and the child may want each to be there. But it could be embarrassing for the child to appear to have two separate families. The parents may decide that it is only sensible for them to present themselves as still a family unit. They may thereupon, perhaps despite themselves, slip back into a rather careful version of their marital relationship. Some couples become accustomed to such ventures, at least through their children's school years.

Family holidays and celebrations—Christmas, Thanksgiving, Easter, Passover, the children's birthdays—pose different problems. A temporary reunion of former husband and wife at such an event would not be simply a matter of public presentation. Some former husbands and wives do join together on some family occasions. As I noted in Chapter 4, being alone on family holidays —especially Christmas—can be excruciatingly painful, and it may not be only for the children that the father may temporarily rejoin his former family.

Reactions to temporary family reunions were remarkably varied. Some thought them successful; for others they were distressing. The man or woman, in these latter instances, might afterward be emotionally exhausted and resolved never to do it again. The temporary reunion had made it only too evident how much had been lost.

Those who had moved on from separation to divorce and remarriage seemed to do somewhat better than others. One man, remarried, traveled to the city in which his former wife now lived to celebrate his son's fourth birthday with her and the boy. His former wife was now engaged to remarry. The man met the husband-to-be and then took his former wife and son out for an afternoon of kite flying. He stayed through the evening, slept on a mattress dragged into the front room of his wife's apartment, had breakfast with his wife and son, and then returned home. He thought the visit had gone well. But a man who had taken his former wife, who was still alone, and twelve-year-old daughter to dinner on the daughter's birthday said later that it had required two stiff drinks after he returned to his own home before he recovered from the feelings of guilt and bitterness the dinner had produced.

# 10

# The Meaning of the Separation for the Children

The first week or so my daughter cried herself to sleep about every night. She didn't want to go to school because it would be written all over her face. I made her go to school. I made her face it immediately. And I told her teachers so they were aware of it. And then she got over it, when she knew that everything was going to stay the same basically. I didn't change, and basically she could see her father.

Maybe six weeks after the break, I was taking a bunch of books into the library, and one of them was about what to tell your child about a divorce. My daughter read the title and said, "Don't worry, Mom, I'm over it now."

My son is older, in high school. Now my son is quite different from my daughter. My daughter was able to vent her feelings. My son is very cool. You could see tears in his eyes, but he wouldn't let it out. Even though I said it is good to cry if you feel that way, he didn't. So he was the one I worried about.

I don't think he got over it. We had one heck of a year. For the rest of the year we weren't too happy with each other. Mind you, he's just going into adolescence and all. I took him to see a social worker because I thought he needed some help. Essentially what she said was that he'd seen the way his father had treated me and he was picking that up. And I was reacting to him in terms of his father. And it was a bad scene.

(Woman, about forty, two children, aged fourteen and nine)

### Telling the Children

Parents find all sorts of ways to tell their children that they are separating. Many take pains to reassure the children that they are still loved by both of their parents and that the only reason for the separation is "Mommy and Daddy aren't happy together." They may try to make the separation understandable while protecting one another's relationship to the children.

**I simply say, "It didn't work out. Your father has been a very wonderful father," which I do believe. "As a husband, it didn't work out. As your father, he can come here whenever he wants to be your father, but he can't come here and be with me as a husband." And that seems to make sense to my children.**

**(Woman, two preteen children)**

Some parents are less protective of one another. One man told his three-year-old son that Mommy liked another man better than she liked Daddy and that was why Mommy and Daddy weren't living together. For months afterward the wife was furious at what she believed, probably correctly, to have been an attempt to turn the child against her.

Occasionally, parents appear reluctant to tell even older children very much at all. They may treat the separation as something that concerns only them, the effect of which on the children is almost incidental.

**What he told them when he left was, "Children, I'll now be seeing you on Sunday." That was his total statement. The older said, "Of course we'll see you on Sunday. We see you every day." It was the younger one who said, "Wait a minute. I think what Daddy means is he'll be seeing us only on Sundays." Well, then he admitted it: Yes, that is what he meant. And you know, he didn't discuss it with the children. The children didn't know what questions to ask, and as long as they didn't ask, he wasn't going to answer.[1]**

**(Woman, about thirty)**

For some children the news of parental separation comes as no surprise. They may have overheard quarrels in which the challenge of separation was made, and perhaps accepted. Or they may have witnessed physical battles after which they themselves wondered why their parents did not separate.

---

[1] In the great majority of separations the man leaves and the woman remains with the children. In this chapter, unless I indicate otherwise, I assume this to have been the case.

I talked with my youngest daughter. She had got right in the middle of a very bad scene. I asked her what she thought about our breaking up. She seemed to think that if it is going on like that, obviously it wasn't good for us to be together.

(Woman, three children, youngest eleven)

For other children the news that their parents are separating comes as a shock. They had been protected by their parents from the parents' quarrels and mutual dissatisfactions. If ever they had been asked about the matter, they would have said that their parents' marriage was happy. Now, suddenly, they are told that their home is to be broken up.

The reactions of children to the news of the separation vary, depending not only on their understandings of their parents' marriage, but also on the ages of the children, their temperaments, and the parents' behavior and attitudes. Age in particular makes a difference: very young children may recognize the father's absence, but be unsure what separation means; adolescent children may be bitter that their parents have not practiced the highly moral behavior they preach.

Not only do the parents' behavior and attitudes toward the children influence the children's reactions, but also the children's reactions inevitably affect those of the parents. It can be devastating to a parent to see a child made deeply unhappy or to become suddenly the object of a child's anger, just as it can be reassuring to a parent to see a child emerge from a first period of upset more mature and self-confident than before. Most parents worry about the long-range effects their separation will have on their children. For some, fear of the damage separation might do their children caused them to postpone it; for others separation may have been hastened by the belief that the unhappy marriage was inflicting greater damage.

In the next two sections of this chapter I shall consider, first, children's reactions as seen by the parents, and, second, some preliminary results from an ongoing clinical study of children's reactions. I shall then turn to the issue of what may be the persisting effects on children of parental separation and divorce. Finally, I shall suggest some implications for parents of the findings of research and clinical practice.

### Children's Reactions as Seen by Parents

The immediate response of most children, of whatever age, to the news of parental separation is distress and anxiety. Several parents reported that one or more of their children became tearful. Other parents reported that their children became tense or withdrawn. Most children were clearly upset. This was true even though the home atmosphere might have been uncomfortable for months, and the children present during bitter quarrels.

A minority of children, particularly among adolescents, seemed able to take separation in stride. Some seemed already to have written off the departing parent. In one case the children had grown up witnessing a father's hopeless struggle to sustain his marriage to an alcoholic mother. On being told by the father that there would be a separation, one of the older children asked, "What took you so long?" In other cases children had been so regularly shamed or punished by one of the parents that they had learned to view that parent as hostile to them.

**My second child just up and clicked her heels when I told her. He had really persecuted her since she was a baby. It was a really bad situation. He thought she was homely and inept.**

**(Woman, mid-thirties)**

Most children indicate that they would like the parents to reconcile. Some try to bring their parents together themselves. One little boy wanted his father to invite his mother to join their outings. Other children solace themselves with reconciliation fantasies, both their own and those packaged by the mass media. One boy insisted that his father take him to a movie during their visit together, even though he had already seen it with his mother. In the movie an adolescent girl successfully manipulated her divorced parents into reconciliation. A girl who had witnessed a succession of all-out battles between her parents, although she recognized that they could not continue that way, nevertheless wanted to feel that their break might not be final.

My daughter said, "Mommy, couldn't you do a separation instead of a divorce so that there is a possibility of—you know." A divorce to her was final, whereas with a separation there was at least an element of hope.

(Woman, three children, youngest eleven)

Apart from the desire that the parents reconcile, the concerns children voice tend to be focused on their own situation. They are likely to want to know where they will live, and with whom. They want to know when they can see the departing parent. They may want to know whether they and their siblings will remain together or whether the family will be split up. And they may want to be reassured that they will be cared for if something happens to their custodial parent; that the other parent, even though living apart, remains responsible for them.

Their first concerns answered, children may express a variety of anxieties. Younger children may let it be known that they suspect that they are in some way responsible for the breakup. One little boy said, "Don't go, Daddy. I'll be good." Older children may express uneasiness regarding their future. They may fear that they will have to assume new responsibilities for children still at home, or drop out of school and take a job. They may wonder whether they will still be able to invite friends into their home, and they might worry that the friends will think less of them for no longer having a traditional family.

Ordinarily, the children, although they may object to the parents' decision to separate, accept the parents' decision regarding with whom they will live. Most children want to avoid deciding between the parents; they do not want to alienate either by choosing the other. Occasionally, however, children may be willing to say that they would prefer to live with one of the parents, because they feel greater affinity for that parent or because that parent can provide a situation they prefer: a house instead of an apartment;

the possibility of remaining in their neighborhood, of continuing in their present school or escaping it for another. In a small proportion of cases, older children reject one of their parents; should this occur, it can be a damaging experience for the parent, if not for the child.

For many children the initial anxiety produced by news of the separation seems to subside rather quickly. This may be the more true as the parents appear confident of their capacity to manage the postmarital situation, remain appropriately related to the child, and keep the postmarital situation free of turmoil. Many parents report that their children adapted more quickly to the new arrangements than they did themselves.

I've been very impressed by the fact that my kids are really doing much better than my wife and I in this whole business. It's incredible. I had this idea that they would not be able to handle all this business. They really are doing fine. The worst thing was the middle kid. When I told him we were going to separate he was in tears for a few hours. Then I told him a couple of weeks ago that I was moving out and he was fine, he was smiling.

(Man, about forty)

A woman reported that her daughter, after a period of upset, had quickly regained her balance.

I have probably the most sensitive nine-year-old girl in the world. She was extremely upset. This is a year later now, and she couldn't be outwardly better adjusted or more happy. And it didn't take that long at all. As soon as routine was established, as soon as she accepted it as a fact, and it happens rather quickly when parents are not in the same house . . . she just seemed to adjust so beautifully.

(Woman, mid-thirties)

One woman found that her adolescent children behaved rather coolly almost from the first, as though their parents' separation was of secondary importance in their lives.

As far as the children go, I haven't noticed any reaction, and . . . I ask them once in a while. . . . The children are very self-centered. They have their own friends and their own lives.

(Woman, about forty, children fourteen and sixteen)

But other children are obviously affected. They display any of a wide variety of symptoms, ranging from those of unarguable emotional origin, such as nail biting, nightmares, or hyperactivity, to those about which the parent cannot be sure, such as an increase in minor accidents or the development of a rash.

My daughter started to break out in a little rash. That's the first thing I noticed. The other thing I noticed, she was putting on a very good front, being very brave. For the first week or so she did cry. Now she doesn't wish to talk about it too much.
(Woman, mother of a nine-year-old girl)

My daughter's outside activities are keeping her busy. But I do see her go off into a trance. And she doesn't speak about it. She refers to it as "when that thing happened."
(Woman, mother of a ten-year-old girl)

It was almost like they were clutching in a way that they never did before, because if Mommy fails them, what then? Their father has left them. Financially, I am the main support. He won't even pay the medical bills. My two daughters both have stomach trouble from their nerves.
(Woman, mother of three children aged ten to seventeen)

Some children seem to deal with parental separation by identification with the absent parent. Through such identification they attempt to replace the absent parent with themselves. This too is a symptom of separation's impact, but one whose consequences for the child are less likely to be unfortunate than symptoms, such as tantrums or pathological withdrawal, that are likely to damage the child's relations with others.

My nine-year-old girl is going through a business where she seems to be taking my role in the family. She's acting as the family judge now. She intervenes with the other children, telling them what is fair and so forth. That is what I did. I don't know whether this is something I should try to discourage or whether I should just stay out of it.
(Man, father of a nine-year-old girl and two younger children)

Children may become angry at the parent they believe to be responsible for the separation. One boy, about fifteen, whose parents were disputing his custody, was asked with which parent he would like to live. "If they go ahead with this," he said, "I'm going to be so mad at both of them I won't want to live with either." He said this grimly, and he meant it.

One must feel sympathy for any parent who is the target of a child's anger, but perhaps more if it is the parent who has custody, for that parent must live with it.

My son is very angry with me. And I think at first I felt very guilty because I had precipitated his Daddy going away and felt a certain amount of guilt for that. So I couldn't really deal with his anger in just an honest way. I feel less guilty now and so I feel better able to meet him. I feel better about it, but he is still angry.

(Woman, mid-thirties)

Anger toward the mother is apt to be expressed directly, as belligerence, or indirectly, in negativism, balkiness, or persistent opposition.[2] Anger toward the father may be expressed in similar ways, or it can be expressed by the child's refusal to see the father when he comes to visit, or to accept his invitations.

My boys are angry with my husband because he has left and they feel he's left for a whole new family. He happens to be in Connecticut and he has a whole new group of friends. They have been to visit him. They just feel that he has deserted us and he has all new friends. And they get angry—they are very angry at him. It's too bad because they don't want to go to see him at all. They won't go at Christmas or vacations. I try to encourage them to go, but they won't. And I don't force them. You can't force teenagers to do anything.

(Woman, late thirties, three teenage children)

The anger of children toward a parent can continue indefinitely. Perhaps the children's anger elicits parental irritation which in turn sustains the children's anger; or perhaps anger leads to emotional distance, which then prevents corrective experience. At any rate, some parents have reported that their children remained angry

[2] Goode reported that almost half his sample of mothers said that their children had become "harder to handle" at some point after their separation. See William J. Goode, After Divorce (New York: Free Press, 1956), p. 321.

with them for years. One mother, after several years of trying to cope with a now adolescent daughter's anger, sent her to boarding school. Though after paying the tuition she was nearly destitute, the alternative was a nearly unbearable life.

Most parents, fortunately, do not find their children persistingly angry at them as a result of their separation. Indeed, Goode reports that not quite half his divorced mothers believed their divorce at the worst did not damage their children, and about a third believed that their children were the better for it.[3] For clues regarding which children come through unscathed, we may turn to a study that used clinical interviews to investigate the emotional responses of children to their parents' separation.

## Children's Reactions: A Clinical Study

Judith S. Wallerstein and Joan B. Kelly have been conducting a study in California since 1970 of the reaction of normal children, aged 2½ to 18, to their parents' separation and divorce. They invited parents filing for divorce to bring their children to a counseling service whose aim was to help the children cope with the divorce. Some sixty couples, parents of 131 children, accepted their invitation. The children and parents were seen three or four times by an experienced family therapist during a six-week counseling period and then again a year to eighteen months later. Although the study is still in process, preliminary reports have been published.[4]

They corroborate parents' reports in that they find that al-

---

[3] Goode, *After Divorce*, p. 317.

[4] Judith S. Wallerstein and Joan B. Kelly, "The Effects of Parental Divorce: Experiences of the Preschool Child," *Journal of The American Academy of Child Psychiatry,* in press; Joan B. Kelly and Judith S. Wallerstein, "The Effects of Parental Divorce: I. The Experience of the Child in Early Latency; and II. The Experience of the Child in Late Latency." (Digest) *American Journal of Orthopsychiatry,* 45 (March 1975): 253–255; Judith S. Wallerstein and Joan B. Kelly, "The Effects of Parental Divorce: The Adolescent Experience," in *The Child in His Family: Children at Psychiatric Risk,* ed. E. James Anthony and Cyrille Koupernik (New York: Wiley-Interscience, 1974), vol. 3, pp. 479–505.

though most children, irrespective of age, are upset at first by parental separation, somewhat more than half return, by the end of a year, to normal development. At that time they appear essentially undamaged by the separation. They are likely still to remember its pain, and may regret that their parents decided on it, but they have recovered. Some, indeed, seem to have been benefited by the separation.

The great majority of preadolescent children are intensely upset at the time of the separation. Often they become tearful and profoundly sad. Children too young to report their feelings may show by fearfulness, by a return to toys they had previously outgrown, or by a new possessiveness that they have lost confidence in their surroundings. Children slightly older are able to talk about their sadness and insecurity and may connect them to loss of their fathers. Children still older may try to escape their distress through activity, or may sequester their unhappiness so that they allow themselves to be unhappy at home but are in good spirits at school. Accompanying these reactions may be other forms of upset: regression to earlier modes of functioning, sleep disturbances, somatic symptoms such as cramps or asthma.

Adolescents also find parental separation intensely painful. Many react as younger children do, with sadness and obvious upset. But some seem able to protect themselves temporarily by distancing themselves from the separation. They assume a stance of "That's their problem, not mine." Although later they may be able to admit that they hadn't really felt that way, at the time they seem cool and detached. This distancing seems to enable them to maintain their balance during the difficult period immediately following the separation, after which it may give way to warm and sympathetic concern for both parents.

Anger because of the separation is common at every age. Very young children may become generally irritable or may have temper tantrums. Slightly older children may express their anger in aggressive play and fantasies, which then may be followed by sleep difficulties and nightmares. Children of school age often direct their anger toward the parent they blame for the separation, although younger school age children who blame the mother may be propitiating toward her, despite inner reservations, lest she expel them too. Somewhat older children, because of the need to retain confidence in at least one parent, may cast one parent in the role of hero or heroine and the other in the role of villain. Adolescent children are more nearly capable of wishing a plague on both their houses.

It seems to be especially younger children who blame themselves for their parents' separation. Children four or five may confidently explain the separation as due to their noisiness, or naughtiness, and be unable to accept reassurance that they are mistaken. (They may, perhaps, prefer the guilt of believing they caused the separation to the anxiety that would follow recognition of their powerlessness to control the conditions of their lives.) Older children are less likely to feel responsible for the separation. Adolescents may, perhaps, feel guilty not about having caused their parents to separate, but rather about having aligned themselves with one parent against the other.

Adolescents may have special reasons for anger with their parents. They may be angry because their parents have made their growing up more difficult by disrupting their home. They may also believe that the parental separation is disgracing, and feel shamed by it; some withdraw from friends rather than have to confess to it.

Adolescents and older preadolescents may question their parents' moral worth. They may condemn one or both of their parents for having behaved childishly or for having failed in other ways to meet their own standards for behavior. Adolescents may suddenly note their parents' frailties and undergo what Wallerstein and Kelly call "precipitous deidealization of the parent." Insofar as the adolescent had rested his or her own self-esteem on identification with that parent, the adolescent may not only feel angry for having been disappointed but also feel set adrift, without internal guidance.

Older children and adolescents may be disturbed by their parents' new interest in dating. Adolescent daughters, in particular, may be made anxious by recognition of their father as someone with sexual interests and capacities and may more or less tactfully arrange to see the father less frequently and then preferably in the company of a friend. Some adolescent children appear encouraged by the more open sexuality of their parents to act on their own sexual impulses before they might have otherwise. Others become jealous of a parent's dates or resentful of a parent's dating.

Almost all children want the separation to be undone. Young children may pretend in school or to themselves that their father is still with them or that he secretly rejoins them when they are otherwise alone. Preadolescent children may express longing for their father's return and anguish at his absence. Some launch campaigns to prevent their parents from becoming involved with someone new.

A small proportion of children of every age beyond the very youngest display none of these unhappy early reactions. These tend to be children whose preseparation homes had been beset by turmoil or whose fathers had treated them harshly. Some among them respond to the separation of their parents with relief.

A year after the separation, over half the children studied had returned to normal developmental progress; they were no less lively than they had been before the separation; they were as self-confident as ever; and they were free of any increase in troubling symptoms. Among the youngest children who made adequate recoveries there may have remained a greater than usual need for an adult's attention and caring, but nothing more. Among some older children the parental separation fostered a level of empathy and compassion for the parents unlikely to have appeared under other circumstances.

A fourth of the children had already been having trouble in school, at home, or elsewhere at the time of the parents' separation, and a year later were neither better nor worse. Somewhat under a fourth of the children became progressively more troubled after their parents' separation. They continued to be sad; their self-esteem had decreased; their relations with others were ungratifying and superficial. Their social and emotional lives seemed to have been persistently impaired by the separation.

Different factors appeared to make a difference in outcome for children of different ages. For young children, the quality of parenting seemed of primary importance. Young children seemed to require that their mother—or other caretaker—be both competent and caring; that she not be so overwhelmed by the new demands on her time and energy that she could not attend to their needs; and that she be loving enough to make the child feel secure and worthy. Young children seemed to do badly when their primary caretaker was enmeshed in continuing turmoil, or for other reasons preoccupied with her own life. They also did badly when that caretaker was disparaging of them.

For older children not yet adolescent, the presence of siblings seemed often to help: siblings gave them someone else with whom to work out what was happening, someone else to rely on, and someone else to share the burdens as well as the gratifications of growing up in a single-parent home. Supportive relationships outside the home also were helpful to older children: it was useful for them to be doing well in school or to be popular with their friends.

Most important for adolescents, especially older adolescents, seemed to be the resilience and integrity already established in their developing characters. Those adolescents who were doing well at the time of their parents' separation seemed much better able than others to cope with the separation and more likely than others to return soon to their normal developmental progress.

It seemed important for children of all ages that their fathers continue to play a role in their lives. Although the father whose contact with his children was restricted to visitations was rarely able to compensate for deficiencies in the relationship of the mother and the children, many fathers nevertheless were able to enrich their children's lives and to contribute to their security.

### Life Without Father

What is it like to grow up in a single-parent home? I once talked with a group of ten adolescents all of those parents had separated years before. Their mothers were now participants in a group similar to Seminars for the Separated. In our discussion of life without father, a few themes were especially prominent.

A first theme developed by these adolescents was that their mothers depended on them for support. A number of the children said that they were pleased that their mothers depended on them less now that they had found other women to turn to. One girl said that her mother had previously treated her more like a sister than like a daughter. Another girl said that her mother frequently talked her problems over with her, and then worried that she was burdening her. Actually she didn't feel her mother to be a burden—she liked being helpful. A boy said that his mother was still upset about her separation, that any little thing bothered her, and that he did his best to help her keep her spirits up.

Another theme expressed by these children with the same mixture of pride and complaint was the extent to which their mothers nagged them. One girl, fifteen, almost adult in appearance, said with rueful affection that now that her father was out of the house, "She has nobody else to nag, just me." Not all the children agreed that their mothers nagged them; one girl said that her mother was still in touch with her father and was "always on the phone to him about something, so I don't have her all to myself."

Several of the children saw their fathers fairly often; a few hardly saw their fathers at all. Two children, siblings, had no recollection of the father who had deserted them when they were infants. One boy's father was alcoholic, and embarrassing to the boy and his family. The boy hated him and wished he would stop showing up. The other children who saw their fathers expressed a kind of affectionate disapproval of them. One girl pictured her father as dashing but preoccupied with his own affairs. At another point she developed a lengthy indictment of the freedom of men in our society. Other children, too, seemed simultaneously to admire their fathers and to disapprove of them.

In the comments of the two children who had been deserted by their father, sorrow was more marked than anger. One of the children, a quiet, attractive girl, told this story:

**I have this daydream, that I'm going to get married in a big church wedding. There are lots of people there and I'm coming down the aisle,**

all dressed in white. And then I look over at where my father should be, because I should be holding his arm, and there is nobody there.

## Effects on Children's Personalities

Many studies have compared children growing up in mother-headed households, most of them the product of divorce, with children growing up in two-parent households.[5] Few of these studies found differences between these groups of children. And where differences did exist, they did not always favor the children of two-parent households. In particular, one study found that adolescents whose parents had earlier separated seemed to have arrived at greater security and happiness than had a comparison group of adolescents who said that their parents were still married, but unhappy.[6]

A very specific worry of parents of boys who are growing up in mother-headed households is that in the absence of their fathers the boys may fail to learn male roles. The parents may fear that the boys in their younger years will be passive, unaggressive, and effeminate, and later in their lives may prove inadequate as husbands and fathers. We might ask how realistic these worries are.

Careful study of boys whose parents had separated suggests that it is not necessary that there be a father in the home for the boys to learn the nature of the roles, responsibilities, and behaviors ap-

[5] Two useful summaries of research on the effects of growing up in a mother-headed household are Henry B. Biller, "Father Absence and the Personality Development of the Male Child," *Developmental Psychology* 2 (March, 1970): 191–193; and Elizabeth Herzog and Cecelia E. Sudia, *Boys in Fatherless Families* (Washington, D.C.: Department of Health, Education, and Welfare, 1971).

[6] Judson T. Landis, "The Trauma of Children When Parents Divorce," *Marriage and Family Living* 22 (1960): 7–13. There are methodological flaws in this study which must be kept in mind when interpreting its results. The late adolescents who were its subjects were asked to rate their own happiness, then those whose parents were still married were asked to rate the happiness of their parents' marriages. It would seem plausible that adolescents who rated themselves as unhappy would be more likely to rate their parents' marriages as unhappy, whether their parents' marriages were especially bad or not. Such a tendency could account for the findings.

propriate to men. Children apparently can learn our society's expectations of men quite well without having a man in the home, just as children of immigrant families learn English even though the language in their home is different.[7] Children apparently learn values in the same way that they learn role expectations. There is fairly consistent evidence that boys who grow up without a father are just as likely to want to assume masculine roles as boys who grow up with their father in the home.[8] Indeed, some boys who grow up without their father in the home seem to give special effort to adopting behaviors and outlooks that they define as male.[9]

Still other studies suggest that any older man in the house, and not only the father, can provide a model for boys to emulate. Father-absent boys who grew up with older brothers more closely resembled boys from father-present families in their development of traditional masculine traits than did father-absent boys who grew up without older brothers.[10]

The age of the boys at the time of parental separation has been shown to have some importance at least for their self-concept. Boys whose parents separated when the boys were quite young—not yet five—seemed later to be somewhat less certain regarding their possession of traditional masculine traits than were boys who were older when their parents separated.[11]

It is difficult to judge whether growing up in a fatherless home increases the chance a boy will adopt a homosexual orientation. Un-

[7] Joan Aldous, "Children's Perceptions of Adult Role Assignment: Father-Absence, Class, Race, and Sex Influences," *Journal of Marriage and the Family* 34 (February 1972): 55–65.

[8] A. Barclay and D. R. Cusumano, "Father-Absence, Cross-Sex Identity, and Field Dependent Behavior in Male Adolescents," *Child Development* 38 (1967): 243–250. See also R. G. D'Andre, "Father-Absence and Cross-Sex Identification" (Ph.D. diss., Harvard University, 1962).

[9] Walter Miller, "Lower-Class Culture as a Generating Milieu of Gang Delinquency," *Journal of Social Issues* 14 (1958): 5–19. See also Joan McCord, William McCord, and Emily Thurber, "Some Effects of Paternal Absence on Male Children," *Journal of Abnormal and Social Psychology* 64 (1968): 1424–1432.

[10] Paul Wohlford, John Santrock, Stephen Berger, and David Liberman, "Older Brothers' Influence on Sex-Typed Aggressive and Dependent Behavior in Father-Absent Children," *Developmental Psychology* 4 (1971): 124–134.

[11] Henry B. Biller and Robert M. Bahm, "Father Absence, Perceived Maternal Behavior, and Masculinity of Self-Concept Among Junior High School Boys," *Developmental Psychology* 4 (1971): 178–181.

doubtedly, there are many determinants of homosexuality, some having to do with very early physical developments, such as endocrine balance during gestation and infancy, others having to do with the interpersonal situation of childhood, and still others having to do with the interpersonal situation of early adulthood. There is good evidence, based on careful study of men in psychiatric treatment, that one set of determinants in homosexuality is what the investigators called "a close-binding intimate" tie to the mother, combined with a hostile, distant, or nonexistent tie to the father. It was found that this complex of intensely close relationship with the mother and distance from the father seemed to occur about as often in homes in which both parents were at least nominally present as in mother-only homes. Since there are fewer mother-only homes in the general population, this may suggest that those we have constitute especially fertile ground for development of the complex.[12] But actually we do not know whether parental separation facilitates its development or whether development of so odd a configuration in an intact family is conducive to parental separation. There may be some slight association between a boy's growing up in a mother-only home and his later homosexual orientation, but the mother-only home may not be causal. This, taken together with the fact that unwavering homosexual orientation is unusual, suggests that single parents need not assume that their male children are seriously at risk.

There has been little work on the issue of the effect of growing up in a mother-only household on a girl's sexual development. One intriguing study suggests that adolescent girls whose parents' marriages ended in divorce are unusually desirous of masculine attention and approval.[13] The same desire for masculine attention and approval has been described to me by separated mothers of small boys. Perhaps all children of separation, both girls and boys, feel some need to regain the presence of a father figure.

A number of studies have shown that children whose parents have separated are on the whole more anxious than children from

12 Irving Bieber et al., *Homosexuality* (New York: Basic Books, 1962).

13 E. Mavis Hetherington, "The Effects of Father Absence on Personality Development in Adolescent Daughters," *Developmental Psychology* 7 (November 1972): 313–326.

intact families.[14] However, it does not appear that parental separation inevitably produces insecure children. Much seems to depend on the mother's competence in managing her situation. Children whose mothers seemed to be functioning effectively appeared not unduly anxious.[15]

As has been noted previously, although parental separation tends to be temporarily disturbing to children's security, a stable and well-functioning parent within the home can make it possible for the children to proceed normally with their development. There might be several reasons for this. First, for children to feel secure with just one parent in the home, that parent should appear strong enough to surmount adversity and steady enough to be reliable. Second, a competent and self-confident parent encourages children to be competent and self-confident themselves by demonstrating the worth of this approach to life. Such a parent clearly believes that problems can be mastered, and this may encourage the children to develop the same belief, the same approach, and eventually the same effectiveness. Third, a competent parent probably is better able to reestablish a stable, relatively stress-free environment for the child.

There are some respects in which children who grow up in single-parent homes seem superior to children who grow up in two-parent homes. One of these is verbal development. A number of studies suggest that the greater participation of the children in the management of the single-parent home and their greater closeness to the mother tend to enhance their verbal skill. This effect seems more marked among boys than among girls, perhaps because girls from two-parent homes are as likely as those from single-parent homes to be close to their mothers.[16]

---

[14] Among studies that report this association are the following: Biller, "Father Absence," p. 191; Frank A. Petersen, "Relationships Between Father-Absence and Emotional Disturbance in Male Military Dependents," *Merrill-Palmer Quarterly* 12 (October 1966): 321–331; Hetherington, "The Effects of Father-Absence."

[15] See Petersen, "Relationships Between Father-Absence and Emotional Disturbance"; see also Landis, "The Trauma of Children."

[16] For example, a study of men in two entering classes at Stanford University showed that students whose fathers were away from their homes for at least one of the years of their childhood scored higher than other students in verbal aptitude, and no lower in mathematical aptitude. See Edward A. Nelson and Eleanor

## Are There Persisting Psychological Disabilities?

The evidence now available does not warrant the conclusion that children whose parents divorce are more likely later in their lives to have emotional problems than children whose parents do not divorce.[17] Certainly if there is an association between parental divorce and emotional disturbance, it is not a strong one. Yet we know from observation and from clinical studies that parental separation is severely upsetting to almost all children. How can this apparent inconsistency be explained?

First we might recall that most children regain their developmental stride after parental separation despite their initial upset. Some, indeed, benefit. Among children who do not resume normal developmental progress, some were already having difficulty in school or elsewhere and simply continue to have difficulty after the separation. For these children the separation did not make things worse. We might suspect that such troubled children are more likely to exist in families headed for separation than in other families, but perhaps the difference is not great. These children who are not ultimately harmed constitute three-fourths of the children of separation if we can extrapolate from the Wallerstein and Kelly data. We might suppose that while parental separation will be a critically important incident in their autobiographies, in the long run it will be only one of many determinants of their well-being and is likely to be outweighed by the others taken together.

Some children, however, do appear to sustain persisting injury as a consequence of parental separation. Yet, for many of them, vulnerability to persisting disturbance preceded the separation. Their relationships with adults and peers already carried the potential for unhappy development, or their ways of dealing with

---

E. Maccoby, "The Relationship Between Social Development and Differential Abilities on the Scholastic Aptitude Test," *Child Development* 31 (March, 1967): 234–250. See also the reference to the study by Bernard Mackler and Morsley Giddings that appears in Herzog and Sudia, *Boys in Fatherless Families*, p. 55.

17 Some studies suggest that there may be an association; other studies fail to find one. See the review of relevant research in Herzog and Sudia, *Boys in Fatherless Families*, pp. 55–56.

reverses were already questionable. Although their parents' separation might have precipitated their difficulties, they might well have had some sort of difficulty had their parents stayed together.

This is not to say that parental separation always has benign or neutral effects on the children. No doubt some children who might otherwise have lived nearly symptom-free lives suffer persisting psychological damage as a result of parental separation. But such children seem a distinct minority.

Children who are already vulnerable to persisting disturbance may be a particularly interesting group. More than other children, they are children at risk when a separation occurs. I have on a few occasions acted as a consultant for a psychiatric clinic in relation to children whose difficulties seemed in some way associated with parental separation. Two children, in particular, struck me as exemplifying this sort of vulnerability.[18]

Let us call the first child Eddie. His parents had never been happy with one another. They separated repeatedly until, when Eddie was eight, they separated permanently. Eddie's oldest brother, whom he idealized, was seventeen when the parents separated, and able to go off on his own. The remainder of the family, including Eddie's mother, his next older brother, a younger brother, and Eddie himself, moved to a small apartment in a new neighborhood. Eddie thus lost, all at the same time, his father, his oldest brother, and his friends.

A year later Eddie was already troublesome. He was disruptive in school and rebellious at home. He sometimes was devoted to his mother, at other times angry with her. At one point he stole a ring from a neighbor's apartment and brought it to his mother as a gift. The mother, frightened that this presaged a life of crime, tried to have him seen at a nearby mental health clinic, but nothing worked out. The mother had her hands full with the other children and could not summon the time and energy necessary to obtain for Eddie the attention he needed.

Here two vulnerabilities display themselves. First, Eddie's practice of bringing his distress to the attention of others by breaking their rules was bound to land him in trouble, whether his parents

[18] Here, as elsewhere in the book, I have changed potentially identifying details.

separated or not. Then, in addition, Eddie's mother had too much to deal with, given the resources at her command, to be effectively helpful to him.

Two years after the episode of the stolen ring Eddie was an active member of a group of older boys who were widely known through the neighborhood as delinquent. Eddie found in the gang some of the security he had not been able to find at home. But one day the police called on Eddie's mother to tell her that Eddie and two other boys had broken into a neighbor's house. Eddie's mother was again frightened and now decided that Eddie was beyond her control. She called Eddie's father, who had by this time remarried, to ask him to take Eddie. The father's new wife was understandably hesitant, but agreed to try it for a while.

There was constant friction in Eddie's new home between Eddie and his stepmother. The father rarely entered arguments on Eddie's side; he seemed more concerned about the stability of his new home than about Eddie's needs. Eddie ran away and was picked up in a distant city. At that point the father called the psychiatric clinic for help.

Eddie's troubles, clearly, were responses to his multiple losses: the breakup of his home, his change of neighborhood, his removal from the delinquent gang. Had there been no separation, Eddie might have had a less unhappy childhood. But it was not just parental separation that produced Eddie's troubles; it was also the inability of Eddie's parents, for whatever reason, to offer him the support he needed, and the faultiness of Eddie's own methods for dealing with distress.

The second child, whom we can call Jane, was sixteen when I met her. Her parents at that point had been divorced about five years. After the divorce, Jane and her older brother initially lived with her mother, but two years later her mother agreed that they should live with their father, partly because the older brother would then be attending a college near the father's home.

The father was a lonely man and was pleased to have his children join him. He enjoyed talking with Jane, who rapidly became his closest companion. This was a role she had previously played with her mother. She found the role both restrictive and gratifying: it kept her at home more than she would have liked, but she enjoyed knowing how important she was to her parent.

Jane felt uncomfortable in her new school. Although she seemed to others to be friendly and sensible, she felt that the other girls were more feminine than she, interested in different things, and therefore uninterested in her. She had only one close friend, and when that friendship ended, she felt herself entirely lost at school.

One day Jane found herself in a sudden, unexpected argument with a teacher, over whether she would be permitted into a class she wanted to take. She was in the midst of explaining why she had a right to enter the class when she suddenly stopped, turned on her heel, and walked away. She felt herself to be unreal. She saw the ingratiating, apparently effective self she presented to the world as having no relation to her. She had no idea who she really was.

Jane's vulnerability was her willingness to enter into what might be called "premature maturity," together with her parents' willingness to support that adaptation. The danger in premature maturity is that the child or adolescent relinquishes age-appropriate interests in order to assume more nearly adult responsibilities. The child may eventually feel that despite his or her apparent maturity there remains within an unattended, much younger self. Or the child may discover, as did Jane, that no genuine self has been able to develop.

Had Jane's parents remained together, Jane might never have felt called on to act as a parent's companion. Perhaps then she would have been able to develop a self more expressive of her own strivings and feelings, which would have seemed more genuine to her. But the attraction toward becoming whatever person others wanted her to be, irrespective of her own wishes for herself, might have expressed itself under any conditions.

## Some Advice

Certain general principles can be formulated that may help separating parents help their children. They are general principles only, and specific cases may have features that make their application inadvisable or impossible. In any event they should be treated as tentative. They represent attempts to apply the research results reviewed earlier in this chapter or to draw lessons from clinical experience. But developing principles for behavior from research results is an uncertain art, and extrapolations from clinical experience, while often useful, are insecurely based.[19]

1. *Children, even very young children, should be kept informed, without overwhelming them with information they cannot assimilate.* Wallerstein and Kelly found that even among children too young to understand what divorce meant, those who were told that Daddy was going to live elsewhere were less distraught than those whose fathers disappeared without explanation.[20] Children should be told enough to explain the father's departure. Failing to do so imposes on the children not only the experience of familial disruption but also the burden of working out for themselves why it happened.

White lies and minor evasions are probably inadvisable. Studies of children who are seriously ill or whose families have suffered severe loss invariably find that the children are more aware of threats to their well-being than adults believe them to be.[21] Children beyond the age of four or five can certainly tell the difference between a business trip the father genuinely has to take and a trial separation. Even if they do not overhear conversations from which it can be inferred that the father may be departing for good, the tension in the home and the preoccupation of the parents will tell them that this is no ordinary business trip.

[19] On many issues clinical experience is all the data we have. Even if this is not the case, clinical experience can produce invaluable insight; indeed it may deal with phenomena that elude more systematic study. But though we do well to take clinical experience seriously, we should also treat its findings as tentative. Clinical experience is, for one thing, personal: my clinical experience is different from the next fellow's. And it tends to be pessimistic: it is based on people in trouble, and though they probably are pretty much like other people, they teach us more about what can go wrong than about what can go right. Finally, clinical experience is peculiarly susceptible to "experimenter bias," which is the tendency to find confirmation for one's own theories, whatever the nature of reality.

[20] Judith S. Wallerstein and Joan B. Kelly, "The Effects of Parental Divorce: Experiences of the Preschool Child"; see also J. Louise Despert, *Children of Divorce* (Garden City, N.Y.: Doubleday, 1953), chap. 3, 4, and 5.

[21] Gilbert Kliman, *Psychological Emergencies of Childhood* (New York: Grune & Stratton, 1965).

Parents who are less than honest with their children encourage their children to develop confused or distorted understandings of threats they cannot avoid recognizing. They also encourage their children to believe that the best way to cope with unpleasant realities is to lie about them, since this is what the parents seem to do.

Parents should try not to weaken the children's self-esteem through their explanations. It is obviously threatening to children's self-esteem to tell them that their mother or father didn't love them enough to remain with the marriage. It can be threatening to their self-esteem in another way to tell them that their mother or father is no good—for, after all, they are the issue of that parent. It is helpful to children if explanations do not incidentally invite the children to condemn their other parent. The children may arrive at such condemnation themselves, but they may do better if they can forgo it. In general, explanations of the separation should as far as possible display respect for the worth of all involved: mother, father, and child.

2. *Children are likely to react to the separation with upset and to need appropriate solicitude.* Very young children are apt to become sad at the loss of a loved figure and fearful that they may lose all the figures on whom they depend. Somewhat older children may be sad or angry or bitter because of what appears to them to be a parental action taken without concern for their well-being. Adolescents may be furious at their parents' interference with the course of their lives.

No matter what age the child is, the parent should try to be understanding and appropriately solicitous. With older children or adolescents this may only mean remaining alert to their feelings while permitting them the space they need to regain their balance. With younger children it may mean spending a good deal of time with them, playing with them, or simply being available to them. If the mother must go to work, it may be equally good to have a steady, reliable caretaker who can provide emotional as well as physical accessibility.

3. *Children who fail to resume normal development within a year of the separation may need special attention.* If a child's sad-

ness, anger, bitterness, or other early reaction to the separation has not faded by the end of the first year after the separation, and if the child is not again functioning in age-appropriate ways within the home, in school, and with friends, something may be going wrong. At this point the parents, together with the child, might try to assess the situation. If there are potentially useful modifications in the parents' relationships with the child that are also practical—the father's taking the child to live with him, for example —they might be considered. If not, a consultation with a professional child therapist should be sought.

4. *A competent and self-confident parent as head of the household is the child's most important source of security.* Children whose mothers maintain an adequate level of functioning seem less likely than other children to be persistently upset by parental separation. Presumably they learn that their mothers are people on whom they can rely, and, in addition, they learn from their mothers how to deal effectively with problems.

Fathers who do not have custody should recognize that they contribute to their children's well-being by being supportive of the children's mother, no matter how much this may go against the grain. The less the mother is burdened by interparental warfare, the more energy she will be able to give to keeping her home stable and happy.

Mothers might recognize that it benefits the children if they use whatever help is available to them. One parent is too few to run a household; indeed, two parents may find the demand on their energies excessive. The single parent should try to use whatever resources are available that may help her function effectively: baby-sitting exchanges with friends or neighbors, paid help or the contributions of older children or kin in the home, all the help the other spouse is able to furnish.

5. *Preadolescent children need a parent's full attention at least part of the time.* It is easy for the newly separated mother to become preoccupied with the tasks of reorganizing her life. In addition to the normal chores of housekeeping and parenting, she may have to find work, establish a new relationship with her husband, build new friendships, and begin a dating life. Yet it is essential

for her children's well-being that she set aside time, preferably every day, during which she can give the children her full attention. Otherwise the children may feel that they have in large measure lost their mother as well as their father.

It should go without saying that children should never be blamed for the separation or told that they are intrinsically bad or that they have the seeds of badness within them. A parent who finds that he or she is unmanageably hostile, punitive, condemning, disparaging, or contemptuous toward his or her children should by all means obtain the help of a family therapist.

6. *Ordinarily, children gain if the noncustody parent remains in the picture.* We do not have information based on systematic research regarding the consequences for children of having greater or lesser access to the noncustody parent. Clinical experience, however, suggests strongly that the father can continue to play a valuable role in his children's lives even though he is no longer a member of their household. He is likely to continue to be a respected and often loved figure. He can function as a guarantor of the children's security should anything happen to their mother. His becoming inaccessible to the children would be a further loss for them, extending the loss they suffered on his departure from their home. All this would hold equally true for the mother, if she should be the noncustody parent.

If the mother remarries, the relationship of the father and the children might have to be reconsidered. The children might want continued contact with their father, but attention would have to be given to coordinating that relationship with their obligations to the new household.

We do not know enough at this point to say that one custody arrangement or system for visitation is superior to another. But it does appear that a consistent pattern, on which the children can rely, is desirable. It may also be desirable if the children are able to telephone or to see the noncustodial parent between scheduled visits; yet they should be encouraged in this only if it does not impose additional stress on the custodial parent.

7. *It is important for the children to retain as many regions of safety in their lives as possible.* Children lose a guarantor of their

safety when their father leaves their home. They should be permitted to retain as many other supports for feelings of safety as is possible, and for a time be protected, if this is possible, from anxiety-arousing situations. This means keeping the children within the same house and the same school, and encouraging them to see the same friends. Changes that would require them to establish a place for themselves within a new group of peers might be avoided: this may mean, for example, resisting a teacher's suggestion that a child be held back in school, and perhaps declining a teacher's offer to skip the child ahead.

A mother might consider returning to her parents' home if this would provide the children with additional guarantors of their security, but she should also weigh the problems the children might have in forming new friendships and establishing themselves in a new school. In addition she might consider the possibility that she would stay with her parents only briefly, after which she would undertake a second move, with additional disruption for the children.

8. *Insofar as there is change, children are likely to profit from parental support in establishing a satisfactory living situation for themselves.* Parents should try to associate themselves, at least in spirit, with their children's efforts to come to terms with their new situation. They should try to help their children feel comfortable with the new household arrangements and the children's new relationship with the noncustodial parent. They should encourage their children to continue their friendships, and stand ready to help as they can. If the children have moved away from their former neighborhood, the parents might try to help their children establish new friendships and might talk with their children about the problems the children may be having in the new school. Even if there is little they can actually do, they can let their children know that the children have their backing.

9. *Children should be permitted to mature at their own pace and neither be encouraged to become prematurely mature nor held back in their development through overprotection.* Appropriate responsibility is unlikely to hurt children and can, indeed, be the making of them. But it seems ultimately disadvantageous

to children for them to become responsible for the emotional well-being of one or both of their parents. Becoming a parent's companion, confidant, or advisor can divert them from the interests and social activities that are more appropriate for their age, to the ultimate detriment of their emotional development.

Some parents go to the other extreme. They try to protect their children from every sort of anxiety, frustration, or risk. Yet such safeguarding can be as dangerous to children's development as can the continuous solicitation of their advice and support. It may foster anxiety and self-doubt by suggesting that the children's personal resources are inadequate to the challenges they may encounter. And the devotion of the overprotecting parent can easily lead children to an exaggerated view of their social worth.

10. *Parents can help their children by establishing satisfactory life situations for themselves.* The self-sacrificing parent, rather like the overprotective parent, must force her children to feel extraordinarily deserving or extraordinarily guilty, or both. In addition parental self-sacrifice is likely to have still other unfortunate side effects.

The children easily come to mean too much for the self-sacrificing parent, both positively and negatively. It is natural for parents whose lives are otherwise empty to attempt to fill them by forming inappropriate relationships with their children. But this can be burdensome for the children and ultimately is likely to be unsatisfactory for the parent. In addition, if the parent devotes all her relational energies to the children, she becomes liable to failures of morale because her life is insufficiently gratifying. But a parent who is depressed can be intensely anxiety-arousing for children who have become almost entirely dependent on her. And eventually she may blame the children for her unhappiness.

I am not advising parents to neglect their children. Rather I am advising them to consider their own well-being as well as the well-being of their children when planning for their family.

OTHER READING

The following book and articles are directed primarily to professionals: Gilbert Kliman, *Psychological Emergencies of Childhood* (New York: Grune & Stratton, 1965); E. James Anthony, "Children at Risk from Divorce: A Review," in *The Child in his Family: Children at Psychiatric Risk*, ed. E. James Anthony and Cyrille Koupernik (New York: Wiley-Interscience, 1974), pp. 461–478; Judith S. Wallerstein and Joan B. Kelly, "The Effects of Parental Divorce: The Adolescent Experience," ibid., pp. 479–506.

The following books seem to me useful for both professionals and parents: J. Louise Despert, *Children of Divorce* (Garden City, N.Y.: Doubleday, 1953); Earl A. Grollman, ed. *Explaining Divorce to Children* (Boston: Beacon Press, 1969).

For parents, a book that reviews with great sensitivity a single-parent father's experiences is Joseph Epstein, *Divorce in America* (New York: Dutton, 1974). A useful book of advice for parents of toddlers is T. Berry Brazelton, *Toddlers and Parents* (New York: Delacorte, 1974), especially Chapter 4, "Parent Alone," pp. 71–98.

For help with the problem of what to tell the children and how to tell the children, parents might consult: Richard A. Gardner, *The Boys' and Girls' Book About Divorce* (New York: Science House, 1970); and Bennett Olshaker, *What Shall We Tell the Kids?* (New York: Arbor House: 1971).

# 11

# Starting Over

When I meet a girl and tell her I'm divorced, I've got four kids, and I'm a thousand dollars in hock—can you imagine what happens? . . . Well, I'm at that point right now where I take one day at a time. And that is a hard switch for a guy like me to make who planned his life not just six months ahead but a year ahead.                                             (Man, late thirties)

I have a new job, managing a real estate office. I can come in late and leave early, so I can keep an eye on my boys at home. And I'm working with two guys who are just great and just to be in the office with these guys who accept me for what I am, I get a kind of support and appreciation. And I get paid. And I moved. And I'm in a church group that is not too churchy, and that has helped me. And I've met a nice guy in the group, and maybe something will develop. But I'm not rushing things. I'm better this week than I was last.                      (Woman, late thirties)

I gave myself one year to pull myself together, to feel that I was on the upswing and starting, creating, and thinking again. And I think I scared myself, because it was almost one year to the day that I started to see this change in my personality, that I was moving in a very positive direction. I think what was most important was my friends and my ability to talk. And I think getting a job. And I think one of the things that was always helpful was when there was some man that I was going out with at the time. And my many friends were most helpful.                      (Woman, mid-forties)

## A Damage Report

Suppose someone separated about a month were to take stock. His or her inventory might begin with a thoroughly disrupted emotional situation, dominated by separation distress, loneliness, and depression, perhaps interrupted by brief intervals of self-confidence and even euphoria. It might go on to note a newly unsettled sense of self that severely diminished his or her capacity to make satisfactory decisions and, combined with restlessness, led to reduced effectiveness at work. It would undoubtedly note disrupted relationships with others, including an intensely ambivalent relationship with his or her former spouse, uncomfortable relationships with kin, and a number of friendships that seemed to be fading away, along with others that appeared still reliable. Relationships with children, though they might have continued, would probably have changed. And finally, the individual's financial state and his or her position in the community would probably have suffered serious reverse.

So much would appear to be in disarray that rebuilding might seem a nearly hopeless task. Yet gradually, almost of necessity, the individual's life will move toward reorganization. Friends are told of the separation, and new relationships begin to develop with them. Kin may at first react negatively to the separation, but then they adapt to it. A new home and a new routine are established. Legal steps are taken to legitimate the new marital arrangement. Even though the individual lives only one day at a time, his or her life becomes coherent again.

Like recovery from any major upset, recovery from separation does not proceed smoothly. A day in which life seems under control may be followed by one in which it clearly is not. Some problems, such as finding a new place to live, may be managed with dispatch; others, such as reestablishing an adequate social life, may not be solved for many months. Some emotional issues may never be fully resolved: After years without conscious desire for the spouse's return, the news that he or she is remarrying may produce new pangs of separation distress.

Actual achievement of recovery might be signaled by two developments. The first is that the individual reestablishes a coherent and stable identity. It may be a new identity, integrating aims and self-definitions different from those of the preseparation identity, but, nevertheless, the individual is once again someone who possesses commitments, goals, and values that remain consistent over time and are sensible in terms of his or her hoped-for future. The second development, occurring concurrently with the first, is the reestablishment of a stable life pattern: a way of organizing relationships with others that may be less than entirely satisfactory but is adequate enough to be self-sustaining.

How long does it take to achieve recovery? My impression, corroborated by the observations of others, is from two to four years, with the average being closer to four than to two. Overwhelming upset may disappear before the first anniversary of the separation, but achievement of a firmly established new identity and new way of life appear to take much longer. Full recovery from separation requires more time than most people think.[1]

There appear to be two fairly distinct phases in movement toward recovery. One is a period of *transition* in which the preexistent pattern of life has been disrupted and a new pattern not yet integrated. The first few months of this period of transition are for many a time of disorganization, depression, unmanageable restlessness, and chaotic searching for escape from distress. In later months individuals are more likely to display a determined attempt to regain their footing, to begin functioning again, and to return order to their lives.

This period of transition seems usually to end within the first year after separation, often by eight to ten months afterward. The second phase, which then begins, is a period of *recovering*, in which the individual has established a coherent pattern of life but has not yet integrated it firmly enough so that it can withstand new stress. During this second phase the individual may usually appear to function as well as or even better than before, but a serious reverse may shatter his or her integration. This phase ordinarily ends from two to four years after the separation with the establishment of a stable and resilient new identity and pattern of life.

[1] During my work with Parents Without Partners I spoke with leaders of the organization about the time required for members to recover from separation. They agreed with my estimate of two to four years before members were fully themselves again.

*Shock*

A distinct minority of separated individuals seem to experience a few days of *shock* and *denial* immediately following the separation. During this period they retain their preseparation routine and pattern of life as though nothing had happened. They do not feel separation distress because they have fended off recognition that the separation has occurred. This response to separation seems most likely among individuals whose separation took them by surprise. Some to whom this happened described themselves afterward as having felt numb; others indicated that they had felt lightheaded, perhaps a bit giddy. The separation appeared unreal, as though they were watching a movie in which they happened to have a role.

*Transition*

Most among the separated enter directly into the phase of transition. This phase is initiated by the disruption both of marital identity and of the relationships that had been dependent on it.

In the transition phase the separated are likely to experience severe emotional upset. They may be oppressed by obsessive review of marital events. Their moods may alternate between despair and elation. They may be unable to hold to a decision. Determination to return to the marriage may be followed by resolution to divorce, which may then be followed by inability to decide anything at all. They may find it almost impossible to get a grip on things. Watching themselves, they may be dismayed by their own behavior.

The following is a description of the first months of transition by a man who had a rather bad time of it:

I had quite a bit of guilt over the whole thing happening, and as a result of that I was really bogged down with it. I was really mentally confused. And I have a department that I try to run, and people are dependent on me for support, so I couldn't stop living. But I can remember the first four months of separation were just horrendous. It was what I call a vacuum period. It was four months of bouncing off the walls. I couldn't eat. I couldn't sleep. I could not work. I'd call somebody I had to go over some papers with and he'd say, "Hi, how are you?" And that would just catch me and I would say, "You don't really want to know, do you?" Fortunately a lot had sympathetic ears, but that's got to be the worst thing in the world to burden people with.

My work just went tashoom. I just was not working. My boss called me in and fortunately he had been through this thing too, so he had a real understanding, and that was very helpful. He just sat down and man to man said, "Look, this is where it's at, and the rest is up to you." And a friend of mine said, "Hey, get hold of yourself. Get some help." I saw a doctor who prescribed some antidepressants or something. I started to eat again, started sleeping. And then once I started eating and sleeping I started to rebuild. The first thing was my job. And then all the other things just fell into place.

(Man, late thirties)

During transition some individuals experience not this "bouncing off the walls" but rather the excitement of new freedom and new possibilities for themselves. But they are likely to be without stable goals or commitments that can direct their activities and, in consequence, may exhibit uncoordinated, almost frenetic, behavior.

The following description of his plans was made by a man who had been separated about three months. Very few of the plans were actually carried out.

My plan right now is to enroll in graduate school, which will be a big switch. And I think I've got to learn to play tennis, because I need the exercise bad. And I have bought a ten-speed bike, and I am going to start doing the bicycle trails. And I really want to get back into sailing. I used to play golf, too, and I want to get back. . . . I plan to do a lot of things that I haven't done in fifteen years.

I plan to go to Europe. I *had* hoped to take my wife. I really planned that for our anniversary next year. It would have been a nice time to do it. I also felt that I would like to take my oldest son. So I am planning a trip for next year, and I could take my oldest son with me.

(Man, late thirties)

Gradually decisions are made that prove both realizable and gratifying. Further decisions are then made in such a way that they will integrate with earlier ones. A coherent, stable, and reasonably gratifying way of life begins to emerge, and with it renewed confidence in the self. The completion of this process marks the end of the phase of transition and the beginning of the phase of recovering.

The following is one woman's description of the transition experience. It is worth noting what helped her—a friends's support, a method for keeping busy, a brief respite, and a return to social engagement.

He told me he was leaving, he wasn't coming back. He was tired of the whole middle-class existence and he wanted an entirely different kind of life. Well after that things were very, very bad. It was just like being kicked in the teeth, you know. It was just all really a nightmare. You know, people would say, "You never smile." I sort of withdrew from everyone, because I thought that if things straightened out, I didn't want to have all that gossip bandied about. It wasn't until about five or six months after he left that I could tell people at work that I was separated. I just couldn't talk about it. I didn't even tell my family. My family heard it as a piece of gossip.

I wasn't comfortable anywhere. I'd leave the house to go out because I couldn't stand being there, but I couldn't stand being anywhere. I really had no place. I think this went on for a long time, although I think in retrospect it was shorter than my memory of it makes it seem. At some point a friend of mine came to stay overnight because we had been invited to a party, and in preparation for her coming I started to clean the house and put things back in order. I had to have a clean bed for her! But it was a matter of about three months of living in squalor and not caring about anything.

One of the things that helped me was to go back to playing the piano. I had played piano in the past, and now I went back to it. I had to learn to read music all over again and learn to use my hands. I would practice for hours, completely oblivious to the passage of time, and before I knew it, it would be time to try to fall asleep. I had trouble sleeping, and I had medication that I took for a while. Now when I play the same piece that I played when I started practicing, the whole miserable thing overwhelms me, how it was.

Another thing that helped me was my sister was offered a job in the West and we spent about four weeks out there, traveling around, and I helped her settle in. Then I began working. Working was very helpful because it made it necessary to get up and go. Having to support myself was part of what was helpful, because these were external pressures which made me get up in the morning and get dressed and leave and function at least for some hours as a reasonably rational person. But for a very long time I would come home from work, get home at five-thirty or a little earlier, and I'd just sleep. I slept my life away. I would come home then and fall asleep fully clothed, exhausted from the strain of having to appear normal, having to deal with people in a rational way, and wake up at midnight, have something to eat, and go back to sleep, then wake up in the morning and go to work.

Things are much better now. Just recently I got an interesting and responsible job. I get up fairly early in the morning, get the house in order, water the plants, and go off for the day. I don't collapse the way I used to.

(Woman, mid-fifties, separated nine months)

The transition phase should be over by about the end of the first year of separation. If it is not, one might wonder whether recovery has for some reason been impeded, and some special effort to initiate recovery—perhaps psychotherapy—might be considered.

### The Phase of Recovering

With the end of the phase of transition, the individual is less vulnerable to depression, mood swings, and other instabilities. He or she may now appear to others to be as well organized and assured as anyone else. However, the appearance is deceptive: There remains self-doubt, the dispersal of which requires energy, and the individual's integration remains fragile. Reverse or adamant opposition may lead to its abrupt collapse; the individual who ordinarily might seem assured and poised may under stress retreat into sullen depression or explode into irrational and destructive anger.

As time goes on, the integration of separated individuals becomes more resilient. By three or four years after their separation, although they may have become different people from the people they were when married, they should again feel comfortable with themselves and be as stable as their nature permits. This is not to say that at this point they will have achieved happiness, but rather that their troubles will no longer be traceable to the separation and its aftermath.

### A Review of Some Strategies for Reorganization

There are alternative ways in which postmarital life can be arranged. As previously mentioned, both women and men can return to their parents' home, perhaps only briefly until they regain their bearings, perhaps for a longer stay. Or they may remain within their own home and attempt in any of a number of ways to reconstruct their lives. They may establish a close and supportive relationship with another person of the same sex, which will become their central adult relationship. Or they may seek to establish a cross-sex relationship that may provide the attachment and sexual gratification lost with the end of their marriage. Or they may seek to establish a life of essential independence of other adults in which, although they may be friendly with many others, no loss of another adult will again disrupt their emotional equilibrium.

Returning to live with parents may provide a breathing space during which the separated individual need not be entirely self-reliant. For the husband or wife with custody, the parents can provide help with the children, although, as I have noted, there is serious risk of a conflict of authority in relation to the children. There also may be constraints on personal freedom, particularly for women.

Some women and men who attended our Seminars for the Separated or whom we met in the course of our research moved to an apartment near their parents' home or to a flat in a house in which the parents also had a flat. By this means, they seemed to gain some of the advantages of having their parents accessible while avoiding the constraints of coresidence. In a couple of cases, however, a woman who had taken a flat in a house her parents owned and in which they also lived felt that she was a bit too close.

Organizing postmarital life around a relationship with an intimate friend seems to provide someone with whom the separated individual can talk, with whom he or she can go places, who understands, and is committed to him or her. The separated individual is still free to become involved in an intense cross-sex relationship. Should an intense cross-sex relationship actually develop, the intimate friendship may be permitted to fade, although the other friend may then feel grief and resentment.

Often there seems to be a certain indiscriminateness about who is chosen to be an intimate friend. It may be a neighbor who happens to be in the same boat, or an acquaintance of long standing who had preceded the individual into separation but to whom the separated person had not previously been especially close. There may be recognition that the friendship, though important, is a product of shared extremity, like the relationship of combat buddies.

Many among the separated seek to replace their lost spouse with a new cross-sex attachment. There are ways in which their lives will remain disrupted even if they succeed. The new boyfriend or girlfriend can hardly solve the problems that will have arisen in their relationships with children, friends, kin, or former spouse. In other ways, however, a relationship with a new attachment figure can be of very great value: separation distress may diminish, self-esteem increase, and loneliness disappear for stretches of time.

Forming a relationship with a new attachment figure has so many attractions that most among the separated will give it at least passing thought. Some, however, feel themselves to have been so burned by their last experience that they are unwilling to enter a new relationship very quickly: They do not want to test their capacity to surmount still another experience of loss. And indeed, those who move from marriage into something new and then lose the something new are apt to feel doubly bereft. They may also lose confidence in their capacity for sensible action.

Other concerns may also make separated individuals cautious about new involvements. Some remain so absorbed in their marriage and in dealing with the aftermath of its collapse that they have no energy for beginning again. Some are so guilty about what went wrong that they feel they have no right to gratification. Some are convinced of their undesirability and hesitate to impose themselves on a new person. And some simply want time without commitment, without anyone expecting anything of them, in order to find themselves; they may be willing to tolerate loneliness in order to have that freedom.

Sometimes the separated seek to gain the benefits of attachment without incurring its obligations. They may move from person to person, permitting no emotional investment to deepen. Or they may involve themselves with someone who is inappropriate for the long term—someone much younger or much older or of a different social class or a different race. In one instance a forty-year-old woman became involved with a twenty-four-year-old man. She felt a certain safety in a socially inappropriate boyfriend: It was evident that the relationship could not continue, and she felt that when it ended less would have been lost.

Some among the separated engage themselves on several fronts. They become socially active, involved with work, and do what they can to find someone new. This energetic moving out in many directions often seems the strategy most likely to achieve a satisfactory new life, though one might be concerned about the coherence of the individual's various explorations.

Others, in contrast, are determined to go it alone. They may decide that they will care for their children and no one else. Never again will they entrust their well-being to the vagaries of others' behavior. Yet this strategy of independence poses high risks of both personal distress and a reduced level of functioning. It makes likely repeated experiences of emotional and social isolation with accompanying loneliness. And unless the individual has extraordinary internal resources and unusual ability to make contact with others quickly should favors or information be needed, it also risks having the individual's life go badly. Autonomy has many attractions, especially after the reverses of separation, but often it is a disguise for withdrawal, and withdrawal is an unsatisfactory approach to reorganizing one's life.

## Perplexities

Irrespective of the strategy of reorganization adopted by an individual, certain issues are likely to prove perplexing. These include how the individual might go about reestablishing a community, how he or she might manage a search for someone new, and whether he or she should consider obtaining professional help. In addition, women who have not previously been employed may wonder whether employment is now desirable.

### Reestablishing Community

Many among the separated feel themselves to have become marginal to their previous network of friends. They no longer have the same interests and concerns. Yet assured membership in a valued network is necessary for a satisfactory life; it is this that fends off social isolation, with all its deficits and discomforts. Where might a newly separated individual find others who might be compatible as friends?

Small towns and family neighborhoods may include only a few similarly situated individuals; and if those few have discrepant routines or tastes, the separated individual may feel out of luck. Yet even in such unlikely localities, a few prospective friends may be encountered at a community meeting, a church group, or a meeting of a Parent-Teacher Association. Cities provide many more settings in which it is possible to meet individuals in similar situations. And within cities a separated individual often has acquaintances who are themselves single, who were perhaps seen infrequently during the individual's married life, but with whom the possibility of a closer friendship might now be explored.

Groups have both deficits and assets. Some separated individuals have constructed friendship networks based on activity-centered groups, such as the Appalachian Mountain Club. Less satisfactory seem to be groups in which the activity focus is weak. Many people report having been alienated, rather than engaged, by groups whose members had come together largely to meet each other.

Nevertheless, there is much to be said for investigation of what might be called, for want of a better term, *supplementary communities.* A supplementary community is one that has continuity despite turnover within its membership, the aim of which is to provide its members of the moment with social linkages in addition to those they may already have in their lives. Parents Without Partners functions as a supplementary community, as do the singles' groups organized by churches and community centers.

The friendship networks within supplementary communities ordinarily are easily entered by a new member. Those already in these networks are themselves in the new member's situation, or were there only recently. And there is likely to be within the larger grouping an ideology of friendliness to newcomers.

There may be other advantages as well in entering supplementary communities. The separateness of the supplementary community can allow it to function as a refuge from daily frustrations. In addition, the consciousness of members of their shared concerns may make them unusually alert to the problems of newcomers. Because the community has specialized in particular concerns, it is likely to have amassed a store of experience and to be equipped to provide at least understanding, and perhaps useful advice as well. It may go farther and offer services tailored to potential members' needs; for example, some chapters of Parents Without Partners schedule children's activities for Sunday afternoons so that men who have their children at that time have somewhere to take them.

But there are drawbacks to supplementary communities. One does not choose the other members, and some may be people with whom one would rather not be associated. And the very self-consciousness of supplementary communities can produce discomfort. Entering into the community can be like an admission that one's own resources are insufficient, and this may be recognized both inside and outside the community. Many members of Parents Without Partners feel diffident or defensive about belonging to the organization.

There is ordinarily little risk in exploring the value of supplementary communities. Relationships formed within them tend to remain apart from other relationships, so if things should go badly in the supplementary community—if, for example, the individual should find other members unpleasant, or the community conflict-ridden—the supplementary community can be jettisoned without the remainder of the individual's life being affected. And there is no reason why people cannot gradually develop a satisfactory life separate from their involvement in the community while continuing to participate in its activities. Indeed, this would seem a reasonable aim for those who do enter into supplementary communities.

## Employment

It may be worth considering employment next, since often among its contributions is access to a community of fellow employees.

Almost all men and many women among the maritally separating will already be employed at the time of their separation. They may find the support employment is able to provide to their sense of worth most valuable. For those women who were not employed previous to separation, entrance into employment might be worth considering.

Paid employment may be especially helpful to women who previously had thought of their occupation as "housewife." Such women are left partially unemployed by separation; they may continue to be mothers and housekeepers, but they have quit or been fired as wives. Paid employment can provide an alternative set of self-definitions to which marital status will be irrelevant. In addition, it can provide a community of others less concerned with the woman's personal life than might be kin and friends. Within this community new friendships can sometimes be made that will extend into nonwork life. Just having this community at work provides an alternative to remaining at home; it makes it possible —indeed, necessary—to get out:

If a woman is out in the working world there is no doubt in my mind that it's a reward of its own. I think a woman going through what I'm going through now, sitting at home with say smaller children, or being hemmed in every day without meeting anybody—

forget it! I mean at least you got to get up, you got to get dressed, you got to consider your appearance, and when you get out you're going to meet people. And by the time you get home, you're kind of tired so that if the night is to be spent alone, it isn't all that traumatic.

(Woman, about forty)

There are still other attractions in work. It can distract one from obsessive review of one's situation. And it can bring in some money, no small matter in the reduced circumstances that follow most separations.

So useful can employment be that one might suggest that even mothers with custody of small children try to arrange part-time work when the children are old enough for nursery school. Indeed, there is no evidence that mothers harm their children by working full time, so long as the children are cared for during the day by an adequate and consistent mother-substitute.[2] The mothers themselves, however, may suffer from task overload. One mother of four small children reluctantly gave up the attempt to hold a full-time job because the demands on her became more than she could manage.

I found it rewarding but also very trying. I was attempting to keep up some sort of social life, to bring up four children, plus being exhausted from all the emotional upheaval. It was really kind of conflicting, you know. I felt like I was being stretched on the rack. How many areas was I capable of doing a good job in, you know? So I feel as if now I'd like to stay home for a while, to put the pieces together.

(Woman, late thirties)

On the other hand, some women seem able to juggle the demands of job, home, and children, with perhaps a bit of aid from neighbors and a sympathetic employer. Another mother of four children, including one not yet of school age, preferred full-time work to the alternative of a housebound existence dependent on the welfare department and the generosity of her kin. She sent her

2 See Mary C. Howell, "Effects of Maternal Employment on the Child," *Pediatrics* 52 (August 1973): 252–263 and (September 1973): 327–343.

youngest child to a day-care center and arranged with a neighbor for the after-school care of the older children. Her employer permitted her to come in late in the mornings so that she could get the older children off to school. She felt that she was a better mother for having something else to do.

### Looking for Someone New

A new partner can be more effective than any pharmaceutical preparation for relief of self-doubt and loneliness. Yet the point at which an individual who has separated becomes available for a new sexual relationship varies greatly. As I have noted, some still-married men and women more or less discreetly indicate their availability in anticipation of a separation that has not yet occurred. Still other men and women withhold themselves from dating for months after their separation because they do not want to risk further rejection, because they believe dating to be beneath their dignity, or because they simply don't know how to begin. A minority at first avoid dating because, to their own great surprise, loyalty to their spouse will not permit them to become interested in anyone new. But in time, if there is no reconciliation, loneliness is likely to force even the most reluctant at least to consider the possibility.

The more cautious approach to finding someone new is for individuals to restrict attention to members of social networks to which they themselves belong, or to people vouched for by kin or friends. The farther individuals move from this strategy, the more they risk repetitive disappointment.

Men and women who are in one another's social milieu are apt to have noticed one another long before a date became a possibility, or to have heard about one another from mutual friends. At the very least they can ask what are others' impressions; social networks maintain informal dossiers on their members to which other members have access merely by asking, "What is he (or she) like?" Each, therefore, will have had opportunity for some preliminary judgment of compatibility which can help in deciding how seriously to take the other. In addition, both are subject to the sanctions of social opinion: Each is aware that the other can

report unacceptable behavior back to their shared friends. Therefore shared membership in a social milieu makes it more likely that
each will act responsibly toward the other. They can, in consequence, more easily trust one another and permit themselves to
become seriously engaged with one another.

There are other advantages in dating within one's social milieu
if one's aim is development of a lasting attachment. A relationship
formed with someone already within one's milieu is more easily
integrated into one's life. The friends of the other person are
already one's own friends, or friends of one's friends. There is also
some assurance of similarity of background, interests, and values.

Under pressure from loneliness, respectable and conservative-
appearing people have explored much more enterprising strategies
for finding someone new, including sending their names to date-
matching services or answering ads in underground newspapers.
The meetings described to me as having resulted from such ventures, while they did not end in disaster, seemed to have been filled
with such wariness that it was counted a triumph simply to have
survived them.

I have been told that one often meets "nice people" in dating bars
and singles clubs. And they do seem to facilitate a certain amount
of sexual adventure. But mutual wariness seems the rule here, too,
just as in dates found through the classified. The man and woman
may doubt not only one another's intentions but even one another's
recital of demographic data. The woman may wonder whether
the man is single or separated, as he claims to be, or rather married
and on a night out; and whether his occupation is the impressive
one he reports. And the man may be skeptical of the woman's
account of her age and personal history.

Women are apt to feel uncomfortable in settings in which their
availability may be assumed. It would seem not only social custom
that makes women loath to appear the initiator in dating but also
their sense that to present themselves as available leaves them vulnerable to disrespect and perhaps misuse.

**I think a woman would go to a lounge with apprehension. She
would have a predetermined notion of what this male who meets**

her is going to think. She would feel, "He thinks I'm a pickup," you know. It would be like you were out hunting, that you are frantic.

(Woman, mid-thirties)

Commercial settings that propose themselves as places to meet the other sex tend to be experienced as threatening by both men and women.

I went into one of these places last week. I guess they call it a dating bar. All I could picture in my mind was a bunch of vultures sitting around on the limb of a tree. Both male and female.

(Man, late thirties)

I went into a dating bar the other night with a friend, and it was one of the most terrifying experiences I've ever had. I came with a date even, and what was terrifying was just listening to conversations like, "My name is Philip, do you feel like talking?"

(Woman, mid-twenties)

Singles' parties may be no better. Much depends on whether those who attend the party can become interested in one another for reasons other than their common search.

I went to a party where there were about forty people, all of them newly separated. It was the most depressing thing I've ever been to in my life. There is this group, a lot of them are newly separated. So this guy decided to have a bash at his pad. Beautiful pad. I lasted an hour and a half and got out of there quick, I couldn't get out fast enough; it was so damned shallow.

(Man, mid-thirties)

In one careful study done of dating among young people not previously married, it was found that first meetings that eventually led to marriage almost always were supported by a social network. Sometimes there was deliberate matchmaking by mutual friends, but even in the very occasional pickups, friends played a role. They might themselves be acquainted with the other person and belatedly furnish an introduction; at least they corroborated the individual's positive appraisal.[3]

[3] Robert G. Ryder, John S. Kafka, and David H. Olson, "Separation and Joining Influences in Courtship and Early Marriage," *American Journal of Orthopsychiatry* 41 (April 1971): 450–464.

It would seem that those whose aim is to establish a lasting attachment might best devote most of their energy to extending their social networks rather than to all-out search for a new attachment. By and large, energy devoted to extending one's network does result in a richer social life. Energy devoted to a search for a new attachment, insofar as it takes one outside one's community, seems likely to produce short-lived relationships. If these are not what one wants, the result may ultimately be a sense of depletion.

Some among the separated report that the only attractive candidates in their survey of possibilities unfortunately are already married. Indeed, they may be friendly with almost no individuals of either sex who are not married. Given such circumstances, the separated may at least briefly wonder, "Why not?" But most share the concerns expressed in the following quotation:

**It's much easier to meet married men than single men. Personally I come across many more married men. But I always ask why should I impose that on myself? I don't want to be number two, but number one. And as far as I'm concerned, in that situation I could only be number two.**

**(Woman, mid-thirties)**

## Professional Help

Many separated individuals become so concerned about their emotional state that they seek professional help. Gurin and his associates [4] found that 22 percent of separated and divorced men and 40 percent of separated and divorced women had sought professional help for personal problems. Others among the separated consult physicians because of conditions, including sleeplessness, lassitude, and vague aches, that have emotional bases. Divorce lawyers often report that their clients seek advice and support as well as specific legal services. The proportion of separated individuals who overtly or covertly seek help with their problems is very large. And many among the remainder undoubtedly contemplate seeking such help.

There are two quite different sorts of help the separated might

[4] Gerald Gurin, Joseph Veroff, and Sheila Feld, *America Looks at its Mental Health* (New York: Basic Books, 1960).

obtain. The first is help in managing the transition from a marital to a postmarital way of life; the second is help in changing themselves. It seems to me that during the period immediately following separation most among the separated would do well to give the first higher priority. My belief is that the emotional upset experienced by most individuals following separation is a response to the separation itself, rather than an expression of deep-seated problems uncovered by the separation. Given this, help in managing the trauma of loss and the confusions of transition might be more useful than help in resolving persisting personal conflicts.

The sort of help I advocate for most among the separated is *support* and *guidance*. A professional furnishes *support* by implicitly or explicitly pledging his skills and experience to realization of the separated person's aims. This is what a lawyer does when he says he stands ready to help his client in every way, what a minister does when he says he will be available for consultation until his parishioner's problems have been resolved, and what a psychiatrist does when he says he will help his patient recognize the best way of realizing the patient's goals. A professional's support is of greater worth than the support of even a respected friend because the professional is likely to be seen as having education, grasp, objectivity, and dedication that make him an especially valuable ally.

In addition to providing support, the professional can help his client make sense of his or her confused situation, and choose among possible lines of action. The professional might do this by outright advice, by encouraging the individual to develop a set of priorities, or just by focusing attention on certain aspects of the situation and neglecting other aspects. This contribution to the individual's ability to grasp and to plan I term *guidance*.

By supplying support and guidance, the professional may reduce the separated individual's vacillation among solutions or end the paralysis that is one expression of anxiety and confusion. The individual, with the professional's support and guidance, may be able more confidently to move in a consistent and desired direction.

Not every professional is equally prepared to provide support and guidance. To be able to help in this way, the professional must be regularly accessible. The work routine of some professionals, including most social workers and psychiatrists, makes possible appointments twice a week or weekly; the work routine of others, including most lawyers, priests, physicians in general practice, and pediatricians, does not. Most members of these latter professions, though they may be extraordinarily understanding and supportive in a first interview, are not able to set aside an hour or two a week for two or three months. In addition, they may have little recognition of the possible importance of continued contact.

There are many professions in which continued contact for the purpose of support and guidance is disdained as "handholding." Some professionals in psychiatry and social work, as well as professionals in other fields, believe it a failing of professional responsibility to do no more. They define support and guidance as superficial treatment that avoids confrontation with the underlying causes of the current situation. They may say to the separated individual something like, "I can help you get through this bad patch, but what good would that be in the long run? You got into this situation because of the way you are; sooner or later you'll be back in another situation just like it. Isn't it important to learn what led you here so that you can change?"

There is almost always some attraction in such a proposal. We have contributed to any situation in which we find ourselves. And there are those who say that when our lives are disrupted, when our identity is in flux and our defenses in disarray, we are most accessible to influence for change. But the issue for the separated to weigh is whether it is more important for them to get their lives going again or to attempt to achieve some fundamental characterological change.

There are those among the separated who are convinced on the basis of observation of themselves that only fundamental change in some aspect of their characters will permit them to lead satisfactory lives. These individuals should enter into change-directed therapy. But for others such therapy seems to me likely to be a distraction at a time when they can ill afford it.

# CHAPTER

# 12

# Legal Matters

It's a kind of terrible and weird feeling. I haven't gone through a divorce, but I've gone through this separation bit, where you go into a court and her lawyer is there and he wants to ask a couple of questions, like how much money do I make each week and what can I afford to spend, and isn't twenty dollars a week enough for me to live on. And then you go into court and this magnificent man is sitting behind a bench and with a stroke of a pen he decrees that you no longer live at such and such an address and you will have reasonable rights to visit the children, but you will now vacate the premises. And the house that you bought, you can't even go there except as determined by your wife.

(Man, early forties)

It takes so long to build up a marriage and so little time to end it. Such a little time. It's almost like your wedding. You plan for months and months and then it's over.

(Woman, early forties,
one week after court appearance for divorce)

### The Relationship with the Lawyer

There are many reasons separated individuals retain lawyers. Some retain a lawyer because they want a specific legal service: a separation agreement to be negotiated, legal pressure to be brought on a nonsupporting husband or on a wife who refuses visitation, or simply a divorce. But others retain a lawyer for all sorts of non-legal reasons. They may want to demonstrate to themselves and their spouse that they are seriously dissatisfied with their marriage: "I saw a lawyer today" can be of decided dramatic value when dropped into an evening's dispute. Or they may be unhappy and confused, and perhaps fearful of the future, and want the reassurance of having talked with someone knowledgeable. Many among the separated see a lawyer initially just for information regarding their legal situation, without any immediate desire to proceed beyond this. Some retain a lawyer almost against their will, because their spouse has insisted that they do so, or because their spouse has retained one and they believe that in self-protection they must follow suit.

Retaining a lawyer is often a new experience for separated individuals. Some may have consulted a lawyer once or twice in connection with purchasing a home or drawing up a will, but many will not have had even this much previous contact. Now it is necessary for them to find a lawyer whom they may eventually entrust with responsibility for restructuring their lives.

Most among the separated begin their search for a lawyer without even knowing that some lawyers specialize in "matrimonial law," as work with the separated is termed. They ask friends, perhaps one who preceded them into separation, for a lawyer's name. If they know a lawyer, they ask him to take them as a client or to refer them to someone who will. If they are without other leads they may try the bar association or take a chance on a name in the phone book. Some of those whose first choice proves faulty eventually become more knowledgeable about the professional scene. But initially there seems often to be a good deal of chance in selection of legal representation.

Participants in Seminars for the Separated who had already had occasion to use a lawyer's services had widely differing evaluations of their experience. Some felt deeply grateful to their lawyer for having supported them through a harrowing time. Others complained bitterly of having been underrepresented and overcharged. My impression is that those who had previously known the lawyer they eventually used tended to be among the most pleased with the relationship that developed. Others who spoke of good experiences were referred to their lawyers by friends who had themselves been clients or by lawyers who did not take divorce cases themselves. Still, not all lawyers' referrals proved good; perhaps lawyers' referrals were most trustworthy if the lawyers knew those practicing matrimonial law but were not involved in exchanging favors with them.

A great many elements appear to contribute to the success or failure of a lawyer-client relationship. Here is a conversation among a group of recently separated individuals about their experiences. Aspects of the lawyer's performance that mattered to them included: the lawyer's trustworthiness as an agent who understood the issues and could be relied on to carry out a commission; the lawyer's acceptance of their aims; the lawyer's accessibility; the lawyer's clarity in discussions; the lawyer's competence and effectiveness; and last, but not least, his fee.

The first speaker's lawyer had been unsatisfactory because he gave the speaker's case too little time.

I'm not satisfied with my lawyer. He is getting the communications garbled. He told me I could pick up my kids at their school on Friday; he said my wife's attorney had told him that would be all right. So I swung by the school and my wife was picking up the kids. She didn't know anything about it. There was no scene or anything, but garbled communications could have created one.

Another thing. I proposed a program for providing my wife's support. Because my business is a little slow right now. And I said, "Give it to the other attorney and see if you can concur or come up with an alternative." So he said, "Okay, I'll read it over the weekend." I called him two days ago and he still hadn't taken it out of his briefcase. He was absent-minded, or too busy.

(Man, early forties)

The next speaker, a woman, had had three lawyers, none of them satisfactory. The first had appeared frighteningly competent, but in pursuit of aims to which the woman could not agree. The second was preoccupied with other matters. The third was simply too busy.

Boy, does that sound familiar. I'm on my third lawyer. Would you believe it? The first one that was recommended to me turned out to be a real barracuda. He even scared me. He was going to take my husband right down to his underpants. And he would have too; I'm sure he would have. So I changed. I didn't really want that. So the second one I got because I called a friend who was a lawyer to recommend a lawyer. And naturally he recommended somebody in his own firm. What I didn't anticipate, the man he recommended was sick and worried about his own situation. If I had stuck with him I'd have been the one who ended up with just about nothing. So I went to a third person who was recommended by [a leading law school] who couldn't even find my papers, he was so busy. So what do you do? I feel stuck. Three strikes and you're out.

(Woman, about forty)

The next speaker, a man, had done well. His lawyer was adequately accessible, committed to him without being overcommitted, competent, and sensible.

I have a lawyer and he is just great. I think you should keep looking until you find one you really groove with. This man was my company's lawyer, although I don't think I'd talked with him more than a couple of hours until this. He makes everything easy and simple. Most things that I've had any problem over, he has settled for me over the phone. I have called him with something that was really driving me crazy. I thought I was in real trouble. And he said, "Well, if this happens, if it goes this way, we'll do this, and if it goes the other way we'll do that, and you don't have anything to worry about."

And that is the kind of lawyer you want. I know the other kind, who say, "Whereas" [and don't tell you anything]. That kind of lawyer you can keep. Or they tell you dirty things to do. Like she said, the barracuda, you know, "You can do this and you'll come out pretty good." That kind you don't want either.

(Man, late thirties)

But different lawyers suit different clients. The description of the woman's first lawyer appealed to the man who spoke earlier. And the woman herself had had second thoughts about having let him go.

*Man, early forties:* What's the barracuda's name? I need a tiger, a real tiger.

*Woman:* He's the top divorce lawyer around this area. He'll cost you about $2,500 in advance. Truthfully, I was sorry I left him after the third lawyer. He has empathy and he makes you feel that he really knows you within an hour.

(257)

It may not be entirely the fault of the lawyer if a separated individual feels misused by him. The separated individual can be a difficult client. Most among the separated come to a lawyer's office with their desires compromised and confused by guilt, anger, and a pervasive sense of failure. Far from being wholehearted in their aims, they may wonder throughout their first interview what they are doing there. Some have formulated no intention at all; they only want to do something about their marriage. Virtually all are intensely ambivalent toward their spouses, so that no matter what course they agree to pursue, they have reservations, contrary wishes, and second thoughts.

O'Gorman, in his study of matrimonial lawyers, found many of them understandably exasperated with their clients. They described their clients as "Subjective, tense, excited . . . emotional . . . acrimonious . . . in a complete turmoil." [1] Some lawyers said that not only did their clients not know much about the law but they also didn't know much about their own minds.

Matrimonial lawyers differ in the role they assume with clients. Some have neither the time nor the desire to deal with the anxieties, confusions, and ambivalences their clients present. They may be willing to undertake whatever course of action their clients seem to wish but can give no more than an hour to review of a client's case and decision on a procedure. From then on they may try to limit contact with the client even if the client can pay for additional time, and certainly if the client cannot. But other lawyers in matrimonial work see themselves as members of a helping profession and are concerned with the ultimate well-being of their clients and perhaps of their clients' families as well. They are likely to be much more accessible.

Some lawyers try to manage anxious clients by telling them as little as possible about how they will proceed, insisting that the clients trust them to do what is best. A number of separated individuals complained that their lawyers kept them uninformed even of their court date until the last possible moment. With some

[1] Hubert J. O'Gorman, *Lawyers and Matrimonial Cases* (New York: Free Press, 1963), 83.

clients this may work well, but with others it only increases their anxiety. These lawyers apparently held to their tactics nevertheless, responding to their clients' calls with bland reassurance that everything was being taken care of or simply not returning calls taken by their secretary or answering service.

Many among the separated are not at all unhappy with their lawyers. Despite the suspicions and readiness to distrust that the separated can hardly avoid bringing to new relationships, there is likely to be so much turmoil in their lives, and they are likely to feel so beleaguered, that they are ready to be deeply grateful to any authoritative figure who offers help. If their lawyer can allay their tensions by providing understanding and support, he may receive their unquestioning confidence. Some lawyers speak not of the exasperating indecision and ambivalence of their divorce clients but rather of their readiness to form positive transferences. Mortlock, in a discussion of his years as a divorce lawyer, writes:

Unhappy women, I have noticed, sometimes tend to form a transference very quickly indeed with the person who seems to offer comfort, relief or stability in a world grown suddenly frightening. . . .[2]

Other lawyers have reported to me that men as well as women among their clients have displayed an unquestioning reliance on them that was suggestive of childhood dependency. Clients who establish such a relationship may tolerate, despite themselves, a measure of patronization. One woman reported that although she resented her lawyer's appallingly smug willingness to tell her what she should be doing with her life, she regularly asked his advice on such matters as what to tell her children about a man with whom she had just become involved.

Sometimes lawyers overrespond to their clients' need. It is tempting to a lawyer to define himself as a knight of the round table riding out to combat evil. Particularly susceptible to rescue fantasies may be a male lawyer consulted by an appealing and attractive female client, but male lawyers also become overcommitted to the defense of male clients and female lawyers to that of female clients.

2 Bill Mortlock, *The Inside of Divorce* (London: Constable, 1972), pp. 99–100.

I had to make up a story on the affidavit. I didn't have to lie, but the problem was I told more truth than I really wanted to, because my lawyer was in the process of separating herself. So it is a little more vindictive than I would have done myself.

(Woman, forties)

There might seem little danger to a client if a lawyer enlists as a true believer in the client's cause. But the client may be more ambivalent than the lawyer recognizes and ultimately less willing to engage in all-out combat with the spouse. And if there are children, the client, and not the lawyer, will have to maintain some sort of relationship with the spouse indefinitely.

It seems possible to infer from comments made about experiences with lawyers some rough guidelines for the separated individual in managing his or her relationships with a lawyer.

It would seem useful, to begin with, that the first meeting between separated individual and lawyer include discussion about their mutual expectations of the relationship. The separated individual ought to think through whether he or she will want the lawyer only to deal with legal issues, or will also want the lawyer as a counselor on other problems that may arise in the course of the separation. And the lawyer should make clear how much time he can make available, and how he will charge for that time. It may be particularly useful to discuss how the lawyer will handle telephone requests for information or advice. It can be dismaying to the separated individual to place a call to his or her lawyer only to discover that the lawyer is too busy to return the call.

The separated individual and the lawyer should reach agreement on the aims of the separated individual. They should agree not only on specific aims in relation to property division, support, and so on, but also about whether the individual and lawyer together want to take away as much as is possible from their negotiations with the spouse, or whether they want to be "fair," even if this means taking away less.

If legal action is to be initiated, the separated individual should learn at least in a general way what will happen, what will be expected of him or her, and what will be the timing of the various events. If the action is to obtain a divorce, then the lawyer might describe the nature of the complaint to be filed, how the spouse will be informed, whether there will be a preliminary hearing and, if so, what will take place in it, what issues will have to be negotiated with the spouse, when the hearing on the divorce action itself might be scheduled, and what will happen in it. In addition there should be agreement that the separated individual will be kept informed of developments.

Finally, there should be agreement regarding fees. If the legal action will be uncontested, it may be possible for the separated individual to be told what the lawyer's total fee will be. In any event, the separated individual should know approximately how much the fee is likely to amount to and how the lawyer will go about deciding it. There also should be agreement regarding the timing of payment: how much of the fee will be required as retainer, how much is to be paid before the final hearing, and how much after all legal work has been completed.

## Legal Services

Despite the many auxiliary services they are called on to perform, there are just four sorts of purely legal services that lawyers have to offer. They can draw on their knowledge of the law to inform and advise. They can manage negotiations with the spouse or with the spouse's lawyer. They can pilot through the courts a petition for divorce or legal separation, or for a particular level of financial support or visitation. And they can serve as an advocate for their client before the judge.

No one is actually required to have a lawyer. Judges and court staff vary in their helpfulness to those who represent themselves, but self-representation is a right available to everyone. Nevertheless, divorce proceedings in many states are complex enough to defeat most laymen's attempts at their management. And even in states in which divorce proceedings have been simplified, a lawyer's help may be desirable, not only for his services as counselor, negotiator, and advocate, but also to insure that the proper papers are completed in the proper way. Of course, the more contested issues there are in a separation, the more a lawyer is likely to be needed.[3]

### Counsel

On what matters can a lawyer advise? To begin with, a lawyer can tell a separated individual what would constitute grounds for divorce in his or her state, whether he or she has such grounds, what would be involved in actually proceeding to divorce or in defending a divorce action brought by the spouse, and whether alternatives, such as separate maintenance, exist. He may be able to advise on the advantages and disadvantages of getting a divorce out of state. He can describe what might be reasonable divisions of property and reasonable levels of child support or alimony, and he should be able to suggest the tax implications of any arrangement. He should be able to suggest what would be construed as reasonable visitation rights. He can estimate the likelihood of winning in a fight over custody and suggest the kind of testimony that might be necessary in order to win. Beyond this, the lawyer may be able to describe the state laws governing modification of decrees which determine whether support levels or custody arrangements can be changed if circumstances change.

Some lawyers also counsel some clients in financial, interpersonal, and emotional matters. And some clients seem very much in need of counsel that goes beyond purely legal issues. An example might be an older woman who had previously relied on her husband to manage her affairs. It may be especially important to these clients that they have the right sort of lawyer.

**My attorney recommended that I work for a complete feeling of independence emotionally. He said I would get it sooner if I handled**

---

[3] Manuals have been written to help residents of California and Maine obtain their own divorces; see Charles E. Sherman, *How To Do Your Own Divorce in California* (Occidental, Calif.: Nolo Press, 1972); and Christine B. Hastedt and Meredith A. Malmburg, *Do Your Own Divorce in Maine* (Ashville, Me.: Cobblesmith, n.d.).

my own affairs. And that meant everything: rent, housing, heat, car, Blue Cross, all the things that you do on a family basis. The first thing he told me to do was to open my own checking account so that I would know where I stood when it came time to make up a tax return. But he recommended everything in the beginning be done in such a way as to foster my feeling of independence. And I followed his advice and it has worked out well.

(Woman, late forties)

On matters that may have bearing on negotiations, lawyers may advise both men and women to live in certain ways. A good many lawyers caution their clients to use discretion in their relations with someone new, both because they do not want their clients to be vulnerable to a charge of adultery and because, as I note below, obvious involvement with someone new may weaken a client's negotiating position. Lawyers may also caution their clients against even brief reconciliations, since from a legal standpoint any reconciliation may condone a spouse's earlier offenses. Lawyers may go even further, and recommend to their clients that they route through them whatever communication with the spouse might be absolutely necessary.

## Negotiations

The issues that exist to be negotiated between a couple after the end of a marriage are largely determined by the income level of the couple, by whether the wife is employed, by whether there are children, and if there are, their ages. The style of negotiation is largely determined by the character of the couple's postmarital relationship. Often it seems as though a marital style continues through the immediate postmarital period: The husband may, for example, continue to make financial decisions, just as he always did, except now instead of giving his wife housekeeping money he sends her a support payment. In a similar fashion, the wife might continue to be in charge of the children's day-to-day life, able to say when the children are too ill to visit with the husband or are required by their schoolwork to return early from a visit. Sometimes couples carry into separation a marital pattern that, while perhaps loveless, works effectively. There seems little to negotiate about.

He went to see my lawyer, and told him what amount of money he would send, and he is sending that. And he has agreed to show my lawyer all his income tax and stuff like that. It was my lawyer's suggestion, because we weren't arguing over custody or money. My husband was being very generous.

(Woman, about thirty)

Other couples carry into separation a marital style of angry contentiousness. Nothing is agreed to; everything can be disputed. Negotiation, explicit or implicit, may dominate their interaction.

I have already made up my mind I will be better off not asking for custody of the children. But I am not about to tell her this. Because, I'll be very frank, this now becomes a strong bargaining point. There is unfortunately involved in this whole Goddamned mess a whole game strategy.

(Man, mid-forties)

In situations like this one each attorney may be called on to champion his client in a battle of demands. How far the attorneys will go depends on many things, but it may be surmised that when the couple are of low or average income and the fee cannot be very high, the attorneys may try to make do with a single conference, perhaps by telephone, and perhaps a telephone review of the resulting agreement. If the couple is more affluent, negotiations are apt to be more careful and protracted.

The outcome of negotiations may well depend not only on the wishes of the clients but also on the lawyers' appraisals of what would happen if the issue in dispute were to be argued in court. A good many elements may contribute to their estimate. In some states "marital misconduct" may legally be considered in determining alimony and custody. In any event, a client who left his or her marriage, or whose behavior in the marriage was patently intolerable, is apt to do less well in many courts than a client who was unwaveringly virtuous; most lawyers therefore would appraise his or her negotiating position as correspondingly weaker. Within their negotiations the lawyers may remind one another of the elements that make their own case strong and the other's weak. One lawyer had as a client a woman who had left her husband on learning that he was sexually involved with another man. The woman's lawyer said nothing about this until the husband's lawyer noted that the woman's negotiating position was weak since she had voluntarily left a good home. The woman's lawyer then replied, "She had cause," and looked meaningfully at the husband's lawyer, who thereupon acceded to the woman's demands.

Negotiation is in some ways like poker: A weak position may not result in a bad bargain unless the other side is aware of it. Having a new spouse waiting in the wings suggests willingness to give concessions in order to gain the divorce, and so weakens one's negotiating position—unless the other side does not know. For this reason a lawyer may prefer that his client keep a new romance secret, and may be heartened to hear that the client's spouse has not.

Lawyers sometimes feel that their clients fail to appreciate the complexity of negotiations. One lawyer said that a woman client complained that she was receiving less in child support than a friend, though their husbands' incomes were the same. The lawyer said that the bargaining positions in the two cases had been entirely different, but there was no way he could get his client to see this.

It is possible for lawyers to negotiate too hard. In pursuit of the best possible agreement for their clients, some lawyers seem to worsen the postmarital relationships of their clients and the clients' spouses. They may, for example, actively discourage a client from talking with his or her spouse for fear that the client will inadvertently weaken his or her negotiating position, or will in thoughtless generosity make concessions without obtaining anything in return. Or they may take positions more extreme than their client desires in order eventually to achieve an advantageous compromise, but by so doing anger the client's spouse and further alienate the spouse from the client. Some separated individuals reported that until negotiations were at an end, their relationship with their spouse became progressively worse.

**The lawyers got involved and we had that situation where we were told not to talk to each other and there was a lot of mistrust. And it**

just got to be impossible. Like I was afraid anything I said would be used against me. Our communication just stopped completely.

I said, God, I just can't believe that it has come to this, where we have known each other for ten years and we can't say anything at all to each other. But for those two months we could not talk to each other. It was just a battle. He would say, "You're ripping me off. You got the house and the kids and now you are trying to get more money out of me." There was so much bitterness and so much anger and so much mistrust.

Now that most of the legal stuff is settled, things have gotten increasingly peaceful and friendly.

(Woman, late twenties)

Some husbands and wives use their lawyers not so much for negotiation as for intimidation. A woman might ask her lawyer to force her husband to send support checks more regularly, or a man might ask his lawyer to force his wife to permit him adequate visitation. The lawyer might then call the lawyer of the other spouse, or call the other spouse directly, and while he might begin by arguing from the justice of his client's cause, he might also threaten court action. If one spouse has obtained a lawyer who is effective in the role of hired gun, the other spouse may be forced to obtain a defender equal to the challenge.

### The Lawyer as Pilot for a Divorce Action

With some variations because of differences in state laws, divorces for fault take the same course throughout the country.[4] They begin with the lawyer drawing up a complaint or petition for the divorce which states the reasons the divorce should be granted. A copy of this is filed with the court and another copy delivered to the other spouse to inform him or her of the proceeding. After the other spouse has been notified a date can be set for a hearing on the petition. The spouse seeking the divorce will have to appear in court at that time, perhaps with witnesses—depending on the state

[4] Divorce law still differs from state to state, although it does not differ as much as it did only a generation ago, when divorce was readily obtained in Nevada, prohibited in South Carolina, and other states ranged themselves between these extremes. The major difference now is between the increasing number of states that permit "no-fault" actions and those that still do not.

and whether the lawyer thinks that witnesses could be helpful—but ordinarily the other spouse will not have to appear unless he or she wants to contest the divorce or some aspect of the post-divorce arrangements. Between the time of filing and the actual hearing, there may be appearances before a judge to arrange for temporary support or for some other separation-related purpose. At the hearing on the petition for the divorce the judge rules on whether the divorce should be granted and the separation agreement approved. If the petition for divorce or some aspect of the separation agreement is contested, there will be argument between the opposing lawyers, and testimony may be taken from the spouses and witnesses. The hearing for an uncontested case may take no longer than fifteen minutes, for a contested case anywhere from half an hour to a day or longer. If the judge rules in favor of the petition for divorce—as he ordinarily does in uncontested cases—the divorce is now entered in the court records. In most states it takes effect immediately; in the others there is an interval, often six months, during which the couple remain married and can void their divorce simply by communicating their wish to do so to the court.

Someone who knows his way through this system may find it straightforward enough. But to the individual encountering it for the first time, it can be forbiddingly confusing. It should, perhaps, be made easier for couples who are without children, have little shared property, and have no adjudicable disputes to obtain a divorce without a lawyer. But there are as yet only a few states where this seems now to be practical, and even in these states only a small proportion of divorcing couples seem to manage the procedure all by themselves.[5]

Many states now have some form of no-fault provision in which a divorce can be granted after a term of separation or simply on testimony that the marriage has suffered irretrievable breakdown. The proceedings for obtaining a no-fault divorce are virtually the

[5] In California, a "no-fault" state where it is reasonably easy for a couple to obtain a divorce without a lawyer's help, only about one divorce in twenty is brought without a lawyer, according to one estimate; see Michael Wheeler, *No-Fault Divorce* (Boston: Beacon Press, 1974), p. 122.

same as those involved in obtaining a fault divorce, except that it is the marriage, rather than one of the spouses, that is impugned.

## The Divorce

*As a lawyer I think of divorce as a play, and I write the script and get a cast of characters.*

(Young lawyer)

The divorce ends the state of marriage between a couple. It makes them free to remarry, it changes their tax status, and it changes the way their property will be distributed should they die without a will. In addition, the hearing in which the divorce is granted can be interpreted by the couple as a ceremony that symbolically ends their marriage, just as their wedding began it. It is a ceremony presided over by a judge rather than by a minister, and it takes place in a courtroom rather than a chapel, but it may be no less convincing in defining their relationship as now different.

Many among the separated are determined to bring about this symbolic and legal end to their marriage. They want a break, an end to connection to their former spouse. But there are others who see no particular reason to divorce.

*Neither of us wants to get married again in any foreseeable future, and money has been kind of tight, and there just doesn't seem to be any need to get divorced.*

(Woman, about thirty-five)

There are attractions, too, in letting a marriage continue. The woman just quoted went on to say, "There is a feeling of security in hanging on to that marriage that I cannot yet clearly understand." Some think of their marriage as a sort of empty dwelling to which they may one day return. Others think of it as a contract, the terms of which are now largely ignored but which still imposes certain obligations on the spouse.

I don't like the idea of being divorced. And so long as I'm not being hassled about it, my motivation is very low to pursue it. I'm still afraid of it. I sort of feel more protected not being divorced. I feel like Bert is more responsible for us now than he will be when we are divorced. There's a certain amount of freedom that he'll have when we're divorced. It's funny, but I don't see it as my having more freedom. He could get married, and if he did he would be giving money to his wife. And maybe she might have children. Now he's still tied to us.

(Woman, late twenties)

Some men and women want the restrictions of a continuing marriage. They fear their susceptibility to remarriage and their proneness to marital error. Or they want to be able to fend off new obligations by demonstrating an ineligibility that is not their fault.

I wouldn't say I was a coward. But my marriage keeps me insulated from getting involved and being committed to someone else. I can say, "Gee, honey, I'd really like to get involved with you, but I've got a wife who just won't give me a divorce."

(Man, early thirties)

Some are not so much undesiring of divorce as unwilling to take the necessary steps. It strikes them as likely to be an unpleasant, demeaning process. Even those determined to obtain their freedom may be made anxious enough by the prospect of a hearing to delay seeing a lawyer.

There can be something awesome in the idea of a hearing. The separated person may anticipate, even though informed to the contrary, that his or her moral worth is to be weighed, after which the judge will apportion praise or blame, penalties or reparation. The separated individual may recognize that the judge has the power to decide custody, visitation, and support level. It is easy to assume that he also has the power to decide who was in the right. The genuine power and the symbolic role of the judge may become intermeshed in anticipation.

Lawyers may attempt to teach their clients a different view of the court. They are likely to want their clients to understand that the judge will apply the law on the basis of whatever evidence is made available to him, and that it is the lawyer's task to present evidence that will result in the judicial decision the client wants. Moral worth has nothing to do with it; evidence is all.

No lawyer will admit encouraging a client to concoct a story, although sometimes lawyers will admit to a bit of coaching. Some do say that if they were faced with a client who otherwise would have no legal grounds for divorce they might refer him or her to a colleague, in another firm, whose ethics were flexible enough to accept perjury in a good cause. Nevertheless, virtually all lawyers will permit a client to tell only that part of his or her story that makes as strong a case as possible. A successful, and ethical, lawyer commented:

No client of mine has ever failed to get a divorce, and as far as I know, no client has ever had to lie. . . . I will freely admit that my client will often tell a rather one-sided story, which, because it is not subject to cross-examination, will sound perhaps more convincing than the full facts would warrant. For example, one client neglected to mention that when her husband struck her hard on the arm, she had a butcher knife in her hand with which she was endeavoring to ventilate his chest cavity.

For the separated person, the need to collaborate in a false picture of the marriage can become still another bit of unpleasantness in the divorce process.

I'm getting the divorce on mental and physical cruelty, and it has to be proved. I have to tell a story. I know it is a technicality, but it is not a very pleasant thing to do. The lawyer came up with the story. It is so out of character for what my husband is like. And I'm not an actress.

(Woman, late thirties)

In some states a corroborating witness must testify even in an uncontested case. If the complaint is largely fabricated, the witness must be brought into the conspiracy to deceive the court.

I have to have a witness. I have somebody. She volunteered to do it. The poor woman, what I'm putting her through. She was told that whatever I say, she should say, "Yes, that's the way it happened." It is a hell of a thing to have to do.

(Woman, late thirties)

Most divorce lawyers experienced in a particular court believe they can guess how each judge of that court will approach different presentations. Some judges are sympathetic to men, some to women, some are more nearly unbiased; some want simply to administer the law, others are more concerned with the welfare of those before them, and still others feel it their responsibility to protect the larger society; some respond only to evidence, while others are guided by their intuition, or the clerk of the court, or feelings of friendship toward lawyers they know well.

It is not considered unethical for a lawyer to attempt to steer his case to a judge he thinks likely to react favorably to his client, and lawyers familiar with the routine of a particular court usually can do so, although courts tend to discourage the practice. Opposing lawyers in a contested case who are equally sophisticated about potential judges may negotiate which judge is to hear their case, as well as other matters.

The judge in a divorce case has a great deal of discretionary authority and often rather little guidance which would help him use it wisely. In uncontested cases in which there is a separation agreement, most judges will go no farther than insuring that the law is being observed and that the separation agreement does not violate their sense of acceptable public policy. Contested cases, on the other hand, may present issues of great complexity regarding which the law is largely silent. It is up to the judge to decide what division of a couple's property would be just, or which parent would be better for the child, or what visitation scheme would contribute most to the well-being of all concerned. Such decisions often require the wisdom of Solomon and the fact-finding ability of a first-rate investigative agency. Yet the judge is likely to feel unable to give any case a great deal of time because of his awareness of other cases waiting to be heard. And some questions seem impossible to resolve. In a typical custody dispute, in which each parent seems to have strengths and weaknesses, how is one to know for certain which would be better for the child?

There are some ways out for the judge. There may be a traditional way of resolving an issue, such as giving the mother custody and the father "reasonable rights of visitation," although traditional resolutions of this sort are increasingly coming under criticism. If the facts are in dispute, it may be possible for the judge to assign a court investigator to the case. Now and then a judge exasperated by stubbornly irreconcilable positions on a less than critical issue can send a couple and their lawyers out to the hall to resolve the issue themselves. But the burden on the judges is large. One judge was reported to have said that since he began hearing divorce cases he had become too tense to sleep at night.

Here is a description of a judge's procedure in a routine uncontested case. Most cases are of this sort. The judge was sympathetic but did no probing beyond that necessary to establish the existence of legal grounds for the divorce.

I couldn't have asked for a nicer judge. I think he realized I just couldn't talk to him, I was so upset. It was a little room and nobody was there. Just me and my witness and my lawyer. Nobody else was in the room. The judge asked me just a few questions. What happened, and what day did it happen? And then he said, "All right." My witness was a close friend, and he asked her a few questions. And when it came to the children's ages, he just had to ask me three questions, and that was it.

(Woman, mid-thirties)

Occasionally a judge will become intrigued with a particular case and, even though it is uncontested, will want to know more about it than the necessary minimum. Sometimes lawyers and their clients suspect such judges of being voyeuristic rather than truly concerned. But in the following story the judge seemed to want to avoid colluding with a fictionalized bill of particulars and to learn what had really happened. Worth noting is the judge's apparent willingness to grant the divorce even though, until her witness testified, the woman did not appear to have legal grounds for it.

The judge showed an interest and wanted to know really what was going on. He was really doing his duty and questioning the whole mocked-up story my lawyer had worked out. So he asked me what the real reason was. And I was really taken aback because I heard that you were lucky if the judge didn't sleep through your testimony. He said, "Why are you really doing this? What went wrong?" And all I could say was that we didn't basically get along. He said,

"Okay, what did you fight about?" And I said, "You know, stupid stuff like who's going to take out the trash." He says, "What was the problem?" And I looked at him in exasperation like he wanted me to tell him hours and hours of things in two seconds. And I said, "Maybe I just wanted to be too dominant and he wanted me to be more submissive." And he said, "Well, do you think you're going to be better off now?" I said, "Yes." He asked me a few other questions like that and finally he said, "Well, that's not grounds, but I'm going to grant it anyway."

I sat down and my witness got up to give her piece. She hadn't heard what I had said. And he said to my witness, "Are you one of these liberated women too?" At this point my lawyer stepped in and said, "Look, you may have got the wrong idea." And he went on to explain that my husband was living with somebody else and that he had had affairs and stuff. And then my witness piped in and said, "Yes, I tried to tell her, some of her friends tried to tell her about it over the summer, and she wouldn't listen." And the judge said, "Yes, the wife is the last to know." And he granted it.

(Woman, late thirties)

The divorce hearing has a good deal of emotional impact on the separated individual. Assuming that it is the woman who obtains the divorce, she may afterward be depressed or elated, may cry, may want to go home and go to bed, or may want to express her new freedom, perhaps go out on a date, perhaps buy a new dress. She may feel, resentfully, that her husband has gotten what he wanted, or she may take satisfaction in the thought that she has shown him that she was serious when she first threatened divorce. Many women want to call or to see their husbands after the divorce, to tell them that it has happened. When the ex-husband learns, he may feel guilty that his wife had to endure the court ordeal and may want to comfort her, or, if he had opposed the divorce, may want to tell his wife how hurt and angry he now is.

The divorce, like the separation, turns out not to be the end of the husband-wife relationship. For most couples it is a significant incident, but only an incident, in a continuing if diverging relationship. The divorce effectively says to the partner and to the world that the individual is now legally and morally independent and free to find someone new. It makes reconciliation less likely. But it does not rule out reconciliation: Many couples have remarried after divorce, and still others have chosen to live together again without getting remarried. If there are children, support and visitation continue as before, with all the coordination and conflict they imply.

### Legal Matters When There Is Little Money

Individuals of very low income will not become absorbed in protracted and complex negotiations and so will be spared watching their affection for their husband or wife end in the meanest sort of bargaining. But other factors may enter to insure that they do not come unscathed through the divorce process.

To begin with, it may be difficult for the poor to obtain a divorce at all. Legal Aid offices may be loath to accept divorce work because of the press of cases that seem to be more urgent and perhaps more worthy, and a lawyer in private practice is unlikely to accept a divorce case for much less than $300.[6] Some low-income couples who separate never get divorced because they never are able to pay the legal fees. Should the husband or wife decide to live with someone new, he or she must choose between cohabitation and bigamy.

The troubles associated with low-income separation, however, begin long before any temptation to form irregular new alliances. If the man was the source of the family income, his departure is apt to leave his family with too little money for subsistence, even if he should give his wife a large part of his paycheck every week. The man's wife may turn to her kin for help, or if her children are of

[6] In 1973 the minimum fee suggested by the Massachusetts bar for divorce work (before the notion of minimum fees became suspect as price fixing) was $25 an hour. Experienced lawyers in good firms charged between $40 and $75 an hour. Some lawyers charged much more than this. An uncomplicated divorce action might take ten to twenty hours, including time spent in court. In 1974 the bulk of fees in Boston were reported to be between $600 and $2,000.

Lawyers varied in their policies regarding retainers. Some were reported to want much of their fee paid in advance; many were said to want their fee in full before the final hearing.

school age, she may search for employment. But the wife's kin are apt to be unable or unwilling to assume continuing financial responsibility, and the wife may not be able to earn enough to pay her bills herself, even with help from her husband. The wife may be required to apply for public assistance.

Application for public assistance can be a wearing and humiliating experience. The woman presents herself as an indigent to an overworked staff in a crumbling office. She is required to fill out forms that probe her reasons for failure and then to undergo an interview that extends the probe. Between each step in her processing she must wait, for half an hour or longer, in an uncomfortable outer room, together with others among society's losers. If her claim appears to meet the agency's rules regarding eligibility, she will be sent home to await a social worker-investigator who must decide finally that she is genuinely impoverished.

Many welfare departments, in their administration of the largely federal program, Aid to Families of Dependent Children, require that separated or divorced mothers demonstrate that they have pursued every avenue toward obtaining support from their husbands. In particular the departments require that the applicant mothers have brought their husband's nonsupport to the attention of a court. There are two different ways in which a woman can do this. She can ask a probate court to require her husband to support her and his family; this defines the failure to support as a civil matter, a failure to meet a legal obligation. Alternatively, she can charge in a criminal court that her husband has broken the state law that makes him responsible for support of his family. Either way the husband will at some point be required to answer the charges in court. The nonsupport action may well be even more effective than the protracted negotiations of wealthy couples in insuring that the postmarital relationship will be hostile.

Having agreed to support payments, the man is likely to discover that after sending his wife a reasonable portion of his paycheck—even though it is still inadequate to her needs—he has so little left for himself that, once he has set aside money for food, housing, and transportation, he has barely enough for pipe tobacco. Many low-income men become irregular or delinquent in their contributions to their wives. They make too little money as it is; and if their wives are on welfare, they may recognize that their contributions will only be used to reduce the payments welfare makes to their families, not to increase their families' income.

Generally a man who is delinquent in relation to support payments will not be pursued legally. But it is possible for his wife or a welfare official to bring legal action against him if either should wish to do so. If the support order has been issued as a result of civil action, then the husband can be charged with contempt of a probate court. The court may decide that the husband is able to pay but obstinately refuses, and thereupon may sentence him to up to six months in jail to force him to meet his obligations. The husband can end the sentence by making the payment, and many (although not all) delinquent husbands who see themselves about to be locked away do obtain the money to pay their wives rather than serve the sentence. It is possible, too, for a man to be jailed on criminal nonsupport charges. In that case the sentence would have to be served even if the man paid up after its passing.

Women may, like men, be held in contempt of a probate court or in criminal violation of the support law and sentenced to a jail term. A few women in Massachusetts have been threatened with ten days in jail for willfully refusing to permit a husband visitation rights. But instances of the jailing of women are rare; the threat of jail following separation is for the most part reserved for men who have failed to keep up with their support payments.

Even the middle class may find themselves in trouble with the courts over support payments. There have been instances of professional men who insisted that they could not meet support payments required by their separation agreement and have gone to jail because a judge did not agree with them. In one famous case, a man was kept in jail on repeated sentences of six months for a total of five years and five months because he could not or would not make up back payments of $2,500.[7]

Many nonsupport actions appear entirely justifiable: One thinks of the woman raising her children in poverty while the children's father lives in unconcerned comfort. But the routine requirement

[7] See the *New York Times* story by Frank J. Prial, April 8, 1974, p. 33.

that nonsupport action be pursued by applicants for welfare assistance seems, if not actually punitive in intent, then indefensibly insensitive to the implication of such action for the continued relationship of the husband and wife. Where there simply is not enough income for two households, nonsupport action is surely a last resort, rather than a first step, in working out its just division. And it is not only among welfare applicants that nonsupport actions can lead to abuse. In middle-income situations as well, just as some separated women have been financially abandoned by callous husbands, some separated men have been severely injured by the conjunction of financial difficulties, a vindictive wife, and a determined judge.

# 13

# Dating and Related Matters

There should be something that sounds more mature. "Dating" is like an adolescent term.

(Man, early forties)

We are more sophisticated than we were when we were younger. You had somebody that you were married to for twenty years. To me the term "dating" should be updated or something, you know, to make it more our age.

(Woman, early forties)

I feel like I'm back in my junior year at college, except that I'm a little bit older and I have three kids. I'm back trying to figure out what it is going to be like to go on a date. I feel I'm a better person than I was then, better able to cope, but I think the problems of meeting people are common to anybody in our society. It doesn't matter whether you are twenty-four and single or thirty-four and separated.

(Woman, mid-thirties)

Many among the separated find the term "dating" offensive; it suggests awkward adolescence and reminds them of insecurities they hoped they had outgrown on leaving high school. The term seems incongruous when applied to the behavior of individuals who were married and who have children, responsibilities, and a certain standing among friends and acquaintances. They may prefer terms like "going out with" or "seeing for an evening." Yet "dating" remains the most convenient way to refer to the very common practice of becoming a member of a temporary couple for the manifest purpose of achieving an entertaining evening, and for the unexpressed purpose of assessing the value of a continuing relationship.

Some among the separated, for a time, feel their lives to be too upset to undertake new associations and to risk the possibility of new problems.

I couldn't think about dating for a long time. First of all I wanted to get over the hassling and I wanted to get into my own life and sort of get settled and start building a home again.

(Woman, late thirties)

It's hard to go out when you're going through all that emotional turmoil. When I was first separated I tended to stay alone in this cabin I have, completely alone, with a dog.

(Man, mid-thirties)

And some are unsure of their attractiveness or even acceptability to a potential date. The process of marital breakdown may have depleted their self-esteem, and their status as a separated person may in their minds further establish their unacceptability.

Coming out of a separation leaves you with a feeling of worthlessness, failure, things not quite right. How can a person who is feeling like this feel good enough about themselves to feel that someone else would want them? You feel, "I am horrible. I have failed." How can you, having such low self-esteem, possibly get into a dating situation?

(Woman, late thirties)

Yet most among the separated, whatever their ages, enter into dating at some point. Hunt estimates that 75 percent of separated individuals begin dating in the first year after their separation, and over 90 percent begin before the end of their second year.[1] Among those recently divorced mothers in Goode's study who had neither remarried nor begun to go steady, more than half were dating at least as often as once or twice a month.[2]

A most important reason for dating is its effectiveness as a remedy for loneliness. During my work with Parents Without Partners I once observed a man who had been slumped in a chair, the image

[1] Morton Hunt, *The World of the Formerly Married* (New York: McGraw-Hill, 1966), p. 110. Hunt describes admirably the processes of dating, from the search for a prospective date through the date itself and its personal and relational aftermath. See also pp. 76–202.

[2] William J. Goode, *Women in Divorce* (New York: Free Press, 1965), p. 258.

of dejection and helplessness, suddenly brighten when an attractive woman stopped to chat with him. What may have taken place was that the man was reassured by the woman's presence and attention that potential attachment figures existed and he could engage their interest.

Making a date may do even more to reassure an individual that his or her world is not barren; it may permit him or her to hope that the date itself may be the beginning of a new attachment. But making a date may be more effective in allaying loneliness than the date itself. The date in anticipation makes hope possible, whereas the actuality may be a disappointment.

**You know, before we spent that day together I was having this fantasy built up that he was going to save me from this dreadful situation that I was in. But when I saw him I realized he was a nice guy that I could like, but I have certain reservations about.**
**(Woman, early thirties)**

The possibility of new attachment is the most important reason for dating's attractiveness. There are a host of secondary reasons: an evening's companionship, a chance to talk with someone of the other sex, the safe adventure of an outing to a restaurant or movie or play, an opportunity to meet the date's friends and thus extend one's own circle of acquaintances. At the very least dating is activity, something to look forward to and to do. At best it can help enrich one's life.

**What has dating meant for me? A whole new world of experiences, personalities, needs, problems.**

**(Man, early thirties)**

The affirmation of self that may be gained from a date that goes well can contribute to one's self-esteem. The other person may reassure where the spouse attacked, be accepting where the spouse condemned. Just being able to manage dating with reasonable success may contribute to renewed confidence in one's ability to meet other challenges of living alone.

**I always felt my husband was a great man, so smart, and I was nothing. But dating has given me confidence. I'm getting along now.**
**(Woman, mid-thirties)**

I felt great the week I met Ollie. I felt completely lovable. I felt like I deserved things.

(**Woman, about thirty**)

An underlying assumption of dating is that it imposes no necessary obligations on participants beyond spending an evening together. This means that if the evening should prove dull or unpleasant, there is no need to repeat it. If the participants want to see one another again, fine; if not, the relationship can be dropped.

**You get the vibrations in a couple of sessions. If the vibrations aren't right, there is no need to continue.**

(**Woman, early thirties**)

But this underlying assumption of tentativeness, while it is dating's essential characteristic, can be a source of tension. It means that each participant is evaluating the other as a companion and potential intimate, and must tolerate being evaluated in the same way. Dating is like trying out for a job, except that it is not one's competence that is at issue, but one's self. And so the woman gets her hair done, the man his suit cleaned; on meeting each tries to make the best possible first impression, and thereafter display the most engaging self. And each may be concerned that whatever he or she does, it may not be good enough.

**I must admit that every time I have a new date I go through feeling like an adolescent. You know, "Will they like me?" I don't think about whether I will like them. Will they like *me?***

(**Woman, forty, about two years after separation**)

Rejection is a possibility for men even before the date occurs. It is traditionally the man's role to propose the date, the woman's to accept or decline. Even men who, when married, had flirted with women they worked with may feel diffident when it becomes possible to issue an invitation which, because it is in earnest, may be refused.

**Where I work there are quite a few females. And I find that when I was married I was pretty safe and I could get away with all sorts of flippant remarks. But now I want to ask the girl out and I get**

to the point of, "We ought to go out for a drink," and she says, "Yeah," and then I don't know the rest of it. I say, "Well, I'll ask you real soon." She says, "Yeah, don't forget."

(Man, about forty)

The possibility of rejection continues through a series of dates, lessening only as mutual commitment is established. So long as the relationship is genuinely one of dating, rejection of one participant by the other is consistent with its premises. Neither party has the right to be angry if it should happen, no matter the distress it may produce.

I met this fellow at a party and I just knew he was going to call and he did, a week later. And it was really very nice. The first night he came over and brought someone over and we talked. The second night I couldn't get a babysitter, and it was the same thing. The third night I finally got a babysitter and we went out. By that time, I was really pouring my guts out. And it just scared him away. I guess if he had done that with me it would have scared me away too. He called me up—and I knew he was going to say this—and he said, "I don't want to get hurt, and I don't want to hurt you." And I thanked him for calling and saying that, rather than just not calling again. And it was a horrible rejection for me. It was like the pain of being knocked down ten more times.

(Woman, about thirty)

Rejection is wounding to anyone, separated or not. But to someone whose marriage has just ended the injury is all the more severe. The newly separated individual is likely to be already uncertain of his or her acceptability, and to have had as yet too little positive experience in dating to argue against a negative report. In addition, he or she is likely already to feel abandoned and isolated. Rejection then intensifies these feelings.

Individuals try to take precautions against rejection. They try not to expect too much of a dating relationship, though they may in truth be looking forward to the next time they will see the other person. They try to anticipate from the other's words or behavior whether he or she will want to continue. And they learn not to presume too much until things have progressed beyond just dating. They learn, for example, not to drop in on someone without first telephoning.

**One night I was out walking and I passed this girl's apartment. And I stopped over. And there was this guy there. I left as soon as I possibly could. I was crushed, extremely depressed. I was figuring that this girl might be happy to see me, when in fact she wasn't.**

**(Man, mid-thirties)**

Some among the separated are so aware of the impact of rejection that they cannot bring themselves to inflict it on another. But then their unwillingness to reject the other person, added to their own vulnerability to rejection, makes dating extraordinarily anxiety provoking.

**I'm so worried about rejection myself I don't want to be the person who rejects. But it is a tremendous source of anxiety. When I went out last time I was tremendously depressed. I couldn't wait to get home because I knew I couldn't handle it.**

**(Woman, mid-thirties)**

Such individuals may maneuver a date with whom they feel uncongenial into being the rejecter, perhaps by presenting their least attractive selves, perhaps by establishing that their emotions are still absorbed in their marriages. Or they may allow themselves to be drawn into relationships they do not really want, simply from inability to call a halt.

Each date represents an investment of self; it can be depleting to have a succession of dates that amount to nothing. And although it can be rewarding to tell one's life story to an attentive and friendly listener, no matter how many times the story has already been told, later there can be embarrassment and chagrin for having imprudently displayed one's private life.

**If during those dates you've been trying to relate at all, you've spilled out a great deal of yourself. And to go through this same process time after time after time after time is very, very painful.**

**(Woman, early thirties)**

(283)

Some individuals never overcome the feeling that dating is an empty social form. One man said that while trying to maintain a conversation with his dinner companion he would find himself wondering what he was doing there. Another reported that after a series of pointless evenings he simply stopped arranging dates.

I went through a frantic three weeks, going out with people that I found unsatisfactory. Basically people that I didn't know. The problem was that I really didn't get to know someone before I asked them out. In that three weeks I had a series of experiences where I literally felt that I didn't want to be where I was after forty minutes, and if I had had any guts I would have taken another twenty minutes, and that would have been it. And since I have not dated.

(Man, late twenties)

There are other problems in dating. It can be expensive both for the man who believes that a restaurant or drinks are expected of him and for the woman who must pay a babysitter. It takes time and energy to arrange. And even the best date is likely to have a contrived quality. Yet dating in some form seems so responsive to the needs of the separated that unless the person moves quickly into a new committed relationship, he or she is almost certain to experience it at some point.

### Sex and Dating

The role of sexual need in the initiation of dating would appear to be secondary for most among the separated. Women as well as men indicate that they experience sexual deprivation when without a partner, but that the deprivation in itself does not account for their interest in new relationships. In truth, sexual desire may be so intermeshed with other feelings of need, including need for emotional as well as physical contact, for the security of attachment, and for assurance of worth, that it is not possible to ascertain its particular contribution to motivation for dating.

Here is an excerpt from a discussion between two women, each separated after many years of marriage, on the subject of sexual desire and the feelings associated with it:

*First woman:* You know, physical deprivation is one thing. But what I miss at this point is the feelings that you get from sex, the feeling of closeness and warmth, of security. What I miss at this point is just being held, and cuddled.

*Second woman:* I've been celibate for a pretty long time, so I've learned to cope with it, but I'll tell you one thing, the first year I should have gone for help. It was very hard to deal with. I cried many a night over it, and didn't know what to do, to just bargain myself with the first offer, or to try to hang in there, which I did. Being alone in that sexual manner does cause hurt, if you are a normal human being and have desires and wants. But you know you want to be with someone who wants you.

The separated, when they first begin dating, may exhibit an odd combination of sophistication and naïveté. They come to dating after years of marriage, aware of sexual needs and at the same time alert to problems of overinvolvement. But they are unaccustomed to the practice of dating, and often uncertain about others' intentions and their own wishes. Because of their inexperience in the world of single adults, they may have no policy regarding the conditions under which it is appropriate to permit a relationship to become sexual. All the years of their marriage may prove of no help.

I don't like being thirty-six and dealing with all these sexual problems. I haven't had any experience. All I've been was married.

(Woman, separated after fourteen years of marriage)

Quite early in the unfolding of a first or second date they may begin speculating about the desirability of the relationship becoming sexual. Tension regarding whether it should or will, and how the decision will be arrived at, can be a source of anxiety. One woman reported worrying all through a date, "What should I do if he begins coming toward me?" To avoid the possibility she did not invite the man in when he took her home, and then felt guilty for having been rude.

In time, some among the separated develop methods for reducing uncertainty and anxiety. One man was proud of his bluntness: "I lay it on the line. She can say 'yes' or 'no.'" Women may try to be equally clear regarding whether they would view a proposal with favor. Some men and women establish as guides for their own behavior a rough schedule of appropriate intimacies, in which a first date may end with a kiss, but the third date, if there is one, can end with intercourse. Some men and women will permit a relationship to become sexual only if it is grounded in mutual love. Others accept sex if the relationship only promises well. Still others may accept a sexual relationship for itself alone.

Those among the separated who are unsure of the policy they should adopt find little guidance in the rules of sexual conduct maintained by our society. It is not that we in modern-day America have no set of rules; rather, we have too many. The traditional ethic which prohibits all but legitimated sexual relationships can find support in the same community in which there is also support for sexual freedom. Such diversity insures that no ethic will have the support of all. Instead of guidance the separated person encounters ethical relativism, in which a person's behavior can only be evaluated in terms of that person's values and goals. The only source of direction is then internal, and the separated person may be told that when perplexed he or she must consult his or her feelings, and behave in whatever way is compatible with them. Sometimes, surprisingly, this advice proves useful.

**I think when I started dating I was prepared for having different feelings about sex and being very confused about how to act. But I decided I would do what really felt comfortable, and as soon as something was uncomfortable, that would be a very big clue, and I would never go against that feeling. And I have followed that, and so far, no matter what I've done or haven't done, I've never looked back and regretted it. Each time I made a decision on what to do or not to do, I just decided on how it was for me. If I didn't want to, I didn't.**

**(Woman, early thirties)**

One problem with ethical relativism is that it promotes discord between the dating partners. Each person makes his or her own rules, and then asks whether there is a joint policy compatible with them. But what feels comfortable for one partner in a dating relationship may not be acceptable to the other. In particular, men complain that women move more slowly than they do. One man said, "I get told, 'Wait until I get to know you better and really like you.' And my feeling is, for God's sake, what's wrong with now?"

**I was very interested in one girl, but sex outside of marriage was against her religious principles. After a series of frustrating experiences I figured this is not for me, and although I was practically in love with her, I felt I had to break it off for my own sanity.**

**(Man, late thirties)**

Yet it may be entirely appropriate for women to develop an ethic more cautious than that developed by many men. It appears that when women accept casual sex, traditionally a more masculine practice, the experience is likely to leave them distressed. Women, by and large, may simply have greater need for security than do men, at least in our present society.

**I don't see anything wrong with a one-night stand, but any experience like that I've had, I've felt more icky after than I did before. I've felt so alone.**

**(Woman, about forty)**

### Some Implications of Sexual Accessibility

One among the several complexes of meanings that may be associated with sex is assurance of attachment. We tend to assume that if a man or woman feels attachment, and certainly if the man or woman feels a more complex sentiment that he or she would characterize as love, the man or woman will be sexually desiring and sexually accessible. Absence of sexual interest tends to be taken as indicative of absence of interest in other respects as well.

Because of the association of sexual accessibility and attachment, a man or woman may seek to elicit attachment feelings in a dating partner in the hope that this will lead to sexual accessibility, or may enter into a sexual relationship in the hope that this will facilitate attachment. Or there may be reluctance to enter into a sexual relationship for fear that the other may become emotionally dependent on the relationship's continuation.

Because it represents a kind of ultimate acceptance, sexual consent by a person of attractiveness and social worth can be testimony to one's own high value. Yet here again the double standard occurs. It is men, much more than women, who gain reassurance of worth from a partner's sexual consent. Men can confidently interpret sexual consent as acceptance, but women have to recognize men's greater tolerance for casual experiences. For women it is not so much a man's initial desire that is reassuring as his willingness to continue the relationship. The critical issue for a woman may be not whether the man wants to go to bed with her, but whether he calls the following day.

Some men emerge from a soured marriage with depleted self-esteem and, perhaps, enough anger toward women to make them, careless of women's well-being. If the men are attractive and enterprising they may initiate a nearly ceaseless sexual hunt which diminishes in intensity only as their need for reassurance lessens. When they eventually establish a firmer sense of themselves they may have no idea why they were so driven.

**At first I went around screwing everything I could get my hands on. You go through that stage. And then you ask yourself why you did that. And then you realize that sex isn't all you want out of a relationship. And then you can start having normal relationships with people. But it took me a year, a year and a half.**

**(Man, late twenties)**

Women may also go through a stage in which they have many brief affairs. But they seem less motivated by desire to augment their self-esteem than by an almost compulsive search for attachment, facilitated, in some instances, by a desire to demonstrate their anger with their spouse or themselves. And while men may later refer almost boastfully to the time after their separation when they "screwed around," women seem more likely to describe such a time as confused and unhappy.

## Dating, the Spouse, and the Children

I have pointed out several ways in which individuals who enter into dating after a marriage find it a different experience from the dating in which they may have participated earlier in their lives. Practices and expectations among adults who have been married are different from those among younger people. The individuals are older and know themselves better; at the same time, they are burdened by the emotional aftermath of separation. There is still another way in which the postmarital situation is different: The individual has a spouse, and may have children as well.

The separated individual who is not yet divorced is not legally permitted to become sexually involved with someone new, and may be cautioned by his or her lawyer that until the divorce is granted, an affair can be interpreted by the courts as adultery. It is highly unlikely that a postmarital affair will result in anyone's being charged under a state's criminal statute against adultery, but adultery may nevertheless become a weapon the spouse's lawyer can use in negotiations. Many lawyers feel that any evident sexual involvement of their client weakens their negotiating hand. In consequence, they caution their client to be chaste if possible, discreet in any event.

Some individuals pay little attention to this. Even if they are involved in fairly unpleasant negotiations, they cannot conceive of their spouse's holding them to an outmoded standard of behavior. Indeed, the woman may arrange for the husband to have the children overnight, for a weekend, or for a week during the summer so that she can be alone with the man she is seeing. Quite often a husband or wife will take pleasure in reporting his or her dating successes to the other spouse, in the belief that managing well is the best revenge.

The image of the spouse may become a participant in an internal conversation which accompanies and counterpoints the events of a date: "You thought I was unattractive. Well, that's not what he (or she) thinks." If the separated individual feels uncomfortable or compromised, the spouse may be blamed, and the awkwardness of the situation added to the list of indictments with which the spouse is charged.

**I found myself sitting in a bar and I didn't know if I was being picked up or what. And I'd sit there and curse my husband: "I'm thirty-eight years old and you've put me in this position."**

Dating is almost by its nature distancing from the spouse. A first date after the end of a marriage can be something of a milestone: a statement to one's self, and anyone else who happens to be watching, of one's freedom. Almost always it will be felt as a repudiation of the spouse as well as a provisional acceptance of someone new. But the attempted repudiation may be unsuccessful. One man said: "The first time I slept with a girl after I left my wife I thought sure I was going to Hell as an adulterer." And if things go badly, there may be a yearning to return to the spouse in reality. Just the tension of dating may lead to desire for the spouse.

**When I was with him all I could think of was running home to Dan. And then I thought, "But Dan's not there."**

(**Woman, about thirty**)

Should the separated become aware of their spouse's dating, they are likely to require themselves to be accepting despite, perhaps, twinges of jealousy. Generally separated individuals manage to tolerate their spouse's dating, although there are exceptions. A few become intensely jealous. Others become indignant, if not at the dating itself, then at the possibility that the children are being neglected. Women may not want their children exposed to other women, and, to a lesser extent, men may want their children safeguarded from the fathering of other men.

Many among the separated who are parents, especially those who have custody of the children, feel great concern, and often some guilt, in relation to their children. Parents whose marriage is intact need never consider how to explain to their children their own need for companionship, attachment, and a sexual relationship; the separated parent can hardly avoid having to explain all this. Often there is both discomfort and defensiveness in the explanation.

What I've done with my children, upon the advice of a child psychologist, is to explain to them that, "This is my friend, and you are going to be exposed to her." But I only tell them about my going out if they raise the subject.

(Man, late thirties, has custody of his children)

The children may inform one parent about the other parent's dating activities. Although children tend to be protective of each parent when with the other, their discretion sometimes fails.

My husband's been acting up lately and I think it's because the children have let him know that I'm seeing somebody. It's okay for him, but I'm supposed to sit home and tend to my knitting. I think it's really bugging him. He's really been difficult.

(Woman, early thirties)

Separated parents may attempt to guard against the many ways they can imagine that their dating might hurt their children. They may do their utmost to discourage a relationship between their children and a date who may soon drop out of their lives, lest the children experience loss. They may assure their children that the date is not competing with the children for their affection. And they try to continue to act the parent, lest they lose their children's respect.

My nineteen-year-old daughter talks openly with her younger sister about her sexual encounters. A little too openly for my taste. The two of them are educating me. But that is them. If I were to go out and do the same thing, I don't know how they would react. After all, I am their mother.

(Woman, early forties)

Children in fact have no single reaction to a parent's dating. Very young children may object to a parent's leaving them for an evening. Older children may recognize the improvement in their parent's morale and be happy for him or her. Some children of all ages enjoy meeting their parent's dates; other children, again of all ages, are indifferent or uncomfortable with them. The range of children's reactions to a mother's dating may be suggested by the following comments:

My children are thrilled when I bring home men I date because they get all kinds of attention from them.

(Woman, about thirty)

Usually when a guy comes to take me out, they stare at him, or if they are in the front room watching TV, they won't even come out to say hello.

(Woman, about thirty)

I think dating is hard on the children. When I introduce them to somebody, they back off.

(Woman, late thirties)

One might guess that if the parent accepts his or her dating, the children are likely to accept it, too. But most separated parents appear uneasy about its effect on their children, and very uneasy about any sexual relationship that may develop. They try to hide their sexual involvements from their children, with the result that they feel themselves to be living with underage chaperones. A few parents, committed to honesty at least about sex, do tell their children that they now and again sleep with a date the children have come to know. One woman's six-year-old son asked her where a man who had stayed overnight had slept, and she answered, "With me, of course." It would seem from her report and those of other mothers who were nearly as open that children are as able to accommodate to parental frankness as they are to parental dissimulation.

## Changing Needs

Many among the separated, for as long as the first year or even the first two after the end of their marriages, may feel themselves to be emotionally unready to make a permanent commitment. They recognize that they haven't yet become the person they will be, and until they have they want freedom from constraint.

During this period they may date, but they make clear to the people they see that they are not ready to settle down. They may run through a succession of superficial dating relationships. Or they may become involved with individuals who clearly are inappropriate as future marital partners because of age or social class differences. Or they may find someone entirely appropriate for them, but ask that person to understand that they cannot make commitments as yet.

**I said to her, "I love you and I care about you, but I have things to work out first." I have no right to ask her for commitment because I'm not there yet myself. I'm not yet ready in terms of being recovered from my marriage.**

**(Man, late thirties)**

In time most separated individuals become less wary of commitment and more responsive to their need for secure attachment. Their motivations in dating then change. Increasingly a date will become for them an opportunity to see if something permanent might work out.

# 14

# New Attachments

What I will face at some point is whether I will do it all over again. I mean marry someone similar to my husband. And make all the same worst mistakes. That is my greatest concern.
(Woman, late twenties, separated a few months)

As the separated emerge from the changes and confusions that characterize the first period of separation, many become more willing to consider "serious" new relationships. Whereas earlier they felt unready for new commitments, despite loneliness and need for support, now they feel themselves again able to deal with the problems and limitations of a potentially lasting tie with some-one who will become a nearly constant figure in their world.

It is essential to such a tie that the two participants feel *attached* to one another: that they feel comfortable and secure in one an-other's presence; that, for each, knowing that the other is ac-cessible dispels loneliness. Lacking attachment, each would be susceptible to loneliness despite the other's presence, and whether he or she wanted it so or not, would be accessible to the estab-lishment of attachment elsewhere. Each would become impa-tient with the other if freedom to find someone more satisfactory should be limited by the relationship.

There are basically three forms that committed attachment re-lationships may assume, although some individuals establish rela-tionships that seem to be a mix of two or even all three. One of the forms is marriage; the other two are "going together" and "living together." The difference among these forms is in their underly-ing assumptions regarding the bonds between the couple. In "go-ing together" it is understood that the only genuine obligation each has toward the other is accessibility. In "living together" the couple also agree to intermesh their living routines, and to assume the obligations of cohabitants. In marriage the couple assume, in addition to the foregoing, the special marital obligations implicit in becoming one another's "next of kin."

## Forms of Attachment Relationships

### Going Together

This form of attachment relationship is in many ways the simplest. The only bond existing between the couple is mutual attachment; the couple have no obligations to one another other than to be as accessible as possible, given the restrictions that may be imposed by other demands. Nevertheless the bond of mutual attachment ordinarily is sufficient to make the relationship central to the individuals' emotional well-being, and to insure that the couple will spend as much of their time with one another as they can.

The assumptions of going together result in interdependence in emotional matters and independence in other matters. If neither individual has conflicting obligations, the couple are likely to have dinner together regularly and to remain together the rest of the evening, to be with one another most weekend days, and to be in touch by telephone when they cannot actually meet. If either feels the other not to be accessible—if either does not know where the other is during an evening, for example—he or she is likely to become distressed. The man and woman will, however, function autonomously in other respects. They will retain responsibility for their own routines, their own financial economies, and their own homes.

There are many reasons a man and woman may be unwilling to intermesh their lives further, despite mutual attachment. They may be pleased with the relative absence of constraint made possible by going together. Though the woman may invite the man to dinner several times in the week, she does not have to consider his food preferences when shopping, nor to organize her afternoon around shopping for and preparing his evening meal. And though the man may want to help the woman in every way he can, he is not responsible for her bills. The woman's worries regarding her children remain clearly hers, though the man may offer advice and support. Actually this is another reason some women prefer going together to other forms of attachment relationship: It does not require that her children and the man learn to live together.

The absence of obligation and duty makes it possible for couples to do things for one another as gifts, rather than as responsibilities. The woman may feel she is expressing her affection for the man when she invites him to dinner; some women think of sex, too, as something they give. The man may do small repairs in the house, take the woman out for coffee or an evening, or bring her gifts of clothing, furnishings, food, or flowers. But whatever either does for the other is understood by both as a freely offered testimony of affection.

There are still other reasons for the relative attractiveness of going together that may be particularly important for individuals newly emerged from an unsuccessful marriage. They may be unwilling to put so much trust in another relationship that they change their living arrangements to accommodate it. And when their marriage ended they may have pledged that never again would they join their life to another's.

**I firmly believe that I don't ever want to get married. I had such a hassle over money and other little things that became huge, that I would never go into another marriage. It's better to be free.**

**(Woman, late thirties)**

For some individuals, particularly men and women living in settled familistic neighborhoods, the issue of respectability may be important. Respectability may be required for neighborhood acceptance. Its absence may be expressed by slights or subtle disparagements from neighbors, and possibly by the withdrawal of friends and the censure of kin. Traditionally, a woman's respectability has depended at least in part on her being sexually available only to a single man who was legally pledged to her. The bases for a man's respectability may be less specific but seem closely related to his capacity to sustain a household in a reliable and sober manner. There are many settings in our country in which respectability defined in this way does not matter. But in settings in which it does, a woman can lose respectability by appearing sexually available to men who are not committed to her protection, and a man can lose respectability by appearing irresponsible or opposed to morality. In such settings, going together may be the only alternative to remarriage.

Going together is compatible with respectability because the sexual nature of the relationship need not be acknowledged to those who might be shamed, hurt, or irritated by it. So long as the man retains his former residence, is not known to contribute to the woman's finances, is not blatantly an overnight guest, and no pregnancy develops, the woman's reputation remains defensible. And the man, on his part, need not be seen as irresponsible.

Just because going together is organized solely around the expression of mutual attachment, with no other mutual obligations to introduce different and potentially confusing expectations, it is in some ways the least troublesome of attachment relationships. There are few problems of clashing routines, no quarrels over who is responsible for which chores, no conflict over the use of shared resources. The man has his life, the woman hers, and the two lives follow independent courses, although each is the more satisfying because of the relationship.

Yet the awkwardnesses of going together may become evident as the relationship continues. The man or woman must shuttle between separate households. The apartment maintained by one of them may begin to seem a pointless, burdensome, and expensive appendage, especially if little time is spent there. Either the man or the woman, depending on whose household is comparatively unused, may begin to feel his or her life has become uncoordinated: Clothes, books, papers, mail, all are in one place, but life is lived somewhere else.

If the woman has children, the primary site of the relationship is likely to be her residence, since she must be home for the children. The man will occupy the status of a guest. This may gratify him briefly, but its disadvantages eventually will make themselves felt. He cannot request quiet if he wants to read or work, nor demand privacy or a place for his things. He cannot have friends in, with the result that he must see friends on his own, or in a double-dating situation, or give them up. Although he may do all three to some degree, some of his friendships are likely to fade.

Because the two people who are going together cannot rely on their living arrangement to bring them together, each must give thought and energy to planning for shared time. Once together, each may feel constrained to be attentive; neither can quite take the other for granted. This may enrich their relationship, but can reduce the availability of time and energy for other matters. One man who was going with a woman he planned to marry said that he hoped that when they finally lived together he would be able to give attention to something other than seeing her.

### Living Together

Cohabitation as a form of attachment relationship has always been present in American communities, but until recently it seemed restricted to people for whom respectability did not matter—entertainers and some among the rich—and to people for whom respectability, while it mattered, was out of reach, especially those among the poor whose previous marriage had ended in marital separation. Within the last decade cohabitation without marriage has increasingly been adopted as a way of maintaining an attachment relationship by young middle-income couples not yet ready for childbearing and by middle-income couples beyond the childbearing years.

Living together seems to happen in various ways.[1] If there are no children involved, then it may seem to happen almost casually, without extensive discussion, although the apparent casualness may be only a device by which the man and woman retain emotional options despite what each recognizes as a major commitment. The

[1] I am drawing here on Jason P. Montgomery, "Toward an Understanding of Cohabitation" (Ph.D. diss., University of Massachusetts, 1973).

decision to live together may come about after one member of a couple has spent increasing amounts of time at the other's place and decides finally to give up the relatively unused apartment. Among other couples, living together may be precipitated by the need of the man or woman to move from a previous residence. But even then the decision might be made with seeming casualness.

When there are children involved, the decision to live together would appear to require greater deliberation. It must be presented to the children and their acceptance of it obtained. And since responsibility for children almost always requires the establishment of good neighboring relationships, the possible reaction of the neighbors may have to be considered. (My impression, based on a small number of instances, is that if the living-together arrangement appears stable, neighbors do accept it, although they remain intrigued by its difference.)

In living together the couple have added to the obligations based on their mutual attachment additional obligations based on their shared responsibility for a home. They must agree to a division of household labor, after which each will have responsibilities to the other. They may or may not agree to share finances, but a shared residence seems to be enough, when added to attachment, to result in a thorough intermeshing of lives. The couple can now routinely expect that, except for time required by their work, they will be together.

One of the attractions of living together may be that it can constitute a halfway station to marriage. It can appear to make possible the same intermeshing of lives that characterizes marriage, but not be so committing that retreat from the relationship is a major undertaking. Some among the separated speculate that living together might be desirable as a kind of trial marriage.

**I think I shocked a friend of mine when I said, "Under no circumstances would I marry again unless I've lived with a guy first." I said there is too much at stake, it is too painful if things go wrong. And how do you really know somebody unless you do that?**
**(Woman, late thirties)**

Yet living together may not in reality provide a trustworthy preview of marriage. The assumptions of marriage, as I point out below, are more complex than those of living together. Inability to manage living together may be a reliable indicator of inability to manage marriage as well, but success in living together does not, I think, guarantee success in marriage.

There seems to be greater latitude in the way in which couples who are living together develop a division of labor than is the case for couples who are married. Often each partner in a living-together arrangement accepts major responsibility for the tasks that are traditional to his or her sex, just as they would if they were married: The woman accepts major responsibility for cooking and perhaps light cleaning, the man for heavy work and work requiring skill with tools. But in living together there seems to be more readiness to depart from this traditional role allocation. Couples seem more easily to establish a division of labor that is quite symmetrical, in which tasks are shared equally or there is a regular alternation in responsibility for tasks. Most couples who live together seem to define themselves not as quasi husband and quasi wife but rather as two equal partners, each responsible for contributing to a shared household.

If the woman has children, the man may form a relationship with them midway between the one he would have formed if he were only going with the mother and the one he would form if he married her. The man is now more than a guest in the household; he is instead one of its principals, with at least the limited authority over the children that would be possessed by any adult member of the household. He can demand that they be quiet; he can break up their quarrels; he can interrupt dangerous or destructive behavior. But he is not the children's stepfather and there are certain rights he does not have. He cannot assume responsibility for the children's development. He has no right, for example, to limit their viewing of television, or to require that they observe an early bedtime. He certainly cannot argue with the mother's child-raising practices except as they may impinge on him.

The shared household responsibilities of the man and woman change the meaning of the services they perform for one another. If they decide their division of labor in such a way that the woman does most of the cooking, then her cooking becomes an obligation and not an expression of affection. No longer can she act the hostess for the man; she may, indeed, feel herself more akin to a housekeeper. Similarly, the man's shopping or work around the house will be defined as his obligation. No longer will he be able to treat these chores as gifts of service.

When a couple who are living together are getting along, each may feel grateful for the other's contributions to their shared household. But each can also become resentful if it seems that the other is doing too little. The absence of traditional roles can make the fairness of the division of labor especially difficult to appraise. Is a man doing enough around the house, for example, if he never cooks and only occasionally cleans? The woman might feel misused in such a circumstance and demand that the man wash the floors—at which point he in turn might feel misused. Feelings of exploitation at the hands of the other seem more easily developed in living together than in other forms of attachment relationships.

Often there are pressures on a couple living together to regularize their relationship by marriage. Kin may be made uncomfortable by the apparent indifference of the couple to traditional notions of respectability. Bank managers and hotel clerks may fail to understand. The neighbors may be friendly, but treat the couple as exotics.

If the couple produce children, they may find living together nearly untenable. There would be more people to explain to, beginning with the obstetrician and continuing with the nursing staff, the pediatrician, and, eventually, the children themselves. There might be legal issues associated with the children's legitimacy: Their right to inherit from their father, for example, might be diminished; in the event of a parental separation the father's right to contest custody, or even to demand regular visitation, would be questionable.

Perhaps more important than any of these concerns, the couple might recognize that the idea of being married has emotional significance for them. Marriage would define their relationship for themselves, as well as for others, as somehow stronger than is the relationship of living together: as a relationship they are pledged to honor through the remainder of their lives.

*Remarriage*

Some young people who have never been married say with admirable confidence that marriage is no different from living together except that the relationship is initiated by a public ceremony and is thereafter registered in the county courthouse. Those who progress from living together to marriage tend to think differently.

Marriage changes the relationship of living together in a number of ways. First, it requires the man to act as a husband, the woman as a wife. These are widely understood social roles that imply, within the home, the assumption of tasks appropriate to one's sex and, in public, the maintenance of a respectable and sober demeanor. These social expectations may not affect the essential self lodged in the core of the man's and woman's personalities, but they affect very much how the man and woman are treated by others, and may also affect how they behave.

There is also in marriage an implication of permanence that is lacking in living together. Others are more likely to count on the relationship continuing; its ending therefore tends to be more disruptive of social relations. The married couple ordinarily display their own belief in the permanence of their union in many ways, not the least significant of which is the pooling of their funds. The couple who have only been living together are more likely to display uncertainty regarding permanence by maintaining separate savings accounts.

The separation distress that follows ending a living-together arrangement may be as severe as that which follows the ending of a marriage; indeed, there may be a special bitterness, since friends and kin may fail to credit its intensity. But there may be other ways in which it is emotionally easier to end living together. In particular, the individual's identity is less likely to be shattered if it is not a marriage that ended: The individual will not have to get used to being an ex-husband or ex-wife after believing that being a husband or wife was a permanent status.

The assumption of permanence in marriage stems from the introduction of a new bond, one implied in the vows traditionally made by each individual "to love and to cherish" the other, "for

richer or poorer, in sickness or in health"—no matter what—
until the relationship is ended by death. In making this vow each
pledges to contribute to the other's welfare even if the other
cannot reciprocate, and to do so for life. But this is exactly the
expectation we have of our kin. After making their marital vows
the man and woman are understood to be one another's family.
Indeed, they become one another's closest family—one another's
next of kin.

As a corollary of the kinship implication of marriage, it might be
noted that it is only through marriage that in-laws can be obtained.
When a couple live together the relatives of one are unrelated to
the other; should they marry, the relatives of one become the relatives by marriage of the other.

### Research Findings Regarding Remarriage

Most among the separated remarry. The likelihood of remarriage
is greater for younger people, but remains high even for individuals
who divorce in their forties. For example, in the 1960s, among
those aged between thirty-five and forty-five at the time of their
divorce, almost 60 percent of the men and about 40 percent of the
women had remarried within four years.[2] At the present time it
appears about five-sixths of divorced men and about three-fourths
of divorced women eventually remarry, and the rate has been going up steadily.[3] Most of those who separate and proceed to divorce can, therefore, look forward to eventual remarriage.

Women with several children sometimes think of themselves as
having little chance for remarriage. As one said, "It is going to take

[2] Calculated from U.S. Bureau of the Census, "Social and Economic Variations
in Marriage, Divorce, and Remarriage: 1967," in *Current Population Reports*, Series
P-20, No. 223 (Washington, D.C.: Government Printing Office, 1971), Table 8,
p. 56.
[3] Paul C. Glick, Presentation to Seminar on the Single Parent, Center for Policy
Research, Cambridge, Massachusetts, April 1974. See also F. Ivan Nye and Felix M.
Berardo, *The Family: Its Structure and Interaction* (New York: Macmillan, 1973),
p. 506.

a pretty special guy who will want to take on four kids." Yet it turns out that women with several children are about as likely to remarry as women of the same age who have few or no children.[4] We can only surmise why this is, but it suggests that a man's desire to marry a woman is based primarily on his relationship with her, and is relatively unaffected by the magnitude of the familial responsibilities that would come with marriage.

There do seem to be special problems in remarriages in which there are children. Inclusion of a stepfather will require reorganization of what had previously been a single-parent household. The mother and children must once again redefine their relationships, just as they did when the father left the home. And while the children may gain in security from having a new man on the scene, they are likely to lose some autonomy. At the same time that they are pleased that they no longer need concern themselves with maintaining their mother's morale, they may be resentful because of their increased distance from her. The extent to which the stepchildren accept the new stepparent appears critical to the happiness of a remarriage.[5]

The most important predictor of a remarriage's success appears to be its acceptability to other individuals in the lives of the prospective spouses. A remarriage that not only has the approval of the two spouses' children, but also has the support of their kin and friends, appears especially likely to be successful.[6]

Remarriages made soon after divorce seem liable to a somewhat larger budget of troubles than remarriages made after a more lengthy interval. There would seem to be merit in the frequently expressed reluctance among the separated to plunge into new commitments immediately on emerging from the old ones.[7]

Most divorced men and women appear to be happy in their second marriages. Survey studies show that those in second mar-

[4] Paul C. Glick, *American Families* (New York: John Wiley, 1957), p. 138.

[5] See Jessie Bernard, *Remarriage: A Study of Marriage* (New York: Russell and Russell, 1971), p. 362.

[6] Ibid., pp. 357-360. However, there are methodological shortcomings in this study such that some of its results should be treated with caution. In particular, it is possible that the informants who at the time of the study appraised their remarriages as unsuccessful exaggerated others' initial opposition to them.

[7] Ibid., pp. 357-360.

riages report about the same level of happiness as those in first marriages.[8] This may be a paradoxical finding, since the rate of divorce in second marriages is considerably higher than the rate of divorce in first marriages.[9] The paradox can be resolved if we assume that while there are no more unhappy second marriages than unhappy first marriages, unhappy second marriages are more likely to be ended by divorce. It seems reasonable that the previously divorced would be less tolerant of an unsatisfactory marriage: They have already demonstrated their willingness to accept divorce as a solution to marital difficulty. In addition, they know how to do it; they know the way to the courthouse.

A small proportion of the divorced may indeed have a difficult time with marriage. Some among them may be less willing than others to accept permanence, or they may be more prone than others to quarrel with intimates or more reckless than others in their choice of mates. Yet the preponderance of happy second marriages suggests that such individuals are a distinct minority among the separated.

In any event, judging the marriageability of the divorced by the success rate of second marriages is not entirely fair. Second marriages may be subject to stresses from which first marriages are relatively free. There may be ex-spouses sniping at the new relationship; children of the earlier marriages may introduce complications within the home; and both kin and friends may be cautious in their acceptance of what they may think of as a replacement spouse. It is remarkable, given all this, that so many second marriages do well.

### The Likelihood of Making the Same Mistake Again

Many among the separated worry that they may be condemned by the vagaries of their own personality to repeat in a relationship with someone new the events of their former marriage. They worry

[8] Ibid., pp. 108–113.
[9] See Thomas Monahan, "The Duration of Marriage to Divorce: Second Marriages and Migratory Types," *Marriage and Family Living* 21 (May 1959): 134–138.

that despite their best efforts, they will be attracted to someone who will turn out to be as irresponsible or hostile as their former spouse, just as the woman who has divorced one alcoholic is popularly supposed to be fated to make her second marriage to another. Or they may fear that in a second marriage they will themselves act to duplicate the events that made their first marriage intolerable; that they will become overdependent, or prove inconstant. They may take some reassurance from the findings that second marriages are on the whole no less happy than first marriages. And yet, they may wonder, what is to prevent them from making the same mistakes again?

This large question has within it three narrower questions, each of which can be addressed separately. First, do we always become attached to the same kinds of people? Second, do we behave in similar ways in new relationships? Third, do the relationships take the same course?

We cannot say with confidence what leads individuals to become attached to one person and not to another. We might guess that the attachment of individual A to individual B is facilitated insofar as individual B maintains proximity, displays interest in individual A, and displays as well the other components of courting behavior. But no matter what individual B may do, there is no certainty that individual A will become attached to him or her. There are many instances in which individuals have failed to form attachments to others who were perfectly eligible and available and then have become attached to someone quite inappropriate, not out of perversity, but because attachment to the apparently more appropriate person was emotionally impossible, and attachment to the other almost inescapable. One woman could not bring herself to accept an ardent suitor approved of by her family, but then against her will fell in love with the husband of a close friend.

Individuals seem able to become attached only to a limited range of others. Loneliness undoubtedly extends that range, but the range seems nevertheless to remain limited. Just what characteristics are required in the other for attachment seems to vary from individual to individual, and may also vary for a given individual over time. Some seem responsive to physical beauty, others to moral or physical strength, still others to gaiety or reliability or the capacity to elicit the admiration of others.

**One tends to like the same type of person. I like an outgoing person. I'm used to someone that at parties will speak up and do things. I have gone out with one or two people that are quiet at a party, and it bothers me. I expect people to show their feelings by laughing and talking.**

(Woman, early forties)

Most individuals, however, find that they can form attachments on more than a single basis, with more than a single sort of person. The following experience is, I believe, quite usual:

**I was worried at first, before I started going out, that I was doomed to make the same mistake. Now I'm not really that worried. My girlfriend is 180 degrees opposite from my wife. She looks different and her outlook is different. Her likes and dislikes are different.**

(Man, late thirties)

A new attachment figure will assuredly be different in significant respects from a former figure, even if we have again become involved with someone who is an essentially angry person or an essentially unrealistic one. We interact with whole personalities, not isolated characteristics, and whole personalities are each unique.

Will *we* be the same sort of person in a new relationship? Will we, in a new relationship, express the same uncertainties and ambivalences, ask for the same sorts of reassurance, have the same fears, respond in the same way to frustration? My belief, based on limited observation and some theory, is that very largely we will.

The sorts of things that provide us with gratification, and the ways in which we deal with difficulty, are unlikely to change dramatically despite the passage of time. We can expect that in any relationship we will remain ourselves, with all our strengths and frailties. Nevertheless, we are not preprogrammed automata. We do learn. Our experiences in separation may have increased our awareness of ourselves and our needs, and perhaps made us more capable of tolerating frustration. We will be older, too, when we

(307)

enter a new relationship, and hopefully more mature and more in control of events.

Will the same things happen again? Will the same plot recur in our new relationship? Are we fated, for example, always to be rejecting or rejected, always to be a leaver or one who is left? The answer would seem assuredly to be "No." Most of us have had more than one attachment relationship and can prove to our own satisfaction how little we repeat the same relationship by comparing these attachments to one another. It takes great determination to make a second relationship follow the same course as a first.

Even though we may be attracted to the same things in others, what we look for may have little to do with the kinds of relationships we develop. A woman who was attracted to extroverts may have chosen someone in her first marriage who became alcoholic; she may well be attracted to someone new who is equally extroverted but for whom alcohol is no problem.

And even though our own tendencies, including those which have an irrational component, remain very much the same, they may be reacted to differently and in consequence give rise to different relational experiences. For example, a need for privacy may lead to accusations of remoteness in one relationship, but be admired in another as self-sufficiency. For another example, some individuals, once they recognize how much an attachment figure means to them, become anxious about his or her reliability, and to test it display the least acceptable aspects of themselves. Their first spouse may have had no tolerance for this demand for unconditional acceptance, but a new person may react by shrugging off the unpleasantnesses and displaying undiminished fondness.

**I have a friendship with this guy that has gone on for a long period of time. Every once in a while we will have a conversation and I will expect certain responses, because that is what I am conditioned to. And his reactions are entirely different to my husband's. He's just a different person, that's all. So with one partner you can do everything and say everything wrong, but with another partner it's fine. So you shouldn't give up hope because you batted out once.**

**(Woman, late twenties)**

All in all, it seems unlikely that the difficulties of a disastrous first marriage will be repeated in a remarriage. This is not to say that a second marriage will be free of problems; problems are inescapable in any marriage, as they are in any human collaboration. But there is every reason to expect a remarriage, especially one that has the support of others in one's life, to work out well.

# Afterword

I can look back and say that it was the right thing to do. But it
sure hurt while I was going through it.

(Woman, divorced four years)

Separation seems to me like being packed off to a foreign country
in which one is constantly confronted by new customs and new
practices, and constantly thrown off balance by the strangeness of
others' reactions. But in separation there has been no customs
shed to warn that the setting will be new, and there is no foreign
language to signal the possibility that others may behave oddly. Instead, the separated see the same people and the same places as always. Those who once were friends continue to define themselves
as friends; everything is still the same. And yet everything is
different.

I hope this book may have served as an analogue to the guide-
book one might have read to gain understanding of the foreign
country of my image. I hope, too, that the experiences of others reported within it may have established that the journey, though uncomfortable, is both manageable and of limited duration.

# APPENDIX

## Seminars for the Separated

> When I first pulled up to that rickety-tickety old building, I thought, "What the hell am I doing here?" And when I walked in, and all these people were sitting in this sleazy living room, I thought, "Oh, my God." I wanted to run away. Then I started to recognize that I had the same problems and could relate to these people . . . . I felt desperately lonely at home, but I didn't feel lonely in the group.
>
> (Woman, mid-thirties)

Seminars for the Separated, as we offered it, consisted of eight meetings held weekly, each meeting lasting about two and a half hours. Its aim was to help recently separated individuals manage the emotional and social challenges of marital separation by providing them with information regarding the experiences they might encounter, by making available concepts and theoretical frameworks that might help them interpret these experiences, by describing others' experiences, and by making available a setting in which they could talk with others in their situation.

How much of the format we used is actually necessary to the effectiveness of the seminars we do not know. For example, it might be equally good to have seven meetings, or nine. We decided on eight meetings after experimenting with both fewer and more and finding that fewer made for too rushed an experience and more seemed unnecessarily dragged out. But others might come to a different decision.

We began each new series of seminars by introducing the staff. Besides myself, the staff might include four or five postdoctoral fellows at the laboratory, and perhaps a graduate student from the psychology or education departments. Each of us stated our name, profession, relationship to the program, whether we had ourselves been separated, and our present marital status. We did not ask the participants to follow suit; we wanted to establish that it would be up to them to decide what they would tell us and one another. Nor did we enter into the details of our own marital histories and situations. We were not group members, and in addition self-disclosure by us would have introduced pressure for matching self-disclosure from participants.

Every meeting except the last began with a forty-five-minute lecture. The lecture was replaced in the last meeting by a brief review and evaluation of the program. Here is an outline of our schedule of topics:

| WEEK | TOPIC |
| --- | --- |
| One | The emotional impact of marital separation, including reactions to loss and problems of identity disorganization |
| Two | The continuing relationship of the husband and wife |
| Three | Reactions of friends and kin to the separation |
| Four | Changes in parents' relationships to their children |
| Five | How the children react to parental separation and how a parent can help |
| Six | Starting over<br>Building a new life<br>Legal matters |
| Seven | Dating and sexual relationships |
| Eight | A review of how Seminars for the Separated has attempted to be helpful, and an evaluation of what it accomplished and failed to accomplish |

After each lecture participants divided themselves into small discussion groups, the membership of which remained the same throughout the seminar. Each group met with its leader for about an hour and a half. The group could talk about the materials of the lecture or about anything else related to separation and its management. In the last seminar meeting, we rejoined one another after the discussion groups for a wine-and-cheese party.

Even though the seminars were announced from the beginning as temporary, the ending of the seminars regularly constituted another disruption of social linkages for individuals who had already had more than enough of such experiences. We therefore suggested, either in the last meeting or in the one before the last, that there be a reunion six weeks after the seminar's end.

The minimum number of participants in a seminar appeared to be four or five; fewer seemed unable to produce enough material to suggest the range of experiences and reactions associated with separation. The maximum size for a discussion group was about ten or eleven participants. With more there would almost certainly be times when someone would be unable to break into the conversational traffic. But more than one discussion group could be formed; we had four discussion groups in one of our series, and three in two others.

## Participants

It was our distinct impression that Seminars for the Separated was useful primarily to those who still were in the transitional phase of separation: who had not as yet made relatively binding choices, and whose new identity had not as yet crystallized. We told individuals who wanted to participate but had been separated ten months or longer that it was likely that they had already encountered most of the issues we would discuss, and that the seminars might seem to them to be a review of past concerns. If after understanding what we had to offer they still wanted to attend, we accepted them if we could not fill our places with individuals separated more recently. We accepted only a very few individuals separated longer than a year and a half. It was my impression that even those separated only a year sometimes felt they no longer had the same concerns as newly separated individuals.

We wanted to enlist the same number of men and women as

participants, and so set aside half our places for men. Our hope was that the seminars would make available to a separated man or woman, from someone other than his or her spouse, the other sex's point of view. Uniformly, however, more women than men wanted to attend. When we filled our places for women we put further female callers on a waiting list. If we did not have enough men to fill the places set aside for them, we accepted women from the waiting list.

It seemed important to have at least two men and at least two women in every discussion group. One man or one woman might be tempted to try to represent his or her entire sex. Having more than a single member of each sex in the group made it easier for individuals to speak for themselves and not as representatives.

We assigned individuals to discussion groups on the basis of the age of their youngest child. Separating participants by their youngest's age produced groups of members similar in a number of respects: The age of an individual's youngest child proved to be roughly correlated with the length of that individual's marriage and with his or her own age. When we had enough childless participants we gave them a group of their own; otherwise we assigned them to groups on the basis of their own age.

At first all participants in our seminars came to us in response to an announcement we had placed in the daily newspaper. Later, as the seminars became better known, individuals came to us because they had heard of us from friends or had been referred to us by a psychotherapist or, rarely, a lawyer. Our announcement in the newspaper stated that the program was still in a developmental phase; was for both men and women among the recently separated; was intended to be helpful to the recently separated through imparting information; would carry a fee; and was being offered by a group within the Harvard Medical School. We included in the announcement a telephone number that could be called for further information.

When we were called we explained at whatever length seemed necessary what the seminars were about. We asked only a few questions: how long the caller had been separated; the caller's age;

the age of the caller's youngest child. Those who wanted to attend were sent an outline of the topics to be discussed.

Except in relation to the length of separation, we did not screen potential participants; that is, we did not attempt to select among applicants those whom we believed were most likely to be able to gain from the seminars, and also be able to contribute to them. In forgoing screening, we remained faithful to our idea that the seminars were an educational service. We would not have screened applicants for any other adult education course; why screen for the seminars?

Three participants seemed at first highly distraught. If we had interviewed them beforehand we might have decided that they would be better served by psychotherapy than by us. Two of the three in fact found the seminars helpful and seemed to become sounder people during the course of the meetings. Their discussion groups had a little trouble with each of them at first, but eventually both were fully accepted. The third was so firmly in the grip of a particular obsession that he could talk about nothing else and could listen to no one. He did not return after the first meeting, to the relief of others in his discussion group. I cannot guess what would have happened had he continued, but some members of his group said they would have dropped out.

Perhaps we should have done some screening. Certainly we had worried moments because we did not. A colleague has argued strongly and convincingly that to the extent that the staff of such a program feels uncertain about its ability to deal with unanticipated problems, they should screen potential participants. They might attempt to discourage from participation not only those who might present them with such problems, but also those who might get little out of the seminars themselves yet interfere with the gain of others.

In the first four or five of our seminars, we tried to call every participant by telephone after every meeting to ask what had been his or her reaction to the meeting. In this way we were able to learn what was going well and what was going badly. We were also able to monitor the extent to which the program was having undesirable side effects for participants. When we began the seminars, we had been concerned that the lectures or discussions might shatter the defenses of a participant whose emotional organization was fragile. The telephone calls made it clear that this concern was unfounded. With the exception of a few individuals who decided in the first meeting that we were about to focus attention on problems from which they preferred to turn their minds away, almost no one said that the experience was unsettling. The few exceptions did not return after the first or second meeting.

Some participants did say that they had cried again or felt depressed again after a meeting that touched a raw nerve. Still other participants were briefly upset because they felt they had been criticized unfairly by another member of their discussion group, or felt that another member of the group was taking too much of the group's time. But these incidents happened infrequently and in no case was anyone seriously upset for more than an evening.

Several participants in Seiminars for the Separated reported that they were undergoing psychotherapy at the same time. I am sure there were other participants in the seminars who were also in psychotherapy but did not volunteer the information. There seemed to be agreement that the two experiences were complementary and mutually supportive.

Our fee was never very high, never more than $45 for the eight meetings. We have helped other groups, including the Boston Paulist Center and the Middlesex County Court, organize programs based on ours that charged still lower fees. Even so, there occasionally were individuals who came to our seminars and those of others who were absolutely without funds, for whom fees had to be reduced or waived.

We think that identifying the staff of the seminars as members of Harvard Medical School had some effect on the kinds of individuals who chose to participate. Having the program sponsored by Harvard may have suggested that it would be appropriate for well-educated individuals. Most, although far from all, of those who participated in our seminars had some college education, and some participants had done advanced work. When the seminars were offered under other auspices, the educational distribution of participants seemed more nearly that of the community as a whole.

## Staff

The experience of the Middlesex County groups and other groups that have offered the seminars program would suggest that the lecturer need not actually be an expert in the areas of separation and divorce, so long as he or she is able to identify the issues that arise within them and offer ways of thinking about those issues. I would anticipate that adequate lectures could be prepared from this book.

Good discussion group leaders seem to come from every background. (The lecturer, in a pinch, may also serve as a discussion group leader.) In our experience it was most important that the discussion group leader be disciplined enough not to intrude himself or herself into discussions unnecessarily, yet also be alert enough, and have enough personal presence, to deal with blocks to group interchange. Clinical training seemed to be helpful, although individuals with a background in clinical psychology, psychiatry, or social work sometimes found it difficult to restrain themselves from offering interpretations or advice. Individuals whose training or experience was in education seemed to do well if they could restrain themselves from teaching.

Professionals seemed often to prefer to lead a group entirely by themselves. But nonprofessionals seemed to do better, and to enjoy the experience more, if they were paired with someone of the other sex.

## Group Management

We impressed on our discussion group leaders that the sole purpose of the group was to provide a setting in which participants in the seminars could talk with one another. The task of the leader was simply to facilitate interchange among participants. We suggested to leaders that they encourage participants to respond to one another by supporting the efforts to contribute of the less forward, by restraining those who threatened to turn the discussion into a monologue, and by insuring that the topic under discussion was one that the participants really wanted to talk about.

When discussions were going well participants gave full attention to one another and were responsive to one another in their own comments. Occasionally, however, participants gave only desultory attention to what was being said; they entered into cross-conversations, or doodled, or permitted their eyes to glaze. Comments followed one another without being responsive to one another; topics shifted abruptly without anyone seeming to mind or even to notice. When phenomena like these appeared, it became the group leader's responsibility to return the discussion to issues of genuine concern to the participants.

In the first or second meeting participants sometimes were too cautious with one another to talk frankly about their situations. Their caution seemed appropriate and there seemed to be no need to encourage that it be dropped. In a couple of cases a member who dominated an early meeting by full confession was troublesome for others, not only because of the claim he or she made on the group's time, but also because he or she was in conflict with the others' desire to feel more confident of the discussion situation before risking candor.

It seemed to be important that a group leader be active in response to the unusual person who talked so much that others in his or her group could feel that no other voice was being heard. When nothing was done about such a situation, group members later complained that the discussion had been dominated by the talkative person. If the compulsive talker was a bit odd, and his or her story had touches of the bizarre, others could feel uncomfortable at finding themselves grouped with this person. It was sometimes difficult for a leader to interrupt a truly effective compulsive talker, but one leader had some success with the device of holding up his hand in a stop signal and saying, "Let me interrupt here to ask what others think of this issue."

At the opposite extreme were those participants who said nary a word. An individual who never talked could make others in the group uncomfortable just because his or her reactions were unknown: The others might wonder what he or she was thinking. Sometimes the previously silent could be encouraged to enter in by the leader's turning to them in an inquiring fashion when they seemed ready to talk. Failing this, a leader might say to them something like, "You haven't said anything so far, and I wonder what you think of what's been said." Our practice, generally, was to do this more in early meetings. No one was required to participate actively who did not want to.

Occasionally men and women who met in a seminar series began seeing one another as dates. The resulting liaisons about which I know have for some reason proved longer lasting than I would guess are most postmarital liaisons. But when two people attending a seminar became paired they tended to participate in the seminar situation not as individuals but as members of a couple; the seminar was simply another setting in which they developed their relationship with one another. Each was always aware that the other was an audience to what he or she might say, and the contributions of both were in consequence modified and might simply be ended.

Infrequently, one member of a group responded to another member on the basis of feelings and perceptions that had their source elsewhere. A man or woman might decide that another member was very much like his or her spouse or was someone he or she wished the spouse had been like; he or she might become intensely competitive with another participant for no obvious reason or might offer advice that was based largely on projection. Leaders sometimes were able to combat this by redirecting the individual's attention to his or her own life. For example, when one man seemed to have identified a woman in his group with his wife and said that the woman sounded hard to live with, the leader encouraged the man to discuss his experiences rather than his projections by asking: "Are you thinking of something that happened in your own marriage?"

## Ending

Most participants in Seminars for the Separated were sorry to see the series come to an end, even when they recognized that there was little more to be covered in the lectures. One woman, speaking for many, said the seminars had become the social event of her week. Leaving the seminars was to her like losing another community.

In the sixth meeting of a series I made it a point to remind participants of the series' approaching end by saying something like, "The next meeting will be the one before the last." My impression was that in the seventh meeting participants tried to sum up the experience and to ready themselves for departure. In the eighth meeting there seemed to be less group involvement.

The party in this eighth meeting gave participants a chance to talk with one another and with staff for the last time before the seminar series ended. Some left the party early: a handshake, a flurry of goodbyes, and they were gone. Others stayed until the very end, when all that was left on the tables were unwashed cups and a few potato chips.

The reunions we held six weeks or so after the end of the seminar reduced the wrench that might have attended a more total break. After the reunion a few participants continued to keep in touch with one another, but most did not.

## How the Seminars Helped [1]

The *information* provided in the seminars helped participants in several ways. It first of all reassured them that they were not alone in their experience—that others, too, found marital separation disabling. Next, it helped them to conceptualize their difficulties and

[1] This is based in part on an evaluation study conducted by Mrs. Dorothy Burlage of the Laboratory of Community Psychiatry.

see them as manageable. The explanations of the source of the problems they were encountering made the problems less anxiety provoking. The informational content of the seminars also made it easier for participants to assess their progress toward recovery, and to judge how long it might be before they were entirely themselves again. Sometimes the information helped participants to think through larger issues of life choices, or more specific issues, such as how to deal with the loneliness of family holidays.

The *community* provided by the seminars helped in other ways. Getting together with other participants constituted a social event of a sort, a reason for getting out of the house. The participants were all in the same situation and so understood one another's problems. Each participant could feel accepted as a valid member of the shared community. Participants could talk with individuals of the other sex, and gain reassurance that the other sex was not entirely rejecting. They also could begin to understand the perspective of the other sex; in the relationship with the spouse anger had made identification impossible.

Finally, the seminars offered *support*. Members of a discussion group ordinarily felt allied with one another in their attempts to regain their footing. The seminar staff obviously was also committed to helping each participant. In consequence, participants were able to feel that there were others with whom they were in touch who both understood their problems and were on their side.

It was our distinct impression that the seminars helped most in getting participants *moving*. In the first few meetings participants generally seemed to us blocked. By the sixth meeting they seemed, often, to have started toward lives they wanted.

# A Selective Review
# of the Literature on
# Separation and Divorce

Until quite recently, little professional attention was given to the emotional and social consequences of separation or divorce. Only novelists seemed willing to explore these issues, and for years their treatments managed to be both romanticized and moralistic. It was not until novelists who themselves had experienced divorce began writing that more realistic protrayals became available. Notable among these were lightly fictionalized accounts of their divorces from each other by Sinclair Lewis and his wife Grace Hegger Lewis.[1]

A few autobiographical accounts of divorce and its consequences began appearing in popular journals during the 1920s and 1930s.[2] These were usually morose descriptions of the discomforts of the postmarried life, with an occasional spirited defense of going it alone. In 1930 Willard Waller, a sociologist, published the first scholarly examination of the social and emotional consequences of marital separation and divorce.[3] His subjects lived in what appears

---

[1] James H. Barnett, *Divorce and the American Divorce Novel, 1858–1937: A Study in Literary Reflections of Social Influences* (1939; reprint ed., New York: Russell and Russell, 1968). Sinclair Lewis's divorce novel was *Dodsworth* (New York: Harcourt Brace, 1929); his wife's was *Half a Loaf* (New York: Liveright, 1921).

[2] Barnett, *Divorce and the American Divorce Novel*, pp. 156–160.

[3] Willard Waller, *The Old Love and the New* (1930; republished with introduction by Bernard Farber, Carbondale: Southern Illinois University Press, 1967).

to be a more moralistic and more insular world than ours, yet his description of the impact of separation and divorce is entirely recognizable today.

A few years after Waller's book appeared, Clarence Schroeder published a Ph.D. dissertation in which he explored the determinants of divorce in the city of Peoria.[4] Skeptical of the reasons for divorce offered in court, he interviewed a few divorced husbands and wives to learn the real reasons their marriages had broken up. Although again his subjects lived in an earlier era of our national history, the emotional and social events they describe are those of separation and divorce today.

Ten years later William J. Goode began collecting data for the first and as yet the only large-scale survey of postdivorce adjustment problems.[5] Because this study continues to be a basic source of information regarding the social and psychological phenomena associated with divorce, and to a lesser extent with separation, it is worth reviewing in some detail.

Goode and his assistants interviewed 425 divorced women with children. All had been between twenty and thirty-eight years of age at the time of their divorce, and all had been divorced in Wayne County, Michigan. Goode selected respondents within groups divorced for different lengths of time. There were four such groups: one divorced about two months, another divorced about eight months, a third divorced about fourteen months, and a fourth divorced about twenty-six months. Each respondent was interviewed just once. Among the many areas explored in the interview were the conflicts that had led to the separation, the emotional impact on the woman of the separation and then of the divorce, the woman's economic adjustment after divorce, her postdivorce friendships and dating, the apparent impact of the divorce on her children, her ties to her former husband, her thoughts about remarriage, and, if the woman had remarried, her experience within remarriage.

[4] Clarence W. Schroeder, *Divorce in a City of 100,000 Population* (Chicago: University of Chicago Libraries, 1939).

[5] William J. Goode, *Women in Divorce* (New York: Free Press, 1965). Originally published as *After Divorce*, 1956.

Goode's study design necessarily imposed limits on the quality of his data. To begin with, his data were provided only by one side of the divorced couple, the wife, although in divorce, more than in any other human event of which I can think, including an auto accident, one cannot guess from the report given by one party the nature of the other party's perceptions. In addition, his data were survey data, with all their limitations as well as strengths. Survey interviewing requires that already formulated questions be asked in a predetermined order by an interviewer previously unknown to the respondent in an interchange rarely lasting more than two hours. Even with the best rapport in the world, respondents can present only a partial and schematized version of complex emotional events. And whether even the most cooperative respondents can be totally frank in the survey situation, given the interviewer's limited acquaintance with their lives, limited time, and limited aims, is still not established.

Goode's data also are *retrospective*, reporting events that took place from one to four or more years before the interview. (Some of those divorced two years prior to the interview had been separated two or more years before their divorce.) Retrospective data dealing with emotional events are extraordinarily unreliable. We all have a tendency to forget or to revise in our memories times and events when we were anguished, distraught, or angry. Goode's data regarding the emotions of his respondents at the time of their separation very likely understate their level of emotional upset, though in truth the data suggest that it was high enough.

Finally, we must keep in mind the character of the sample: younger women with children, living in Detroit, in the years immediately following World War II. We can only guess how their experiences might differ not only from those of men but also from those of older women, women without children, or women whose marriages were not subjected to the social dislocations of the war years.

Despite these deficiencies in the data it presents, Goode's study remains, over twenty-five years after its writing, a standard sourcebook on the emotional and social impact of divorce. This is both testimony to the value of the study and indication that time might be ripe for updating.

Several books on separation and divorce aimed at a popular market have appeared in recent years. One that has unusual merit and has contributed to our basic understanding of separation and divorce is by Morton Hunt.[6] Hunt interviewed marriage counselors and sociologists who had had professional experience with separation, as well as a number of separated individuals, and also conducted a questionnaire study of not quite 200 individuals who were either members of Parents Without Partners or clients of the marriage counselors with whom he had come in contact. On the basis of this information he reviewed in his book the problems encountered by the "formerly married" in reorganizing their lives, especially their problems in dealing with loneliness and with sexual needs.

A number of books have offered the separated advice of one sort or another. Several have focused on the legal aspects of divorce.[7] Others have attempted to provide a sort of handbook for the separating, listing things to be done and suggesting ways of managing.[8] One recent book, which made the best seller lists, attempts to help its readers achieve emotional recovery from di-

[6] Morton Hunt, *The World of the Formerly Married* (New York: McGraw-Hill, 1966).

[7] Raoul L. Felder, *Divorce* (New York: World, 1971); Bill Mortlock, *The Inside of Divorce* (London: Constable, 1972); Marya Mannes and Norman Sherisky, *Uncoupling* (New York: Lippincott, 1972); Barbara B. Hirsch, *Divorce: What A Woman Needs to Know* (Chicago: Henry Regnery, 1973). Useful for Californians and to a lesser degree for citizens of other states is Charles E. Sherman, *How To Do Your Own Divorce in California* (Occidental, California: Nolo Press, 1972). Apparently inspired by this, but with a good deal of additional material relevant to Maine laws, is Christine B. Hastedt and Meredith A. Malmburg, *Do Your Own Divorce in Maine* (Ashville, Maine: Cobblesmith, n.d.). Pennsylvania residents might consult *The Women's Survival Manual: A Feminist Handbook on Separation and Divorce* (Philadelphia: Women in Transition, Inc., 1972).

[8] Carol Mindley, *The Divorced Mother: A Guide to Readjustment* (New York: McGraw-Hill, 1965); Angela Reed, *The Woman on the Verge of Divorce* (London: Nelson, 1970). *The Women's Survival Manual: A Feminist Handbook on Separation and Divorce* (Philadelphia: Women in Transition, 1972) provides a discussion from a feminist perspective of issues related to reorganizing one's life after separation.

vorce.[9] A few autobiographical accounts have also appeared, which may have value in making clear to the separated how much of their own experience has been shared by others.[10]

There are also several books available intended to help parents help their children deal with separation and divorce. I have listed a number of them in Chapter 10, on children's reactions to separation.

Magazine articles on separation and divorce have appeared frequently in recent years. *The Single Parent*, the journal of Parents Without Partners, Inc., has a section reviewing such articles.[11] This journal is itself a most useful publication. In addition to its reviews of magazine articles, it presents original articles addressed to the single parent and reviews of books that single parents might find useful.

[9] Mel Krantzler, *Creative Divorce* (New York: M. Evans, 1974).

[10] Eve Baguedor, *Separation: Journal of A Marriage* (New York: Simon and Schuster, 1972); Joseph Epstein, *Divorce in America* (New York: Dutton, 1974). Epstein combines an account of his own experience with a review of published material regarding divorce in America.

[11] *The Single Parent* is published by the International Headquarters of Parents Without Partners, Inc., Washington, D.C.

# INDEX